Enforcement of Decisions of the Unified Patent Court

A Survey of Participating Member States

AIPPI Law Series

VOLUME 9

Series Editors

AIPPI

Introduction & Contents/Subjects

Books in this series are developed within the framework of the International Association for the Protection of Intellectual Property (AIPPI), a non-affiliated non-profit organization dedicated to the development and improvement of legal regimes for the protection of intellectual property at both national and international levels.

Objective & Readership

The aim is to publish innovative work appealing to practitioners, other users of IP systems and academics.

The titles in this series are listed at the back of this volume.

Enforcement of Decisions of the Unified Patent Court

A Survey of Participating Member States

Edited by

Christof Augenstein

and

Johanna Flythström

Wolters Kluwer

Published by:
Kluwer Law International B.V.
PO Box 316
2400 AH Alphen aan den Rijn
The Netherlands
E-mail: lrs-sales@wolterskluwer.com
Website: www.wolterskluwer.com/en/solutions/kluwerlawinternational

Sold and distributed by:
Wolters Kluwer Legal & Regulatory U.S.
920 Links Avenue
Landisville, PA 17538
United States of America
E-mail: customer.service@wolterskluwer.com

ISBN: 978-94-035-4846-3

e-ISBN: 978-94-035-4856-2
Web PDF ISBN: 978-94-035-4866-1

AIPPI Law Series ISBN 98-888-8020-8

About the Contributors

Dr Christof Augenstein is name partner at Kather Augenstein. He has been active as a litigator for more than twenty years and has become a Certified Specialist in Intellectual Property in 2007, enforcing intellectual property rights such as patents, trademarks, and designs in litigation. His advice, especially in extensive, technically complex patent infringement litigation, is valued by clients around the world. Since several years Dr Augenstein is the Chair of the Standing Committee Q 243 Unitary Patents/Unified Patent Court at the AIPPI. He is also an author and editor of various legal commentaries about the Unified Patent Court (UPC). He is the co-publisher of an international commentary together with other European litigators, author at the Beck-Online Commentary on the UPC Agreement as well as co-author for an international commentary project together with appointed UPC judges. He regularly holds seminars about the UPC at the German Association of Intellectual Property Experts (VPP), and at the Center for International Intellectual Property Studies (CEIPI), at the University of Strasbourg/France, where he is also involved in the training of judges. Prior to co-founding Kather Augenstein, Dr Augenstein worked in various positions at prominent national and international law firms in Düsseldorf, Cologne, Paris and London. He holds a PhD in law from the University of Freiburg/Germany.

Dr Dimitar Batakliev is a Bulgarian patent attorney and Bulgarian and European trademark attorney at PETOŠEVIĆ, an intellectual property firm with offices in the region of Central and Eastern Europe. He has over fourteen years of experience in the field of IP. Prior to joining PETOŠEVIĆ, he worked as a legal advisor at the Bulgarian Patent Office. He advises and represents clients across various industries in trademark, design and patent matters in Bulgaria and provides assistance in other Eastern European countries.

Dr Rainer Beetz is qualified as Austrian and European Patent, Trademark and Design Attorney, as well as UPC representative. He is a partner at SONN IP Attorneys. Rainer advises and represents clients in IP prosecution as well as in contentious proceedings. He regularly appears before the European Patent Office and in Austrian courts. He also serves as an expert judge at the Commercial Court of Vienna and the Austrian Supreme Court. Rainer teaches patent law at the law school of the University of Vienna. He is president of AIPPI Austria and co-founder of EPLIT. In addition, he is a member of the editorial board of Austria's leading IP journal. His academic credentials include a Master's degree in Mechanical Engineering and a Ph.D. from the Technical University of Vienna. He also holds an LL.M. and a postgraduate certificate in IP litigation from Nottingham Law School.

Nicolaj Bording (partner of Kromann Reumert, Copenhagen, Denmark) is an attorney at law specialising in litigation and IP dispute resolution, including in particular cases concerning patents or trade secrets or involving complex technologies. Nicolaj has conducted a multitude of high-profile patent cases and has a wealth of experience within all aspects of patent law. He is also highly experienced in international arbitration of IP disputes and have conducted high-stake trade secrets cases before international arbitration tribunals. Furthermore, he advises on contracts concerning licensing, technology transfer and collaborative research. Nicolaj is also a certified arbitrator. In addition, Nicolaj is the author of several publications on patent law.

Gualtiero Dragotti (Partner of DLA Piper) is a lawyer with over 25 years of experience in handling IP matters, with a focus on patents and the protection of innovation, particularly in the mechanical, life science, chemical, fashion and sports equipment industries. He advises leading Italian and international clients on various non contentious and contentious IP cases, including some of the key patent litigation issues in Italy. He has been teaching IP at the faculty of Chemistry – University of Milan as appointed Professor for over 10 years and since 2017 is a lecturer for the annual 'Industrial Property – Patents' course organised by the Polytechnic University of Milan. He was appointed as a member of the Research Project on Biotechnology under the patronage of the University of Modena and Luiss – Guido Carli International University, with the sponsorship of MIUR. Past President of AIPPI Group – Italy, he is member of the Standing Committee on the Unitary Patent and Unified Patent Court of AIPPI International.

Jules Fabre, Partner, is a member of the Intellectual Property team of Pinsent Masons in France. Jules specialises in intellectual property, with a particular focus on patent matters in the Life Sciences and pharmaceutical sector. He has extensive experience handling complex French and cross border patent and SPC litigations, both in private practice and in-house. In addition to his previous experience in other international law firms, Jules was a Senior Counsel in the European IP and Regulatory Litigation team of Teva Pharmaceuticals, where he coordinated pan-European launch strategies, patent litigations and settlements. This brings an in-depth understanding of the industry from the inside, which enables Jules to provide sound and commercially relevant advice, and a detailed knowledge of patent litigation in the various European jurisdictions. Jules also has a broad experience advising on transactional matters such as collaboration and R&D agreements.

Carlo M. Faggioni is an Italian and European patent and trademark attorney and partner of IP law firm Fumero Srl in Italy. He is graduated in aerospace engineering and before starting profession as patent attorney, he spent some time in the military and civil aerospace industry. Apart from assisting domestic and foreign clients both in managing their patent and trademark portfolio and in the technical support within IP law suites, he has been appointed as court technical expert in a number of civil procedures. He is also a qualified patent litigator within the framework of the Unitary Patent Court (UPC). He is member of the professional associations AIPPI and FICPI and currently member of the board of chartered institute of Italian IP consultants.

Victor Fasmer Henum (assistant attorney at Kromann Reumert, Copenhagen, Denmark) is engaged in litigation, in particular patent and other complex IP disputes. Moreover, he advises clients concerning intellectual property rights and trade secrets.

Johanna Flythström is a Partner at Roschier Attorneys Ltd, in Helsinki, Finland. She is specialized in advising clients in strategic and commercial IP and technology issues with an emphasis on IP and technology disputes and licensing in various technical fields. Ms Flythström has considerable experience in advising and representing clients in multi-jurisdiction patent and technology litigations – both in Finland as well as coordinating multi-jurisdictional disputes – across a broad range of technical fields. In addition to her Finnish LL.M. degree (University of Helsinki), Ms Flythström holds a Master's (M.Sc. (Tech)) from the Helsinki University of Technology (Aalto University), and a post-graduate LL.M. from the University of California, Berkeley, School of Law. She is admitted to practice in Finland and California (Member of the State Bar of California) and is an authorized patent attorney in Finland. Ms Flythström also has strong commercial experience in IP having worked for several years in in-house IP management positions prior to joining Roschier as well as a secondee in the R&D- and IP-intensive context in high technology companies in Finland and in Silicon Valley in the United States (US). She currently serves as an Assistant Reporter General of AIPPI and has served, inter alia, as the President of the Finnish Association for Industrial Property Rights (STY).

Nevyn Fournel is a lawyer at the Paris Bar. Working at specialist patent litigation firm Schertenleib Avocats in Paris, France, Nevyn's practice is focused on complex cross-border disputes, principally in the area of life sciences. She has experience at every stage of litigation, from preliminary injunction through to final hearing and appeal. Nevyn holds several degrees, including a Masters in Private Law from University Pantheon-Sorbonne, where she graduated first in her class, a Masters in IP Law from University Pantheon-Assas, a Masters in International Law and Management from HEC Paris, where she won the prize for best thesis, and a Masters in Law from Columbia Law School in New York.

Mark G.R. van Gardingen is one of the founder partners of the law firm Brinkhof (Amsterdam). He specialises in litigation and providing strategic advice on European patent disputes. Mark's science grammar school education, combined with his Master's in Patent and IP law from Utrecht University, enables him to quickly grasp any kind of technology and translate it into legal opportunities, be it in the field of electronics, chemistry, biochemistry, mechanical engineering, or any other area. Mark's style is personal, energetic, passionate, pragmatic and always focused on the often-broader end result – the 'end game'. Last but not least, it is enjoyable to work with him. The cases Mark works on are often international in nature. Mark has been highly involved in shaping the future of European patents, particularly concerning changes arising from the introduction of Unitary Patents and the establishment of the UPC. He serves as a board member of the European Patent Lawyers Association EPLAW. Additionally, he holds a position on the UPC Standing Committee of AIPPI. Mark is also a member of the IP Advisory Committee of the Dutch Bar and a member of the 'Commission of Eight', which serves as a consultative body for the Netherlands Patent Office and the Ministry of Economic Affairs and Climate. In addition, Mark plays an active part in mock trials for The European Patent Academy, the external education and training arm of the European Patent Office.

Emmanuel Gougé, Partner, heads the Intellectual Property team of Pinsent Masons in France. He specialises in intellectual property law, with a strong focus on patent litigation and technology transfer, dealing with both contentious and transactional matters. By virtue of his admission in England and Wales as well as in France, he has been involved in a range of multi-jurisdictional intellectual property matters, including patents and know how litigations, in particular in the electronics, transportation, as well as pharmaceutical and life sciences sectors. Emmanuel's experience is complemented by his expertise in negotiating and drafting domestic and international technology transfer agreements. Emmanuel has been President of the Licensing Executive Society (L.E.S France) from 2011 to 2015, Chair of the European Committee of LES International from 20019 to 2021 and is now Counsel to the board or LES International. He is Director of the Diploma on Patent Litigation at CEIPI, University of Strasbourg, a leading European Executive program for Senior IP Professionals.

Louise Jonshammar is an attorney at law (LL.M.) in Sweden and Partner at AWA Sweden. She has extensive knowledge and experience within IP law (in particular patent law) and contractual law, and is an expert in supplementary protection certificates (SPC) in Sweden. Louise is very active in the IP community in Sweden; appointed by the Swedish government to serve on the Board of Patent Attorneys (*'Patentombudsnämnden'*) and included and active in the Swedish Justice Department's reference group for patents; as well as serving as President of FICPI Sweden. She is also involved in IP committees within AIPPI International and the industry organisation for Swedish intellectual property companies (SEPAF). She is the author of commentaries on the Swedish patent law and patent decree, and writes and comments patent law and practice on a regular basis. Louise is qualified for representing clients before the Unified Patent Court, leads AWA's Specialist Team Unitary Patent and has published multiple articles on the Unitary Patent and Unified Patent Court, and held online webinars on the topic.

Marc Lauzeral is a lawyer at the Paris Bar. Counsel at specialist patent litigation firm Schertenleib Avocats in Paris, France, Marc's practice is focused on complex cross-border patent, SPC, and trade secrets disputes. Marc has extensive experience at every stage of litigation, from preliminary injunction to final hearing and appeal before French Courts and the Unified Patent Court. In addition to previous experiences in international law firms, Marc was a law clerk for the intellectual property judges of the Lyon Court of First Instance which allowed him to prepare and attend over fifty hearings, and to draft decisions. Marc is a member of the UPC Standing Committee of the AIPPI.

Sophie Lens, admitted to the Brussels Bar in 2005, is a lawyer and counsel at the Belgian law firm ALTIUS. She specialises in intellectual property matters, with particular expertise in trademark and patent litigation, anti-counterfeiting and parallel-trade matters, as well as trade secrets. Her legal practice also includes unfair market practices, advertising, as well as drafting opinions and contracts in IP-related matters. Sophie is an author and co-author of various publications, and frequently participates as a speaker, moderator and/or co-organiser at various conferences and seminars, particularly on IP issues. Sophie is an active member of several associations, including the French association 'Association des Praticiens du Droit des Marques et des Modèles' (APRAM), the 'Association Internationale des Jeunes Avocats' (AIJA), where she is the vice-president of the Intellectual Property, Technology, Media, and Telecommunications Commission, and the AIPPI, where she represents the Belgian group on the Standing Committee on Trade Secrets. Sophie is also the vice-president of the ANBPPI (AIPPI Belgium).

J.C. Sebastian Pinckaers holds an LL.M. degree from the University of California (Berkeley) and a doctorate degree from the University of Amsterdam. He heads Van Doorne's Patent & Trade Secrets team. He is an experienced patent litigator, advises on coordinating and conducting national and European patent litigation and has successfully represented global companies before the Courts of The Hague. He is familiar with patents covering industry standards and the interface with EU antitrust law. For more than twenty years, Bas has been highly involved in promoting the UPC and Unitary Patent system. He is member of the Board of the Dutch Intellectual Property Association (VIE), Secretary of the Dutch AIPPI Group, member of the AIPPI Standing Committee on the Unitary Patent/Unified Patent Court, Member of Union (European Practitioners in Intellectual Property) and EPLAW. Bas has published numerous articles and regularly lectures on subjects related to patent and trade secrets enforcement. He serves as member of the editorial board of the Dutch IP magazine IER (Intellectuele Eigendom & Reclamerecht = Intellectual Property and Advertising Law), in which he has published articles about the UPC and Unitary Patent.

Oswin Ridderbusch is a German and European patent attorney, a registered UPC representative, and a partner at the IP-specialised law firm Vossius with an academic background in biochemistry. His practice includes the drafting and prosecution of patent applications, contentious post-grant proceedings including opposition, revocation and infringement actions, as well as the prosecution and litigation of supplementary protection certificates. Oswin is an author of the handbooks *European SPCs Unravelled: A Practitioner's Guide to Supplementary Protection Certificates in Europe* (second edition, 2021), *Antibody Patenting: A Practitioner's Guide to Drafting, Prosecution and Enforcement* (second edition, 2023), and *From Clones to Claims: A Handbook on Patenting Biotech and Biopharmaceutical Inventions in the European Patent Office and on Enforcing such Patents* (seventh edition, 2023). He is regularly invited as a speaker to international conferences. Oswin is an active member of AIPPI and engages in AIPPI's Standing Committee on the Unitary Patent and the Unified Patent Court.

Christophe Ronse is a partner in the IP & litigation department of ALTIUS and leads the firm's life sciences and patents practice. In particular, Christophe specialises in intellectual property, with a focus on patent law, and healthcare law. He advises and assists national and international clients in complex litigation at the Belgian and international level. Christophe is a regular contributor of legal articles and a speaker at conferences mainly in the field of intellectual property and pharmaceutical law, including delivering the inaugural address to the Brussels Bar Association for the judicial year 2005–2006. He is a member of INTA, LES, EPLAW and was the president of AIPPI's Belgian association from 2011 until 2017. Christophe serves on the board of AIPPI Belgium and on the AIPPI Standing Committee on Pharma and is also a member of the editorial board of ICIP, a leading Belgian legal journal in the IP field. He was appointed deputy judge at the Court of Appeal of Brussels in 2016 and is an active member of the International Bar Association (IBA), presently serving as officer of the IP Committee.

Gonçalo de Sampaio is a partner at J.E. Dias Costa, Lda., an IP firm based in Lisbon, Portugal. He graduated in Law by the Law School of Portuguese Catholic University. During Law School, and under the Erasmus program, he spent a year in the Law School of the Universidad Complutense, in Madrid, Spain. He has been practising for more than twenty-five years, focusing in the last twenty on patent litigation. Besides being a lawyer, Gonçalo is also an Official Industrial Property Agent, after passing the examination of the Portuguese PTO and also a European Trade Mark Attorney before the European Union Intellectual Property Office – Trade Marks and Designs (EUIPO). Since 2015, Gonçalo is the President of the Board of AIPPI (Portuguese Group). Prior to that he was the Secretary of the Board of ACPI (Portuguese Group of FICPI), from 2000 to 2015. Gonçalo is a Member of the Portuguese Bar Association, AIPPI, FICPI, INTA, ICC and LES.

Rainer Schultes is an Austrian attorney at law one of the founding partners at GEISTWERT Rechtsanwälte in Vienna. His practice covers all matters relating to Intellectual Property, in particular patents, designs, trademarks, and unfair competition, with an emphasis on patent litigation. He regularly represents before courts and patent office and also advises on licenses. Having a technical background in engineering, Schultes advises on all points of intersection between technology and law. He has conducted a considerable number of patent litigations in all fields of technology, including life sciences, mechanical engineering, and electronics. Schultes was elected onto the Board of the Austrian Association for Intellectual Property and Copyright. He is member of a number of professional associations, including: AIPPI, GRUR, INTA. Mr Schultes is the author of numerous publications in the field of IP.

Juhani Sinkkonen is a Counsel at Roschier Attorneys Ltd., Helsinki. He is specialized in dispute resolution, with an emphasis on intellectual property disputes. Mr Sinkkonen's other focus areas are marketing & consumer law and regulatory matters. Mr Sinkkonen has trial experience before national courts in a wide variety of matters including IP disputes, private enforcement of competition law, commercial disputes, unfair competition lawsuits, product liability litigation and criminal matters. In addition, he has advised clients in international enforcement of intellectual property rights as well as in proceedings before self-regulatory boards of the industry. Mr Sinkkonen is a member of the AIPPI Standing Committee on Unitary Patent / Unified Patent Court. He holds an LL.M. from the University of Lapland, Finland.

Table of Contents

Foreword

Shoichi Okuyama, President of AIPPI

AIPPI is delighted to introduce another instalment in the AIPPI Law Series, entitled Enforcement of Decisions of the Unified Patent Court. With the recent launch of the new unitary patent system and the new Unified Patent Court ("UPC"), it is timely for us to be able to publish a book on the practical aspects relating to the UPC.

Indeed, a lot has been presented and discussed in terms of the procedural and legal aspects of the UPC. It is important, however, to look at the enforcement of UPC decisions in each country once they are handed down. This book is expected to give readers very important insight and practical guidance on what would happens when UPC decisions are to be enforced at the national level. AIPPI expects that this book will an important source of information in the library of all UPC users.

Since its foundation in 1897, AIPPI – the International Association for the Protection of Intellectual Property – is the world's leading non-profit association dedicated to the development and improvement of laws for the protection of intellectual property. It is a politically neutral, non-profit organization based in Switzerland, with over 8,100 members worldwide from 131 countries across all continents. AIPPI members include lawyers, attorneys and agents working across all fields of intellectual property in corporate and private practice throughout the world, as well as academics, judges, government officials and other persons interested in intellectual property. AIPPI promotes the protection of all types of intellectual property through comprehensive analysis of existing and proposed intellectual property laws and policies, and formulates proposals to harmonize intellectual property laws and their application.

AIPPI would like to cordially thank Christof Augenstein, the Chair of the AIPPI Standing Committee on Unitary Patent / Unified Patent Court, Johanna Flythström, an assistant to the Reporter General, who is responsible for this book in the Bureau, and the volume editors of this book, for their work and dedication in the creation of this book. Furthermore, AIPPI also expressly thanks the chapter contributors, all of whom are active AIPPI members, for their dedication and diligence. Without their involvement and hard work this project would not have been possible.

Wolters Kluwer has been instrumental in the development of the AIPPI Law Series and the launch of this book. AIPPI very much appreciates the wonderful partnership with the publisher and acknowledges its ongoing support in this fruitful enterprise.

Shoichi Okuyama
President of AIPPI
September 2023

Acknowledgements

This book would not exist without the expert contributors: We would like to express our sincere gratitude to all the chapter contributors who shared their expertise and their valuable time to make this book a reality. A special thanks to members of the AIPPI Standing Committee on Unitary Patent / Unified Patent Court for sparking the discussion on the enforcement questions.

We would also like to thank all the members of the AIPPI Bureau for seeing the importance of this timely topic and in particular Reporter General Dr Ari Laakkonen for his initiative on this book.

We wish to express our sincere thanks to Simon Bellamy and Steve Lambley of Wolters Kluwer for their professional guidance and support throughout this process.

European patent litigation landscape is in an exciting phase with the launch of the UPC: While the long-awaited reform has only just become reality, it is the choices of the users and the practice of the Court that will shape the system. We hope that this book will provide its readers practical guidance in navigating the new system.

Christof Augenstein
Johanna Flythström
September 2023

Chapter 1

Enforcement of Unified Patent Court Decisions

Christof Augenstein and Johanna Flythström

The very purpose of the Unified Patent Court ('UPC') is to harmonise the validity and infringement proceedings of European and Unitary Patents to avoid contradicting decisions by national courts. At the end of such proceedings, the UPC issues an enforceable court order, which must be enforced against a non-complying party.

Regulation 1215/2012 about enforcement of decisions in Member States of the European Union ('EU') has been modified for the enforcement of UPC decisions. Its new Article 71d(2) states that the Regulation 1215/2012 only applies in relation to Member States that do not participate in the UPC. For the enforcement of decisions in Member States that participate in the UPC system, the Regulation 1215/2012 does not apply. As a consequence, UPC decisions are directly enforceable in Member States without any further measures.[1]

§1.01 UPC IS COMPETENT TO ENFORCE ITS ORDERS

Article 82(1) UPCA states that decisions and orders of the UPC are enforceable in all Contracting Member States. Therefore, the UPC itself has the competence to enforce its decisions and they will not be transferred to national courts for that purpose. If a party has failed to comply with such an enforceable order, the first instance panel who has previously handled the matter may decide on penalty payments, Rule 354.4 of the Rules of Procedure of the Unified Patent Court ('RoP UPC'). The regulation refers to procedural rights of the parties as set out in Rule 264 RoP UPC. This again indicates that the UPC itself is competent for the enforcement of its decisions.

---

1. Article 71d(2) of Regulation 1215/2012 reads:

   > However, where recognition and enforcement of a judgment given by a common court is sought in a Member State party to the instrument establishing the common court, any rules of that instrument on recognition and enforcement shall apply instead of the rules of this Regulation.

According to Article 82(3) UPCA the law of the Contracting Member State only applies for the enforcement procedures in the respective countries 'without prejudice to this Agreement and this Statute'. According to Article 24 UPCA, the UPCA prevails over national rules. Therefore, the question is which areas are covered by the UPCA and which areas are to be supplemented by the laws of the respective contracting Member State.

Article 82(4) UPCA states that the party not complying with an order of the UPC may be sanctioned by a recurring penalty. Likewise, Article 63(2) UPCA says that non-compliance with an injunction is subject to a recurring penalty payable to the UPC. So, for the enforcement of injunctions, the text of the UPCA indicates that the competent division of the UPC will set the amount of recurring penalties to make a party comply with an injunction.

Article 82(4) UPCA is not limited to a particular order of a division of the UPC. Thus, it could be applicable to various orders of the UPC and might not be limited to injunctions. It would also be possible to apply recurring penalties to any orders included in a first or second instance decision. Thus, claims for information, rendering accounts, destruction or recall of products can also be enforced by imposing recurring penalties on the defendant.

[A] Harmonisation by the UPC

This view supports international harmonisation within Europe. A decision of the UPC is generally effective in several Contracting Member States. It is the very purpose of the UPC to facilitate European-wide patent protection. Enforcement of infringement decision is the ultimate goal and final relief for the patentee whose patent has been infringed.

It would contradict this very purpose if the subsequent enforcement of a decision after a harmonised procedure depended on different requirements. Applying different national requirements would create uncertainty and multiply the efforts and costs for a patentee. There might be a vast variety of different requirements to comply with before decisions can be enforced according to national procedural rules. For instance, Rule 354.4 RoP UPC has been included 'last minute' in the 18th draft of the Rules of Procedure requiring that penalty payments must be provided for in the order. This inclusion in the order is a requirement also set out by the German Code of Civil Procedure before an injunction can be enforced. There might be other requirements according to national laws of Contracting Member States not foreseeable by the patentee and the UPC because they cannot know in advance in which country the defendant will breach an order. In the meantime, until the UPC remedies this particular requirement, the defendant could continue with its infringing activities.

If national procedural rules would generally apply with respect to the enforcement, the remedies against an order would vary from country to country. A further issue is remedies against decisions during the enforcement procedure. For instance, the German Court for Civil Procedure foresees different remedies according to the alleged mistake of the enforcement body. This would result in different levels of protection for the defendant. Moreover, it would be unclear which would be the competent authority for such a remedy. Either the national courts as indicated by the then applicable national law or again the UPC. Consequently, if national law applied, those national authorities would have to decide about the correct enforcement of a decision a different court had issued. Many national laws assign the enforcement to the same court that had issued the previous order for good reason, because this court is in the best position to evaluate whether its orders have been respected.

Moreover, representation might not be allowed by the representative of the main proceedings at the UPC. Lawyers in Contracting Member States are normally not allowed also to represent clients at foreign courts. In particular, patent attorneys with an European Patent Litigation Certificate might not be allowed to represent clients in many of the Contracting Member States before those local courts. This would result in additional costs for local counsel and coordination of several national enforcement proceedings.

Even though recognising that Article 82(4) prevails over national rules, for instance, the German draft implementation law emphasises the competence of national courts for the enforcement and even attributes the enforcement of injunctions to the specialised German infringement chambers. This suggests that the German legislator generally assumes that the enforcement will be done by the national courts rather than the UPC itself. However, there is no real conflict even if the UPC recognises its own competence, as these rules would simply have little application, but would not contradict or impair the UPC's enforcement measures.

[B] The Application of National Laws

Only in those cases in which a recurring penalty is inappropriate or useless does a national law apply.

For instance, if a debtor does not pay an already imposed penalty, further penalties might be useless. In those cases where the creditor wants to collect money from the debtor, the enforcement procedures of the country in which the money is situated would apply. The UPC would then act according to the precise national rules to collect those funds for the creditor. This is not as burdensome as enforcing a decision with different requirements, as the creditor needs to identify the assets of the debtor anyway. Those assets are generally situated in a particular country. It will depend on the particular asset the creditor wants to exploit, whether the UPC itself will be the competent court. If, for instance, the creditor wants to seize receivables, the UPC can itself act according to the respective national laws.

The UPC can also instruct a bailiff to seize goods. Only in those cases in which the proprietorship of particular assets is registered by national courts does the UPC require the assistance of national courts. The UPC has no competence to change those registers. This must be done by the respective national court. Then, only national remedies against mistakes of this particular court are available.

Another possibility to apply national rules is the enforcement of set recurring penalties, if a party even fails to pay these. Again, the UPC then depends on national rules. In Germany, the Federal Office if Justice (*Bundesamt für Justiz*) will be competent to collect these penalties as the competent authority.

This book intends to provide an overview of precisely these national procedures. This first chapter aims at providing an overview of the enforcement of orders at the UPC itself.

§1.02 ENFORCEMENT OF ORDERS

Enforcement is generally done with penalty payments. They are mentioned in Article 82(4) UPCA and Article 63(2) UPCA for permanent injunctions. But Article 82(4) UPCA is not limited to certain decisions or orders. According to this provision any order is enforceable by recurring penalties.

Part III, Chapter IV of the UPCA confers general powers on the UPC. Article 56(1) UPCA clarifies that those powers can be imposed by the UPC. The appropriate means is an order. Therefore, provisional measures during the course of the main proceedings can also be imposed on a party by way of an order. Some of these orders may also be reasonably enforced by recurring penalties. Such measures include:

- order to produce evidence, Article 59 UPCA;
- order to preserve evidence and to inspect premises, Article 60 UPCA;
- freezing orders, Article 61 UPCA;
- provisional and protective measures, Article 62 UPCA;
- corrective measures in infringement proceedings, Article 64 UPCA;
- communication of information, Article 67 UPCA.

For all of these orders the UPCA can provide appropriate means for enforcement. This system of enforcement by recurring penalties replaces national rules for enforcement of injunctions and other actions.

§1.03 AUTHORITY TO ENFORCE UPC ORDERS

According to Rule 354.4 RoP UPC the competent body within the UPC is always the first instance panel of the division that has heard the case at first instance level. This makes sense as this division is already familiar with the case and is therefore in the best position to decide whether the respondent has complied or has not complied with the UPC order. That also means that even if a case was already decided by the Court of Appeal, applicants always need to go back to the first instance court even if the first instance court has not granted the order in the first place but its decision was reversed by the Court of Appeal.

Thus, if a defendant has missed to challenge the competence of the local or regional division in question or of the UPC in general before, the applicant has no choice and must go again to the very division that has issued the enforceable order and might not change its mind and go to the court that is actually competent.

§1.04 GENERAL REQUIREMENTS FOR ENFORCEMENT

There are five general requirements for enforcement at the UPC:

(1) attachment of the decision to the principal order;
(2) notification of the claimant to the UPC which part of the orders are to be enforced;
(3) a certified translation if enforced in a country where the language of proceedings is not an official language of this country;

(4) service of the order on the defendant by the registry, including translation if needed;
(5) handover of a security if and as determined by the UPC.

[A] Attachment of the Decision

The requirement that the decision must be attached comes from Article 82(1) second sentence UPCA. That means any order to be enforced must be accompanied by the decision itself. It should be noted that only the order, and not the full decision needs to be translated.

[B] The Notification to the UPC

Further general requirements come from Rule 118.8 RoP UPC. The first requirement is that the claimant must notify the UPC which part of the orders she or he intends to enforce. This provision is part of the disposition principle. The party can freely choose whether it makes use of the possibility to enforce the decision. It is at the full discretion of any claimant to decide. That means without the claimant's explicit notification there is no basis for the enforcement of a UPC order.

[C] Certified Translation of the Order

Another requirement originating from Rule 118.8 RoP UPC is the provision of a certified translation. Of course, the translation is only necessary if the order is intended to be enforced in a Contracting Member State, in which the language of the proceedings is not an official language. That also applies to orders of local divisions using a language according to Article 49(2) UPCA, i.e., an official language of the European Patent Office. For instance, if a claimant wants to enforce an order of the Dutch local division issued in English on the territory of the Netherlands, this same order needs to be translated into Dutch. If the language regime within one Contracting Member State differentiates between regions, the plaintiff needs a translation for the region in which the order shall be enforced. This is because national rules can impose further requirements here.

Moreover, only the order to be enforced needs to be translated. It is not necessary to translate the whole decision including the reasons. Therefore, it might be advisable to describe in detail the infringing embodiments in the motions to the UPC. With that the claimant can ensure that the order itself is sufficiently specific to allow, for instance, a bailiff to identify the goods to be seized without consulting the reasons of a decision. This is reflected in the *Guidance on Decisions in an Action for Infringement with Counterclaim for revocation* published on the website of the UPC.[2] There, the order to take corrective measures according to Article 64 UPCA starts with a description of the defendant's infringing activity.

---

2. https://www.unified-patent-court.org/sites/default/files/upc_documents/guidance-for-use-of-template-cfi-decision-ia-with-cfr_en.pdf, p. 4.

For the translation, Rule 118.8 RoP UPC refers to Rule 7.2 RoP UPC, which deals with translations in general. According to this provision a certified translation is only necessary when so indicated in the Rules of Procedure. Rule 118.8 RoP UPC is precisely such an exception. It explicitly requires a certified translation. This is justified as the wording of an enforcement order is much more important than other documents in the proceedings at the UPC.

[D] Service of the Order by the Registry

Another general requirement for enforcement is the service of the notice and, where applicable, a certified translation of the order. This obligation comes again from Rule 118.8 RoP UPC. The text only refers to the notice with which the claimant informs the UPC, and the certified translation. That means that the order itself in the original language need not be served. However, as the order in the original language of the proceedings is included in the decision that is attached for the enforcement anyway, the defendant is again made aware of what the claimant actually enforces. Moreover, the claimant most likely will make sure that the notice with which he or she informs the UPC will make clear which orders are to be enforced. To this end it seems advisable to cite the order to be enforced again.

Service will be done by the Registry by electronic means. The order will be served upon the defendant's representative. According to the Rules of Procedure there will be always a representative of the defendant available, since a change in representation is only valid, after the new representative has informed the UPC, Rule 293 RoP UPC. Rule 293 RoP UPC also specifies that until the reception of the notification of the new representative, the former representative is responsible for the communication between the UPC and the party concerned. That means even if a representative decided to stop representing his or her client, she or he must still accept the service of enforcement orders. They are then correctly served.

[E] The Provision of Security

Article 82(2) UPCA explicitly mentions the possibility that the enforcement of the decision may be subject to the provision of a security. Rule 118.8 RoP UPC refers to Rule 352 RoP UPC, the latter repeating the UPC's discretion to ask for security as a condition for enforcement. The purpose of the security is to ensure compensation for any damages suffered. The Article explicitly mentions damages because of unjustified injunctions.

[1] Discretion of the Court

It must be noted that requesting a security is at the discretion of the UPC. There is no general rule that particular orders would require a security in any event. So, the UPC can issue preliminary injunction orders without any security. It is also not mandatory to require securities for first instance decisions on a regular basis. Even the enforcement of a decision by default can be made subject to the provision of a security, Rule 355.4 lit (b) RoP UPC.

This may surprise litigators as there are some countries in which security is mandatory to cover potential damages. But the provision gives the UPC flexibility.

The purpose of security is to cover potential damages that result from the enforcement of decisions that are later revoked, Rule 352 RoP UPC. The reason is that a defendant should not take on the risk of insolvency of a claimant who enforces a decision that turns out to be not justified, since the defendant's compliance was not needed from a legal perspective. However, if there is no or very little risk that the claimant will become insolvent, it might be questionable whether a security is needed at all. This applies in particular as the security must very rarely actually cover damages a plaintiff can no longer pay, but rather creates options for defendants to get away with the infringing activities without any penalties. For instance, defendant's representatives regularly doublecheck a bank guarantee as to whether the individuals who signed the document have a power of attorney to do so. Defendant's litigators very often also question the particular language in documents. Thus, the bank guarantee creates lots of discussions, which might help a defendant avoid paying penalties and thus create obstacles and pitfalls for plaintiffs.

Therefore, to secure efficient enforcement and respect of UPC orders, the UPC might not be inclined to request securities on a regular basis. That does not mean that if there are indications that a plaintiff might not be able to reimburse potential damages, the UPC should request the security. Fair justice requires that if such indications are present, the defendant needs this protection.

[2] Discretion is not Unlimited

The UPC's discretion is not unlimited. Ignoring a request for security by the defendant can always be brought to the attention of the Court of Appeal. Rule 220 RoP UPC provides for remedies even if the court of first instance has not allowed an appeal. In this case a party can file a request for Discretionary Review of the Court of Appeal. With this instrument the Court of Appeal has always access to any order the court of first instance has issued and with which a party is not satisfied.

Orders of the Court of Appeal need no security. They cannot be lifted so that there is no possibility that the party may suffer damages because an order might be subsequently revoked.

If a party wants to challenge the issuance of a security, the easiest way to challenge might be a request according to Rule 352.2 RoP UPC. There, it is explicitly said that the UPC can release any security by way of an order.

[3] Amount of Security

Because of the purpose of the security its amount depends on the potential damages that a defendant may reclaim in the event that a first instance decision is subsequently revoked. With respect to these damages Article 82(2) UPCA says that it should cover compensation for any damage suffered, in particular the consequences of injunctions. Likewise, Rule 352 RoP UPC says that the security should cover legal costs, expenses and any other likely damage resulting from the enforcement.

Supposing that the duration of appeal proceedings is also approximately one year, the security should envisage damages for this period.

As there is no differentiation between the damages, potentially all expenses must be compensated. Potential damages in particular include losses for a stop in production, costs for recall or storage of the goods before definitive destruction. The author believes that the value of the disclosed information should also be taken into account. So far, in particular German courts only take into account the effort that is needed to compile information, but no value for the information as such. Even though such a value might be hard to determine, it is nonetheless true that if such information is disclosed, in particular to a competitor, the recipient of such information most likely will gain an advantage. Imagine the situation where a competitor received the profit calculations of an infringer. This competitor might then be in a position to adjust any offer in a tender just below the offers of the defendant. This might lead to a significant loss of further business.

As it is at the discretion of the claimants to enforce any order of the UPC, the Court can likewise request a security only for some of the orders. As a consequence, the Court would also be free to split the security between to the individual orders. Thus, a claimant should also be allowed to submit the security only for the orders she or he wants to enforce and has given notice according to the second requirement (see above §1.04[B]). It is common practice at German courts to define portions of the overall security for the enforcement of the claim for information and rendering accounts on the one hand and for injunction recall and destruction on the other hand.

It should also be noted that in the event of a limitation or revocation of a patent, the final judgement cannot be revoked. The enumerated reasons for a rehearing according to Article 81 UPCA do not include the revocation of a patent. However, if a patent is subsequently amended or revoked the UPC may order upon the request of the defendant that this decision ceases to be enforceable, Rule 354.2, third sentence RoP UPC. With that mechanism a defendant can also prevent the further implementation of an unjustified decision.

[F] No Distinction between Order to Cease and Desist and Other Orders

The author is of the opinion that these requirements including the requirement for security if ordered apply to all orders the UPC might issue. Given the Guidances on the UPC website[3] one might be of a different opinion. There, enforceability between the order to cease and desist is distinguished from other orders the UPC can issue. The respective passage is:

> Enforceability of orders [Article 82(1) UPCA, Rules 118.8, 350.2 RoP UPC]:
> - The order to cease and desist is immediately enforceable.
> - The order is/the orders are enforceable only after the claimant has ...
>   - notified the Court which part of the orders he intends to enforce and the notification has been served on the Defendent [and/or]
>   - a certified translation of the orders in the official language of a Contracting Member State in which the enforcement shall take place

3. https://www.unified-patent-court.org/sites/default/files/upc_documents/guidance-for-use-of-template-cfi-decision-ia-with-cfr_en.pdf.

has been provided by the claimant and served on the Defendant [and/or]
- a security has been given by the Claimant to the Defendant ... [as determined by the Court in accordance with Rule 352 RoP UPC].

Whereas the first bullet point declares that the order to cease and desist is immediately enforceable, the second bullet point lists the general requirements including the requirement for security if ordered. The author strongly believes that this cannot mean that orders to cease and desist fall under a different regime than other orders. Neither Rule 118.8 RoP UPC nor Rule 352 RoP UPC distinguish between orders to cease and desist and other orders. Therefore, these requirements must apply to orders to cease and desist just as they apply to any other. Thus, if the UPC orders a security, the order to cease and desist can only be enforceable if the security has been given to the defendant.

[G] Enforcement by Recurring Penalties

[1] Wording in the UPCA

The English wording of Article 82(4) and Article 63(2) UPCA is very clear as it speaks of 'recurring penalty payment'. The German wording however only speaks about '*Zwangsgeld/Zwangsgelder*' which does not necessarily mean that they are periodic. The French wording '*astreinte*' is also used in French procedural law. As in France orders are enforced by periodic penalty payments, it seems that this French word also rather suggests a periodic penalty payment. All language versions have the same value, Article 88(1) UPCA. So, the author concludes that the Agreement rather suggests periodic penalty payments as the English wording does not leave any doubt, whereas the German and the French wording do not exclude periodic payments.

[2] Wording in the Rules of Procedure

Rule 354.3 RoP UPC speaks in all three languages about periodic penalty payments. The French as well as the German version repeat the word 'periodic' in their respective language. Therefore, it seems to be very clear that no lump sum payments can be ordered but only recurring penalty payments are available.

[3] Possibility to Use Different Basis for Recurring Penalties

French decisions regularly distinguish between penalty payments for injunctive relief and other orders, such as a claim for information or rendering of accounts. Whereas penalty payments for injunctive relief are calculated on a per-unit basis, penalty payments for other orders are calculated per day of delay.

[4] Guidance from the UPC

The guidance published on the UPC website suggests such a distinction as well, as it includes the two possibilities to calculate periodic penalty payments per unit or per day of delay. However, the form also shows a third possibility to determine a penalty payment, which is a lump sum. The first bullet point does not refer to any countable item.

> Any failure to comply with the order … [e.g. to cease and desist] will render the Defendant liable to pay to the Court a penalty of …
>
> up to … EUR [or]
>
> up to … EUR per item [or]
>
> up to … EUR per day for each day the Defendant fails to comply with this injunction
>
> [as found appropriate by the Court; different penalties may apply with regard to different orders].

Thus, there is some confusion as to whether under particular circumstances the UPC might also be entitled to enforce orders on the basis of lump sum payments instead of recurring penalties.

[5] Threat of Penalty Payments

According to Rule 354 RoP UPC any periodic penalty payment must be provided for in the order. That means without mentioning the penalty payments in the order to be enforced, penalty payments are not available. In such an event the UPC must first issue an additional order including this threat of penalty payments which must be then again served upon the defendant. Therefore, it seems advisable to include such threats of penalty payments already in the decision, as foreseen by the guidance published on the UPC website.[4]

[6] Amount of Penalty Payments

The amount of the penalty payments must be proportionate to the importance of the order, Article 82(4) UPCA, and have regard to the importance of the order in question, Rule 354.3 second sentence RoP UPC. The importance of the order is mainly defined by the plaintiff's interests as she or he is the one suffering from the infringement. Therefore, these interests might be more important than those of the defendant. In any event, the penalty payments must be so significant that the defendant cannot afford to continue the infringing activities by not complying with the UPC order. Therefore, the capabilities of the defendant also need to be taken into account as a very wealthy defendant should not consider that it might be worthwhile not to respect the UPC orders.

4. https://www.unified-patent-court.org/sites/default/files/upc_documents/guidance-for-use-of-template-cfi-decision-ia-with-cfr_en.pdf.

§1.05 OVERVIEW OF PROCEEDINGS

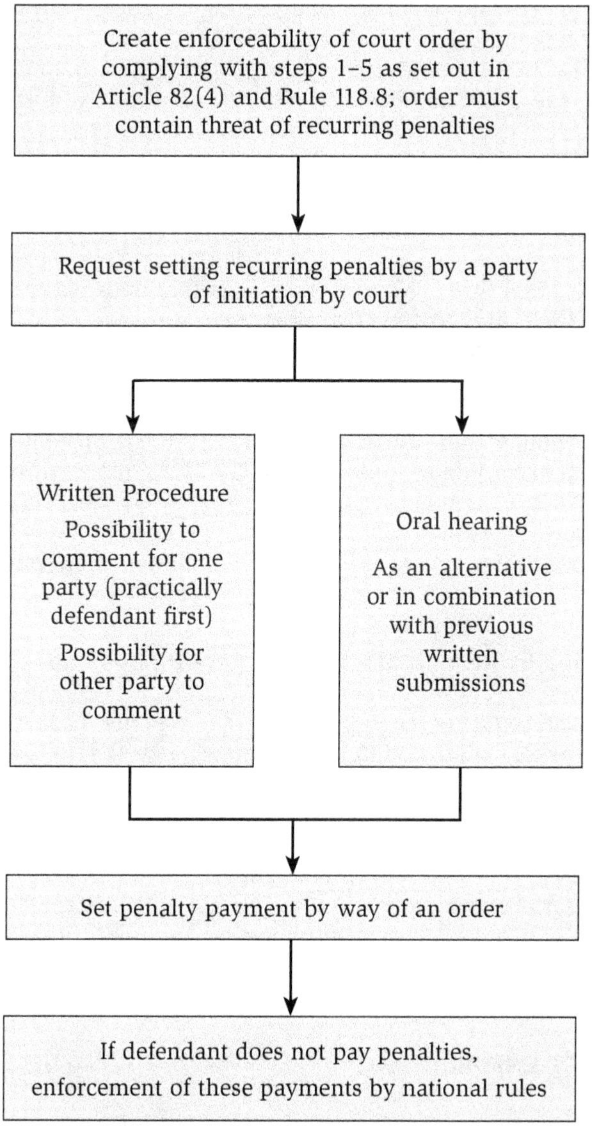

[A] Proceedings According to Rule 264 RoP UPC, Right to be Heard

There is no specific enforcement procedure within the Rules of Procedure or the UPCA. Only Rule 354.4 RoP UPC refers to the procedure according to Rule 264 RoP UPC. Rule 264 RoP UPC relates to the right to be heard. Rule 264 RoP UPC allows the

UPC to choose from various options. The very basic one is whether the UPC requests written submissions within the specified period of time or invites the parties to an oral hearing on a fixed date. Thus, the oral hearing is optional but not excluded. If a date for the oral hearing is set Rule 264 RoP UPC says that such a hearing can take place either by telephone or videoconference. With the referral to Rule 105 RoP UPC it is clear that if the UPC has taken the alternative of an oral hearing, the parties can request a hearing in court, Rule 264 third sentence RoP UPC in connection with Rule105.2 RoP UPC. Every hearing will be recorded, see Rule 106 RoP UPC.

[B] Requirement to Hear Both Parties

In addition, Rule 354.4 RoP UPC further requires that both parties are heard. This means if the UPC decides to take the alternative of a written procedure there is not only one possibility for the submission as foreseen in Rule 264 RoP UPC, but also a second possibility for the second party. The UPC is then also free to grant the party submitting the first written submission another possibility to comment. Therefore, even though there is no specific enforcement procedure the UPC may use the procedure according to Rule 264 RoP UPC for a more substantial exchange between the parties. This might even take some time, however it is clear that the enforcement procedure cannot go through all of the steps of the written procedures that are foreseen for infringement actions or other actions determined in the Rules of Procedure.

[C] Initiation by Request of a Party or the UPC

The enforcement procedure is generally triggered by a request of a party. However, the UPC can initiate it on its own motion. The author expects that the second alternative will only rarely be used. It is difficult to imagine that judges of the UPC by themselves will look for violations of their enforced orders. So, from a practical perspective the judges of the respective panel need to learn about any violation.

From a strategic perspective this could open new possibilities for competitors. If a competitor learns that a party is not respecting an enforceable order, this party may request the UPC take appropriate measures to make these competitors stop using a particular technology. The UPC might then act on its own motion and make the defendant stop violating the UPC orders.

§1.06 COST OF ENFORCEMENT

With respect to the cost for the enforcement procedure, Article 69 UPCA applies likewise. This means that the losing party also has to reimburse the successful party reasonable and proportionate costs for the enforcement procedure. There is no limitation that Article 69 UPCA would only cover main proceedings and not other proceedings such as enforcement proceedings. It is true that the administrative committee has not yet set a ceiling for the reimbursement on an enforcement case. If the ceilings are meant to apply for the first instance including potential enforcement measures this would be highly unfair, because then the party might not get reasonable costs for the enforcement as the violation of the order is the sole responsibility of the defendant.

§1.07 LEGAL REMEDIES AGAINST DECISIONS

It can be derived from Rule 354.2 RoP UPC that the UPC has the power to revoke its own orders. Therefore, if circumstances may have changed or it turns out that an order has not been justified, the UPC could on the basis of its own powers revoke it. Likewise, a court could always take back that measures that it has granted beforehand, at least if such a measure is not yet binding. This might be particularly relevant if measures are taken by the Court of Appeal, since decisions of the Court of Appeal are not appealable at all. Thus, such an '*actus contrarius*' might be the only option to make the Court of Appeal rethink a particular measure. With respect to security, the UPC can declare upon request of one party that the security will be released, Rule 352.2 RoP UPC.

An appeal against enforcement decisions is possible pursuant to Rule 220.2 RoP UPC, see the final sentence of Rule 354.4 RoP UPC. As enforcement measures are not listed in Rule 220 RoP UPC, an appeal might be possible with the consent of the court of first instance or as a request for discretionary review. Thus, the party not agreeing with an enforcement measure can appeal or requested discretionary review so that in any event the Court of Appeal might review the case and decide it differently.

Chapter 2

Austria

Rainer Schultes and Rainer Beetz

§2.01 SOURCES OF LAW FOR ENFORCEMENT

Decisions and orders of the Unified Patent Court ('UPC') are directly enforceable according to Article 82 of the Agreement on a Unified Patent Court ('UPCA') in connection with Rule 354 of the Rules of Procedure.

The Austrian rules for the enforcement of court decisions are contained in the Act of 27 May 1896 on Execution and Security Proceedings (Execution Code – 'EO'), as amended by Federal Law Gazette I No. 61/2022.[1]

According to Section 1 EO, the enforcement of monetary claims as well as of acts, tolerations or omissions by judicial execution requires an execution title. Execution titles are, inter alia, final judgments and other judgments and orders of the civil courts rendered in litigation established in Austria, if further legal action against them is excluded or if a legal remedy suspending execution is not granted and final orders and decisions of the civil and criminal courts imposing fines or penalties on parties or their representatives.

Pursuant to Section 2 EO acts and deeds of those authorities or public bodies which, although located abroad, are subject to a domestic authority shall be deemed equivalent to Austrian acts and deeds, which are established in Austria. Acts and deeds which are established on the basis of an international agreement or a legal act of the European Union shall also be deemed equivalent to such acts and deeds.

1. Unofficial translations of the provisions quoted in this chapter can be found here: https://geistwert.at/en/the-most-relevant-austrian-law-provisions-for-the-enforcement-of-upc-decisions-in-austria/

[A] Subject Matter Jurisdiction

According to Section 3 EO, 'the district courts in civil matters (execution court) shall have jurisdiction to grant and perform execution'.

[B] Definiteness of the Execution Order – Confirmation of Enforceability

Pursuant to Section 7 EO, execution may only be granted if the execution order indicates, in addition to the parties, the object, type, scope and time of the performance or omission owed. Execution may not be granted before the due date of a claim and before the expiry of the time limit for performance specified in a judgment or in another execution order. If the due date or the end of the period for performance is not specified in the execution order either by stating a calendar day or by stating a starting point of the period that is fixed in terms of the calendar, or if the enforceability of the claim is made dependent in the execution order on the occurrence of a fact to be proved on the part of the entitled party, namely on a previous performance by the entitled party, the occurrence of the facts that are decisive for the due date or enforceability according to this must be proved by means of public or publicly certified documents. Any confirmation of enforceability granted unlawfully or in error shall be set aside by the court that granted it, either *ex officio* or by order on the application of one of the parties. The order shall be served on all parties. If the confirmation of enforceability for an execution title has been granted unlawfully or erroneously, applications for revocation of the confirmation shall be filed with the authority from which the execution title originated. The application for setting aside the confirmation may be accompanied by an application for discontinuance of enforcement or for deferment.

[C] Objections to the Claim – Opposition Action

Objections to the claim in favour of which execution has been granted may be raised by way of a complaint according to Section 35 EO in the course of the execution proceedings only insofar as they are based on facts which cancel or inhibit the claim and which occurred after the execution title on which these proceedings are based came into existence. If, however, this execution title consists of a court decision, the point in time shall be decisive up to which the obligated party was able to make effective use of the relevant facts in the preceding court proceedings. If the objections are granted with final effect, the execution shall be discontinued.

[D] Objections to the Grant of Execution – Action for Impugnation

If the obligated party disputes that the facts relevant for enforceability of the claim have occurred, according to Section 36 EO it can defend by filing a complaint with the court in charge of the enforcement. The same applies if the creditor seeking enforcement has waived the initiation of enforcement at all or for a period that has not yet expired for the time being.

[E] Third-Party Objection – Excessive Interest Action

An objection to the execution may also be raised by a third person by way of a complaint according to Section 37 EO, if the person claims a right to an object affected by the execution, such as the legitimate proprietor of the object.

[F] Cessation, Limitation and Deferment of Execution

Except for the cases mentioned above, the execution shall be discontinued, if the execution title on which it is based has been declared invalid, revoked or otherwise declared ineffective by a final decision; if the granted confirmation of enforceability has been rescinded; if the execution is not covered by an execution title or the latter lacks confirmation of enforceability; or if the declaration of enforceability of a foreign execution title has been rescinded.

[G] Obtaining Fungible Acts

If the obligated party has to perform an act which may be performed by a third party, the court granting the execution shall, on application, authorise the petitioning creditor to have the act performed at the obligated party's expense (Section 353 EO). The creditor may request that the obligated party be ordered to make a down payment.

[H] Obtaining Non-fungible Acts

The claim to an act which cannot be performed by a third party and the performance of which at the same time depends exclusively on the will of the obligated party, shall, pursuant to Section 354 EO, be enforced by fines or by imprisonment for a total period of up to six months. Before the first fine is imposed, the obligated party shall be warned by the court that fines will be imposed in case of non-compliance.

[I] Obtaining Acquiescence and Forbearance

Cease and desist orders shall be enforced pursuant to Section 355 EO by way of fines to be imposed on the obligated party by the execution court for each infringement after the execution title has become enforceable. For each further offence, the execution court shall, upon application, impose a further fine or imprisonment for a total period of up to one year. The amount of the fine or imprisonment shall be determined according to the nature and gravity of the offence, taking into account the economic capacity of the obligated party and the extent of the obligated party's participation in the offence. An order imposing a fine or imprisonment shall also state the reasons for determining the amount of the penalty.

At the request of the plaintiff, the obligated party may be ordered by the execution court to provide security for the damage caused by further infringement.

[J] Request for Fines – Sentencing

When applying for enforcement, the petitioning creditor, pursuant to Section 358 EO, shall contemporaneously send a copy of the request directly to the obligated party. Unless there is imminent danger, the court shall give the obligated party the opportunity to make a statement on the grounds for the penalty, before imposing fines. The obligated party may object to the amount of a penalty if he/she has not already been heard before the decision is taken.

[K] Fines

According to Section 359 EO, a single fine shall not exceed EUR 100,000 per application.

If the fine has been wrongfully imposed before the penalty decision becomes final, the amount received shall be repaid to the obligated party upon request.

[L] Damages for Wilfulness

The petitioning creditor, according to Section 363 EO, shall be liable for wilful enforcement.

[M] Issuance of a Declaration of Intention

If the obligated party has to make a declaration of intent, this declaration, according to Section 367 EO, shall be deemed to have been made as soon as the judgment has become definitive.

[N] Costs of Execution

According to Section 369 EO, the costs for the enforcement (according to the Austrian Lawyers' Tariff, Rechtsanwaltstarifgesetz – RATG) shall be imposed onto the obligated party.

The new Section 14f[2] of the Austrian Introductory Law on Patent Treaties ('PatV-EG') provides that the decisions and orders of the UPC under Article 82 UPCA shall be deemed equivalent to Austrian decisions. Enforcement shall take place without a separate declaration of enforceability under the same conditions as in the case of an executory title established within the territory of application of this Act.

Explanatory remarks on the draft amending the PatV-EG:

> Section 14f clarifies by reference to section 2 (2) of the Execution Code that no further declaration of enforceability in Austria is required.
>
> The enforcement of decisions and orders of the Unified Patent Court follows the same rules as apply to the enforcement of domestic titles.

2. Federal Law Gazette I/51/2023 of May 19, 2023

Pursuant to Article 54(3) of Regulation (EU) No. 1215/2012 of 12.12.2012 on jurisdiction and the recognition and enforcement of judgments in civil and commercial matters (OJ L 351 of 20.12.2012, p.1.), as amended by Regulation (EU) No. 542/2014 of 15.5.2014 amending Regulation (EU) No. 1215/2012 (OJ L 163, 29.5. 2014, p.1), the party seeking enforcement may, if necessary, be required to provide a translation of the judgment. There is therefore no provision to this effect in the PatV-EG.

§2.02 OVERVIEW OF AUTHORITIES EXECUTING ENFORCEMENT IN AUSTRIA

[A] District Court ('*Bezirksgericht*') – Main Competence for Enforcement

In principle, applications for execution (except for security and provisional proceedings) must be filed with the general district court, which is the district court being in charge for the obligated party (there are 115 district courts in Austria). This local jurisdiction, i.e. the question of which district court the application is to be filed at depends on the domicile of the obligated party in the case of execution for injunctive relief and in the case of execution for pecuniary claims (in the case of pecuniary claims, alternatively also on the place of jurisdiction of the obligated third-party, i.e. the person against whom the obligated party has claims). The district court that keeps the respective land register is responsible for the execution on rights recorded in the land register (real estate). In the case of execution on patents and patent applications, thus, if a patent shall be pledged, the first act of execution is the entry of an executive lien into the patent register. Since the patent register is maintained at the Austrian Patent Office, which has its seat in Vienna, the jurisdiction of the execution court in this special case is also based on the Austrian Patent Office's physical location (see, e.g., Jakusch in *Angst/Oberhammer*, EO· 3rd edn, Section 18 EO, margin no. 12/1 (as of 1.7.2015, rdb.at)). In conclusion, most judgments and injunctions in patent matters are enforced at the local district court at the defendant's place.

[B] Vienna Commercial Court ('*Handelsgericht Wien*')

The Vienna Commercial Court has exclusive competence for lawsuits in patent matters. This includes competence for provisional proceedings, which are part of the enforcement proceedings and execution for securing. Thus the Vienna Commercial Court is the pendent to the UPC in patent infringement proceedings. Judgements or provisional injunctions of both, the UPC and the Vienna Commercial Court are to be enforced at the district courts (see above).

[C] Regional State Courts (Regional Courts for Civil Law Cases)

The Regional State Courts usually are courts of first instances for civil matters, such as the Commercial Courts for commercial matters. However, they also act as appeal Courts for decisions of the district courts. Thus, decisions of the district courts on enforcement are to be appealed to the Regional State Courts (there are 20 in Austria).

[D] Higher Regional State Court of Vienna ('*Oberlandesgericht Wien, OLG Wien*')

The Vienna Court of Appeal is competent for the enforcement of (national) fines. It is also the venue for appeals against decisions of the Austrian Patent Office and the Vienna Commercial Court.

[E] Supreme Court

An appeal to the Supreme Court ('OGH') shall only be admissible if the decision depends on the resolution of a question of law which is of major importance for the preservation of legal unity, legal certainty or legal development, for example because the Court of Appeal deviated from the case law of the Supreme Court or such case law is lacking or inconsistent. Under this prerequisite, (appeal) decisions of the Regional State Courts can be directly appealed to the Supreme Court as the third instance.

§2.03 GENERAL REQUIREMENTS FOR ENFORCEMENT

A prerequisite for enforcement is a confirmation of enforceability. A decision is enforceable as soon as no legal remedy is possible that has a suspensive effect. Confirmation of enforceability must be distinguished from confirmation of legal effect (thus the decision being legally binding with no further possibility of appeal). A decision is legally binding when no further (ordinary) appeal is available.

The confirmation of enforceability is issued by the court that issued the execution order. The order for enforcement of the decision according to Article 82(1), 2nd sentence UPCA should suffice as an enforceability certificate: Rule 354 of the Rules of Procedure which relates to Article 82 UPCA stipulates that decisions and orders of the UPC shall be directly enforceable from their date of service. Pursuant to Section 7 EO, an incorrect confirmation of enforceability must be set aside by order of the court that issued it (thus also by the UPC).

Enforcement shall take place upon application of the party seeking enforcement (the 'petitioning creditor') (with the exception of fines, which shall be enforced *ex officio* by the Vienna Higher Regional Court). The application is filed electronically via the Electronic Legal Transaction ('ERV') system. However, the execution courts can request the original title (judgement or provisional injunction). Electronic signatures are accepted.

The official language in Austria is German. The proceedings before the Austrian courts are in German. An exception is the allowance of English before the Austrian local chamber of the UPC. Nevertheless, the party invoking a judgement or seeking its enforcement is required, pursuant to Article 54 para. 3 EU Regulation No. 1215/2012, to provide a translation of the judgement/decision. Although many judges are familiar with English, it is recommendable to provide translations or partial translations in order to avoid deficiencies which may give rise to an appeal.

According to Section 52 EO, representation by an attorney at law is not obligatory in the first instance of enforcement proceedings, but it is on appeal. In the latter case, representation or the assistance of a local attorney is required pursuant to

Section 5 European Lawyer's Act (Europäisches Rechtsanwaltsgesetz, Federal Law Gazzette I/27/2000).

In the case of an injunction pursuant to Section 355 EO, the petitioning creditor must also send the application for authorisation of execution of the cease and desist title (preliminary injunction or judgment) and any application for a penalty pursuant to Section 358 EO directly to the obligated party. Unless there is imminent danger, the court shall, before imposing fines, give the obligated party the opportunity to make a statement on (exclusively) the grounds for the imposition of the penalty, unless a statement on an essentially identical application is already known by the court. As a result, such a statement needs to be requested only once and not repeated for any enforcement request (unless they are made at very different times, so that the situation of the obligated party might have changed). The statement of the obligated party under Section 358 EO does not serve the question of whether the application for execution is justified, i.e. whether a title violation has occurred at all, but shall only provide the execution court with information about the financial status of the obligated party to allow setting the appropriate level of fines.

In Austria, any civil enforcement is made upon request of the prevailing party, except for the enforcement of the fines, if not paid. However, public authorities (health funds, public administration, administrative courts, the Ministry of Finance, etc.) can also revert to enforcement (see, e.g., Section 1 lit 11 to 14 EO). Thus, also the UPC can request enforcement of its decisions *ex officio* based on R 354.4. Like any other party so entitled, the UPC will direct its request for enforcement to the competent district court.

In order to secure pecuniary claims, the performance of execution acts may be granted upon application even before the entry into force of the judgment or before the expiry of the time limit set for performance, if it is certified that the recovery of the pecuniary claim would otherwise be considerably impeded or that for the purpose of its recovery the judgment would have to be enforced in states in which the enforcement of the claim is not secured either by international treaties or by Union law (execution to secure = to secure pecuniary claims).

On the basis of final judgments of first or second instance courts against which an appeal or revision has been lodged, execution acts to secure pecuniary claims are also permissible without this certificate if the creditor seeking enforcement provides security, which is to be determined by the court at its own discretion, for the damage threatening the obligated party as a result of the execution acts. The execution may not be commenced before proof has been furnished to the court showing that the security has been provided.

If the party in jeopardy has been ordered to furnish security when an interim injunction is issued, the furnishing of such security is a prerequisite for the enforcement of the interim injunction.

Should a provisional injunction subsequently be revealed to be unfounded (e.g. because the patent was subsequently declared invalid), the defendant has a claim for damages irrespective of the preliminary injunction seeking the party's culpability.

§2.04 OVERVIEW OF PROCEEDINGS

Pursuant to Section 54(2) EO, the application for execution must be accompanied by a copy of the execution order confirming its enforceability.

The execution procedure for satisfaction consists of four steps:

- request;
- approval;
- execution (seizure);
- recovery.

The execution to secure consists of three steps:

- request;
- approval;
- execution (seizure).

In provisional proceedings, the execution to document a condition by means of an interim injunction is carried out in the following steps:

- request;
- approval;
- enforcement.

In the most common injunction execution in patent litigation, the party seeking the injunction (the petitioning creditor) first obtains the confirmation of enforceability from the title court. This enables it to file an application for authorisation of execution, which is very often combined with an application for fines. For this purpose, the party seeking enforcement asserts a violation of the injunction.

In the case of an execution of a cease and desist claim, the petitioning creditor must serve the request for fines on the obligated party in advance, pursuant to Section 358 EO. This ultimately serves as a warning to the obligated party to stop the title-breaching conduct without having to wait for the execution court's decision.

The execution shall be granted solely on the basis of the submissions of the party seeking enforcement. Penalty applications shall also be granted solely on the basis of the plea of the party seeking enforcement. The execution court only examines whether the obligated party's conduct complained about is covered by the enforced title. The allegation of such conduct shall specify the time and place of the alleged violation.

If the conduct complained about is covered by the title, the execution court shall – after hearing the obligated party on the reasons for the sought fines – determine a fine by order. These fines are not criminal penalties, i.e. not penalties in the sense of criminal law and also not retributive penalties, but rather coercive penalties. Pursuant to Section 359 EO, the fines may not exceed EUR 100,000 per application. Typically, the fine is significantly less for a title's first-time violation and is gradually increased by the execution court for repeated violations. Imprisonment may also be imposed, but only after pecuniary fines proved to be ineffective for stopping the obligated party's breaching conduct. According to Section 361, imprisonment may not be imposed for longer than two months. In practice, imprisonment is virtually never imposed.

If several penalty applications targeting one obligated party are jointly decided in one decision on a fine, a fine of up to the maximum amount per application and thus a multiple of this amount in total may be imposed (but not more than EUR 100,000 multiplied by the number of applications for fines to be decided).

The enforcing party may file one request for a fine per day, even if the obligated party has violated the title several times. All infringements in the past are covered by one fine, so that even in the case of infringements extending over several days, only one fine (with a maximum fine of EUR 100,000) may be imposed if only one enforcement motion was lodged.

Fines are enforced *ex officio* by the Vienna Higher Regional Court. The legal bases are Section 1 para. 2 and Section 12 of the Judicial Collection Act ('GEG') as well as Section 234 of the Rules of Procedure for the Courts of First and Second Instance ('GEO'). The fines may not be forfeited or deferred by way of pardon. Applications to remit or defer fines imposed with final effect pursuant to Section 355 para. 1 EO – contrary to Section 9 para. 5 GEG 1962 – are to be decided by means of a decision in the 'judicial administration proceedings' pursuant to Section 9 para. 4 GEG 1962 in a (corrective) interpretation of Section 9 para. 5 GEG 1962. If the execution of the injunction is postponed due to an impugnation action, this constitutes a reason for postponing the collection of the fine (see, e.g., Klicka in *Angst/Oberhammer*, EO, 3rd edn, Section 359 EO, margin no. 3 (as of 1.7.2015, rdb.at).

A refund of unjustly collected fines is possible. Under Austrian law, fines accrue to the Republic of Austria (Article III para. 16 EO-Nov 2000; see also, e.g., Klicka in *Angst/Oberhammer*, EO, 3rd edn, Section 359 EO, margin no. 4) (as of 1.7.2015, rdb.at); Höllwerth in *Deixler-Hübner*, EO, Section 359 margin no. 7, 31st ed. October 2020). In contrast, Article 82(4) UPCA provides that penalty payments shall accrue to the UPC.

In the case of the other types of execution, the realisation is either a public act, as in the case of the execution of movable and immovable property, or a private act, as in the case of the execution of salaries. The public realisation procedure always leads to a public auction of the assets of the obligated party. The assets are auctioned off to the highest bidder and the auction price is paid to the petitioning creditors or distributed among several petitioning creditors.

The petitioning creditor's allegations are not to be scrutinised by the enforcement court but rather to be taken as accurate. The obliged party has to revert to the remedies according to Sections 35 and 36 EO ('Oppositionsklage' and 'Impugnationsklage') for defence. If, according to the petitioning creditor's pleading, there is an infringement of a cease and desist title, the competent enforcement court will impose a court-determined fine upon the obliged party.

For other claims deriving from a title, such as a claim for payment, the enforcement court may order, depending on the request of the prevailing party, an execution on movables, on claims of the obligated party or a seizure of real estate for the purpose of realisation. Patents and patent applications can also be seized and exploited by way of execution via a corresponding registration in the patent register (Sections 34 and 43(1) Patent Act). A prohibition of disposal is issued. The priority of the lien is determined by the date of receipt of the request for registration by the Patent Office. The realisation takes place through forced administration, forced leasing or, if necessary (subsidiary), through forced sale (Oberhammer in *Angst/Oberhammer*,

EO, 3rd edn, Section 331 EO, margin no. 61f (as of 1.7.2015, rdb.at)). In contrast, the seizure of licence rights simply is made by a double prohibition directed to licensor and licensee. If the patent holder agrees, a licence can be independently exploited like a patent right. If the patent holder does not agree, the exploitation can only take place within the framework of forced administration of the enterprise holding the licence (Section 37 PatG; Oberhammer in *Angst/Oberhammer*, EO, 3rd edn, Section 331 EO, margin no. 61f (as of 1.7.2015, rdb.at)).

Legally established claims/legally enforceable titles can be enforced for thirty years.

Figure 1. Process in a flowchart

Injunction execution:

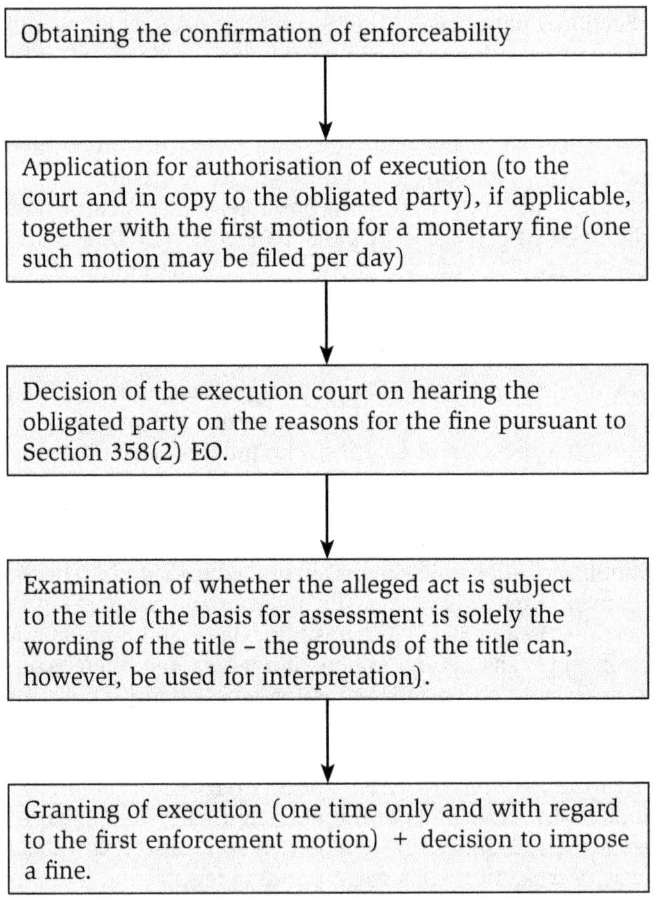

Appeal	Opposition action (§35 EO)	Impugnation action (§36 EO)
Deadline 14 days	Any time	Any time
Ground for appeal: The conduct of the obligated party as asserted by the enforcing party is not covered by the title (in the abstract).	Plea: Patent has expired.	Plea: The obligated party has not violated the title.

↓

Appeal to the Supreme Court on a substantial question of law	Appeal	Appeal
Deadline 14 days	Deadline: 4 weeks	Deadline: 4 weeks

↓

	Appeal to the Supreme Court	Appeal to the Supreme Court
	Deadline: 4 weeks	Deadline: 4 weeks

§2.05 COSTS

In principle, the obligated party shall reimburse the petitioning creditor for all costs associated with the execution. If the obligated party succeeds in averting the costs other than by making full payment or initiating insolvency proceedings, or if it prevails in an interlocutory dispute, the executed acts of execution (seizures) shall be revoked in accordance with the corresponding decision, and the costs already awarded shall be forfeited to the petitioning creditor whereas the latter shall be obliged to reimburse the costs to the obligated party (Sections 74, 74a, 75 EO).

In principle, the winning party shall be awarded all costs incurred for the appropriate prosecution, i.e. court costs (e.g. court fees, expert fees, execution fees) on the one hand and lawyer's fees on the other hand. The reimbursement of the lawyer's fees is calculated according to the statutory Lawyer's Tariff Act (*Rechtsanwaltstarifgesetz*). The lawyer's fees for an application for enforcement are in the range of approx. EUR 700 to EUR 1,000, and complaints in enforcement proceedings range from approximately EUR 2,000 to EUR 3,000. Thus, in patent matters usually only a part of the actual cost is reimbursed. Whether the recorded costs for the involvement of a patent attorney are to be awarded depends on whether his/her expertise was required for the respective service recorded and thus necessary for the appropriate prosecution (OGH 17 Ob 19/08f). This may well be the case in complex issues, such as whether a modified (equivalent) embodiment is still covered by the title (see, e.g., Gassauer-Fleissner/Schultes, 'Der Patentanwalt ist trotzdem zur zweckentsprechenden Rechtsverfolgung notwendig!', ÖBl 2002,58; in this sense also OLG Wien 28 December 2004, 10Ra102/04z).

§2.06 COUNTERMEASURES ON ENFORCEMENT

The entitlement to execution requires not only an enforceable execution title, but also that after the conclusion of the oral proceedings in first instance no facts have been realised in the title proceedings that would cause the title to lapse. If there is a dispute on this question, the obligated party has the option of proceeding against the petitioning creditor with an opposition action pursuant to Section 35 EO or with an impugnation action pursuant to Section 36 EO.

With an opposition action pursuant to Section 35 EO, the obligated party can, for example, defend itself against an injunction execution that is being carried out despite the expiry of the patent on which the title is based.

With an action for impugnation pursuant to Section 36 EO, the obligated party may object that the allegedly title-breaching conduct which forms the basis of the execution being sought out does not violate the title, for example because the allegedly infringing product has been changed to such an extent that it is no longer covered by the title or that it is not infringing any longer.

In these proceedings, the so-called contingent maxim applies, i.e. the obligated party must submit all legally relevant facts known together with the impugnation action. It may not withhold any individual grounds. The same applies to the defendant, who equally must present all facts in the first pleading.

The action for expropriation (action under Section 37 EO) is the action of a third party (person different from the obligated party) who objects to the execution because it interferes with his or her rights. A classic example is when execution is taken against an object that is the property of the third party. In these proceedings, the contingent maxim does not apply.

If the obligated party wins these proceedings, the execution shall be discontinued.

Pursuant to Section 42(1) lit 5 EO, suspension of execution may be ordered upon application of the obligated party. The following conditions are prerequisite for the suspension:

- a ground for suspension pursuant to Section 42 EO,
- legal interest in a suspension pursuant to Section 44(1) EO,
- the suspension must be qualified to exclude a danger of an irreparable or hardly reparable harm for the obligated party,
- the suspension must not jeopardise the petitioning creditor.

§2.07 PARTICULARITIES WITH RESPECT TO SPECIFIC ORDERS

[A] Permanent Injunctions, Article 63 UPCA

Injunctive relief is enforced pursuant to Section 355 EO. The special feature of these claims is that they are based on generally passive behaviour and not on positive action. However, the duty to cease and desist cannot always be precisely distinguished from a duty to act, because the fulfilment of a duty to cease and desist sometimes also requires the elimination of an unlawful condition.

Whereas in title proceedings the question of the scope of the request for an injunction sometimes plays a significant role (should, for example, equivalent embodiments be included in the injunction, impliedly or expressly?), the decision on the application for execution must solely be based on the execution title's wording. However, it must be examined as to whether that wording is sufficiently determined in the sense of Section 7(1) EO. In principle, the subject matter, the type and the scope of the performance owed must be sufficiently precise from the execution title for forbearance or acquiescence. Very general prohibitions, such as any infringement of a patent, even if it protects numerous different embodiments, are deemed too vague and not suitable as an execution order. However, Austrian practice is quite generous in this respect and allows injunctions to suffice which, for example, reflect the infringed claims and specify them in more detail by listing the actually attacked embodiment by way of example ('in particular'). This practice is unproblematic if the obligated party violates the title by distributing the unchanged subject matter of the infringement. However, it poses great challenges to the execution court if the product has been modified to such an extent that it is no longer covered by the title from the perspective of the obligated party. In this case, it is up to the district court to examine whether the modified object is still covered by the injunction. In practice, this sometimes raises complex questions of equivalent patent infringement, which have to be resolved by a district court – which is not specialiszed in patent matters and cannot revert to the know-how of technical lay judges. In this case, the obligated party will defend itself by means of impugnation proceedings and the single judge of the district court will have to clarify this claim – usually with the assistance of a court-appointed expert.

A certain tension arises from the rules of interpretation that apply to execution titles. According to case law, injunctions are to be interpreted taking into account local and linguistic usage as well as the rules of the trade (see, e.g. OGH 1Ob199/73,4Ob 421/81,4Ob551/95, 6Ob40/97v). In contrast, the scope of protection of patents is interpreted according to the Protocol on the Interpretation of Article 69 EPC.

The ending of a cease and desist obligation may be expressly mentioned in the title. If this is not the case, the obligation is permanent and not limited in time, but ends with the expiry of the patent.

A prerequisite for the granting of an execution is a violation of the injunction by the obligated party. In the application for execution, the petitioning creditor must concretely and conclusively allege the violation (OGH, 3 Ob 199/97p). This is necessary so that the court can examine whether the asserted obligated party's conduct actually violates the title and the level of fine it considers appropriate. This information also enables the obligated party to defend itself specifically with an action under Section 36(1) lit 1 EO (impugnation action). Information on the time, place and nature of the offence is required. A mere indication of the date without any other specification is not sufficient. A multitude of infringements must be substantiated by singling out individual acts.

The infringement of the obligated party only has to be concretely alleged, but not proven or certified.

The application for execution must contain the request for a fine, but it is not necessary to specify the specific amount of the fine.

In the case of cease and desist orders based on unfair competition law provisions, the infringement by third persons is sometimes attributed to the obligated party pursuant to Section 18 UWG (OGH 3 Ob 130/77,4 Ob 301/88). The liability of the entrepreneur applies to persons whose acts were done in his/her business interest and in connection with his/her business to the extent the entrepreneur has the legal possibility to ensure that the conduct ceases; the mere factual (and not legal) possibility does not suffice. Although the corresponding case law was issued in relation to the Unfair Competition Act, it can be assumed that it also applies to patent law.

Under Section 358 EO, the petitioning creditor must send the petition for the granting of execution and any motion for imposing a fine directly to the obligated party. This is to be noted on the pleading submitted to the court. This is to give the obligated party the opportunity to react as quickly as possible and to act in accordance with the title.

Defects in the application for execution or the application for fines can be corrected on the relevant court order. The dismissal of an application for execution is therefore only admissible after unsuccessful correction. However, a step for correction does not have to be taken if the application for execution is not conclusive and must already be dismissed for this reason. As a result, the correction of the request for enforcement is only possible if a violation of the execution title is not alleged at all.

The assessment of the fines is within the scope of the discretion of the execution court. It must take into account the breach's degree, severity and persistence. A repeated breach has an aggravating effect. The extent of the participation in the breach as well as the economic capacity of the obligated party must also be taken into account, as well as the benefit derived by the obligated party from the infringement.

Unless there is imminent danger, the execution court shall, pursuant to Section 358(2) EO, give the obligated party the opportunity to comment on the amount of the fines to be imposed. The amount of the fines actually imposed may subsequently be contested by means of an objection or an appeal.

The postponement of injunction executions is possible in principle, also with regard to enforcement acts already imposed. The payment of fines alone is not a pecuniary disadvantage that cannot be compensated or can only be compensated with difficulty, because these are to be repaid when the obligation to pay ceases to exist.

The basis of assessment for the costs of injunction executions is the value of the pursued claim according to the title proceedings. This also applies to requests for fines. The amount in dispute for impugnation proceedings is the amount of the title proceedings and not the amount of the fine at stake.

At the request of the petitioning creditor, the obligated party may be ordered to provide security for damage caused by future infringements. The order of a security is subsidiary and can only be granted in connection with an execution under Section

355(1) EO. A prerequisite for the order of a security is a violation by the obligated party.

[B] An Order to Produce Evidence, Article 59 UPCA

According to the Austrian Code of Civil Procedure, the production of evidence is not enforceable by executive order. If the obligated party does not produce the evidence requested by the court, the court has to take this into account within the framework of the free assessment of evidence. Before the UPC, the same applies, according to Rule 172:

> If the party fails to produce the evidence, the Court shall take such failure into account when deciding on the issue in question.

If the order for the production of evidence can be enforced, the rules on non-fungible acts pursuant to Section 354 EO would apply. The execution according to Section 354 EO is carried out by means of fines. If the obligated party has not complied with his obligation to produce, he is given a deadline to perform the act under threat of a fine, later also under threat of imprisonment. After fruitless expiry of the time limit, the threatened penalty shall be enforced at the request of the petitioning creditor.

As regards witness duties, Section 325 of the Code of Civil Procedure provides for execution in the event that a witness unjustifiably refuses to give information or to take an oath. These legal witness duties are also to be enforced according to Section 354 EO. However, Section 325(1) ZPO makes a separate provision for the permissible duration of detention.

[C] An Order to Preserve Evidence and to Inspect Premises, Article 60 UPCA

Section 384 ZPO reads:

> (1) The taking of a visual inspection or the examination of witnesses and experts may be applied for in order to secure evidence at any stage of the legal proceedings and even before the commencement of the same if it is to be feared that the evidence would otherwise be lost or the use of the same would be impeded.
>
> (2) Such taking of evidence may also be ordered without the requirements of subsection (1) being met if the present condition of an item is to be ascertained and the applicant has a legal interest in such ascertainment.
>
> (3) The application shall be filed with the trial court, in urgent cases, however, as well as if a legal dispute is not yet pending, with the district court in whose jurisdiction the objects to be inspected or to form the basis of the expert evidence or the persons to be heard are located. The application may be made on the record of the court.

The preservation of evidence serves the precautionary taking of evidence before a legal proceeding or before the taking of evidence during a legal proceeding. It has similarities with the provisional procedure for issuing interim injunctions.

As a preventive act of legal protection, the preservation of evidence requires the assertion and at most the substantiation of a special interest in legal protection. This can lie in the fact that there is a threat of evidence being thwarted or evidence being made more difficult to obtain, i.e. in cases where the future taking of evidence appears to be objectively endangered.

Before a lawsuit, the preservation of evidence can only take place upon application, during a legal dispute also *ex officio* by the judge. The application must always be made to the trial court, i.e. the UPC. In urgent cases, if the legal dispute is not yet pending, the district court in whose district the matter is located has jurisdiction.

When an inspection order is issued, the court will appoint an expert to conduct the inspection. The parties and their representatives are permitted to participate in the inspection.

[D] Freezing Orders, Article 61 UPCA

Freezing orders according to Article 61 UPCA can be ordered by interim injunctions which are enforced by the means listed in Section 382 EO. According to Section 381 EO, interim injunctions may be granted to secure claims:

> 1. if it is to be feared that the judicial prosecution or realisation of the claim in question would otherwise be frustrated or considerably impeded, in particular by a change in the existing situation; it shall be regarded as such an impediment if the judgment would have to be enforced in states in which the enforcement of the claim is not secured either by international treaties or by Union law;
>
> 2. if such orders appear necessary to prevent imminent violence or to avert imminent irreparable harm.

For patent matters, the Austrian Patent Act contains a special provision for interim injunctions, namely Section 151b. Unlike the requirements for an interim injunction according to Section 381 EO, the risk of imminent damage or destruction of evidence is not a basis for a claim for securing evidence under Section 151b Patent Act, but only a prerequisite for an order without hearing the opponent (OGH 5. 9. 2017, 4Ob 83/17k). The evidence to be secured need not already be known to the applicants. Article 7 of the Enforcement Directive 2004/48/EC does not require (in contrast to Article 6 of the Enforcement Directive) a designation of specific evidence in the control of the defendant, so that mere measures to find evidence should also be admissible (Koller in *Stadler/Koller*, PatG, Section 151b, marginal no. 49).

Depending on the nature of the individual case, the court may, upon application, order in particular the following as means of security pursuant to Section 382 EO in order to enforce a provisional injunction for freeze (and other claims):

> 1. the judicial deposit of movable property in the custody of the opposing party of the endangered party for the surrender or performance of which the claim asserted by the latter or already awarded to it is directed, or if the property is not suitable for judicial deposit, the ordering of safe custody within the meaning of section 259;

2. the administration of the movable property referred to in para. 1 or of the immovable property or rights to which the claim asserted by the party in jeopardy relates or to which it has already been granted;

3. the authorisation of the party in jeopardy to retain property of the opposing party in its custody to which a claim asserted by it or already awarded to it relates until a final decision on this claim has been made;

4. the order directed to the opposing party to perform individual acts which appear necessary for the preservation of the objects referred to in paras. 1 and 2 or for the preservation of the present condition;

5. the prohibition of individual detrimental acts or of making certain or all changes to the objects referred to in paras. 1 and 2 addressed to the opposing party;

...

7. the prohibition of third parties by the court if the opposing party of the party in jeopardy has to make a claim to a third person for performance or surrender of objects to which the claim asserted by the party in jeopardy or already awarded to it relates. This prohibition shall be enforced by prohibiting the opposing party from disposing of his claim against the third party and in particular from receiving those things and by ordering the third party, until further order of the court, neither to hand over the things due to the opposing party nor to take any other action with regard to them which could frustrate or considerably complicate the enforcement proceedings thereon; ...

This list is non-exhaustive.

[E] Preliminary Injunction, Article 62(1) UPCA

See the above comments on permanent injunctions.

The court may impose a security deposit on the applicant in case of insufficient certification of his/her claim pursuant to Section 390(1) EO. However, a certain degree of certification of the claim remains a prerequisite (König/Weber, *Einstweilige Verfügungen im Zivilverfahren*, 6th edn, margin no. 5.3).

However, even if the claim is sufficiently certified, the court may order the applicant to provide security if weighing the need for security on the one hand and the depth of the encroachment on the legal sphere of the defendant as well as the seriousness of the damage on the other hand is in favour of the defendant (König/Weber, *Einstweilige Verfügungen im Zivilverfahren*, 6th edn, margin no. 5.4).

In patent litigation, the security deposit is imposed in particular if the evidence does not show an overwhelming likelihood of invalidity of the patent, but the invalidity nevertheless appears possible to the court (OGH 19. 11. 2009,17 Ob 24/09t; OGH 19. 11. 2009, 17Ob33/09s).

An insufficient certification of the risk of destruction of evidence cannot be substituted by a security deposit (König/Weber, *Einstweilige Verfügungen im Zivilverfahren*, 6th edn, margin no. 5.5).

Even if an interim injunction cannot be enforced because the defendant is abroad and the foreign country in question does not enforce the interim injunction, but property is located in Austria for court proceedings, the granting of an interim injunction can be made dependent on the provision of security. The defendant should be protected accordingly if he/she 'voluntarily' complies with the interim injunction (König/Weber, *Einstweilige Verfügungen im Zivilverfahren*, 6th edn, margin no. 5.6).

An imposed security can be deposited in cash with the court or in the form of a bank guarantee. A bank guarantee may be limited in time and may also contain the possibility of termination by the bank (with a notice period), but other conditions are inadmissible (OGH ÖBA 1997,735f; 4 Ob 272/98y). In the case of limited guarantees or in the case of termination by the guarantor, it is incumbent on the court to call the security in due time if the period ends before the expiry of the interim injunction and a new bank guarantee is not furnished in due time.

The amount of the security depends on the amount of the expected damage for the defendant, but also on the probability of the existence or non-existence of the claim to be secured.

If an interim injunction is made dependent on the provision of security, but this is not provided within one month (Section 396 EO), the interim injunction definitively does not enter into force. This time limit cannot be extended pursuant to Section 58 EO. This period is not suspended by an appeal by the applicant against the amount of the security (König/Weber, *Einstweilige Verfügungen im Zivilverfahren*, 6th edn, margin no. 5.18).

Court practice is sometimes not uniform with regard to the serving of a preliminary injunction on the defendant which is subject to a request for security. Service after the deposit of the security is unproblematic; in this case, the time limit for appeal is calculated as always from the day of service. The beginning of the time limit for appeal and the admissibility of an appeal is disputed if service is effectuated before the deposit of a granted request for security. According to case law, an appeal is inadmissible until then. The doctrine differentiates according to whether it was apparent to the defendant whether the interim injunction is already effective or not (see König/Weber, *Einstweilige Verfügungen im Zivilverfahren*, 6th edn, margin no. 5.19 ff).

It is practical to serve the interim injunction before the deposit of the security, but with the indication that the security has not yet been deposited, that the defendant will be served with the interim injunction again with the information as soon as the security has been deposited, that the provisional injunction will only then become effective and that an appeal is only admissible from this new service onwards. Although this does not eliminate the unpleasant state of suspense for the defendant in the case of a threatened interim injunction (after all, it depends on the applicant whether he makes the interim injunction effective by depositing the security or not), it at least creates clarity with regard to the time limits for appeal.

Section 391 para. 1 EO provides for the possibility of the defendant paying an exemption amount, if this is sufficient to secure the applicant according to the nature of the case (OGH 16.2.2011 17Ob5/11a). However, this is not the case with injunctive relief for patent infringement (OGH 16.2.2011, 17Ob5/11a).

If the claim for which the interim injunction was granted is finally and conclusively denied to the party in jeopardy, if its application otherwise proves to be unjustified, or if it misses the deadline set for filing the action or initiating the execution, the applicant shall compensate the respondent pursuant to Section 394 EO for all pecuniary disadvantages caused to it by the interim injunction, irrespective of any fault on the part of the applicant. The amount of the compensation shall be determined by the court upon application at its own discretion (Section 273 of the Code of Civil Procedure).

If the interim injunction was apparently obtained wilfully, a penalty for wilfulness, to be assessed by the court with regard to the particular circumstances of the individual case, shall be imposed on the applicant at the request of the respondent.

[F] Seizure or Delivery up of Infringing Products, Article 62(3) UPCA

A seizure or an order for surrender are practically unknown to the Austrian patent process. Seizure is more common in the context of the execution of a movable property, where, in addition to the description by way of a lien, a seizure is also carried out for subsequent realisation. The legal bases for enforcement are found in Sections 346 et seq. EO

Section 346 EO

> (1) If the obligated party has to hand over certain movable property or movable property of a certain kind and if these are in his custody, they shall be taken away from the obligated party by the executing body by order of the execution court and handed over to the executing creditor against acknowledgement of receipt. The enforcement order also covers the recording of a list of assets pursuant to section 346a.
>
> (2) This provision shall also apply if the obligated party is required to deliver securities or a specified quantity of fungible property.

Section 346a EO

> (1) If the property for the surrender or performance of which execution is sought is not found on the obligated party's premises, the obligated party shall state in court or before the enforcement body where such property is located or that he does not possess it and does not know where it is located.
>
> (2) After a declaration of assets under subsection (1), the obligated party may, at the request of the same petitioning creditor and on account of the same claim, be required to make a further declaration of assets before the court only if the petitioning creditor establishes credibly that the factual situation with regard to the holding of the property or the knowledge of the obligated party has changed since then.
>
> (3) Section 47(2) on instruction, inspection of records and confirmation by the obligated party and section 48 shall apply to the declaration of assets.

The same procedure can also be applied to the surrender of movable property held by a third party (Section 347 EO). Objects which are not suitable for a physical handover due to their size, weight, extent, mobility or manipulability or otherwise cannot be handed over with reasonable effort, may be handed over symbolically pursuant to Section 348 EO. For example, the handing over of documents, the taking of possession of tools or keys can be considered as corresponding signs with which the underlying object is considered to be handed over.

[G] Precautionary Seizure of Movable and Immovable Property, Article 62(3) UPCA

Regarding the precautionary seizure of movable property, the same rules as described above apply. It has to be mentioned, however, that no realisation shall take place.

The execution of a claim, which is directed towards the granting, transfer, restriction or cancellation of a right in the land register, is effected pursuant to Section 350 EO by the execution of the entry in the land register.

[H] Recalling from the Channels of Commerce, Article 64(2) lit (b) UPCA

In practice, any recall only occurs in connection with a claim for injunctive relief or removal (OGH 14.7.2009, 17 Ob12/09b), so that, as a rule, the execution pursuant to Section 355 EO is applied for enforcement, which is applied also for cease and desist orders. According to the Austrian Supreme Court in case 17Ob12/09b, a removal may only be ordered if the removal of the unlawful condition is actually within the infringer's power of disposal. If the goods have been handed over and the purchase price has been paid, the seller generally is no longer entitled to dispose of the goods. According to Austrian case law (OGH 21.02.2017, 4Ob141/16p), such a recall can only be ordered in the main proceedings because any performed recall of infringing goods creates a non-recoverable condition.

As a rule, a recall will be a fungible act, namely the recall does not have to be carried out by the obligated party personally, but can also be carried out by the petitioning creditor, for example. In this case, the rules of Section 353 EO apply.

Insofar as the recall from the distribution channels can only be carried out by the obligated party in the individual case, the enforcement shall be carried out according to the rules for non-fungible acts pursuant to Section 354 EO.

[I] Depriving the Product of Its Infringing Property, Article 64(2) lit (c) UPCA

The Austrian Patent Act also provides in Section 148(5) that if the unlawful condition can be remedied other than by destruction or rendering unusable, the infringed party may only request such palliative remedies.

For trade mark law, for example, it was decided that the claim for removal could not only be fulfilled by destroying the entire infringing object, but also by merely removing the trade mark from the goods, because in this way the unlawful condition can be remedied with less destruction of value (OGH 27.11.2001, 4 Ob 265/01a). The claim for destruction can be denied if there is another possibility of removal and the other measures are also reasonable for the right holder (OGH 18.11.2003, 4 Ob 210/03s). A claim for destruction, however, does not have to be denied if the infringing condition can be remedied in a way other than by destroying the goods. Rather, a balance of interest test is applied, according to which the right holder is granted a claim for destruction of the infringing goods 'unless the condition of the goods caused by the infringement can be remedied by other means and the destruction is disproportionate for the infringer or the owner in the individual case'. The balance of interest takes into account (among other factors) the degree of fault, the severity of the infringement as well as the economic significance of the infringement and the damage caused by the destruction. A prerequisite always is that the possibility of remedying the unlawful situation by other measures exists at all (OGH 18.11.2003, 4 Ob 210/03s). These considerations are transferable to patent law. If the infringement, for example, is caused by the storage of files, their deletion will be sufficient for removal. Destruction of the hard disk is not required (cf. on Section 15 UWG: OGH 16.1.2007, 4 Ob 198/06f).

[J] Definite Removing from the Channels of Commerce, Article 64(2) lit (d) UPCA

The claim for recall of the infringing objects is a subset of the claim for removal (OGH 14 July 2009, 17 Ob 12/09b, Transdermal-Pflaster). The claim for removal and the provisions on injunctions are to be interpreted in conformity with Directive 2004/48/EC on the enforcement of intellectual property rights (Enforcement Directive). The recall of goods from the distribution channels is provided for in Section 5 of the Enforcement Directive on measures based on a substantive decision (Article 10), but not in Section 4 (Article 9) on provisional and protective measures. Definite recall in cases where the defendant no longer has the power of disposing of the products subject to the recall can therefore only be ordered in the main proceedings. For a recall that may be the consequence of a preliminary injunction, see above h).

Apart from that, a performed recall would create a non-returnable condition, especially since the defendant would not have a claim against its customers for the conclusion of new contracts after the reversal had taken place and thus impairments (loss of business relations) may remain after the lifting or expiry of the injunction, which cannot be compensated in money without further ado (OGH 21.02.2017, 4Ob141/16p).

[K] Destruction, Article 64(2) lit (e) UPCA

Depending on whether the destruction in the individual case can only be carried out by the obligated party or whether it is a fungible act, the provisions of Section 353 EO for fungible acts or of Section 354 EO for non-fungible acts apply. However, the obligation for the hand-over, surrender, return, restitution, surrender or delivery of a movable object in the obligated party's custody is to be enforced according to Section 346 EO (OGH 3 Ob 189/01t). The demarcation between the different types of execution is mandatory – the creditor is not entitled to choose (OGH 3Ob215/16p). In case of doubt as to whether an act is to be considered fungible or non-fungible, it is to be treated as fungible first, because the execution of fungible acts burdens the obligated party less and leads more easily to the enforcement of the title (OGH 3Ob60/95).

[L] Communication of Information, Article 67 UPCA

The claim for information, like the claim for accounting, is to be enforced according to the rules for non-fungible acts pursuant to Section 354 EO (OGH 3Ob 77/95).

In contrast, the handing over of documents is to be enforced according to Section 346 EO, unless it can be carried out solely on the basis of documents without the cooperation of the obligated party (OGH 3Ob 176/78).

The enforcement of an unjustifiable act under Section 354 EO is only permissible if its performance depends exclusively on the will of the obligated party.

Chapter 3

Belgium

Sophie Lens and Christophe Ronse

§3.01 SOURCES OF LAW FOR ENFORCEMENT

In Belgium, the enforcement of court decisions (including decisions of the Unified Patent Court ('UPC')) is governed by the Belgian Judicial Code ('JC'). In this respect, reference can be made in particular to Part 5 of the JC, which identifies the enforcement measures available in the absence of voluntary compliance with a court decision. Thus, without prejudice to the rules of the Unified Patent Court Agreement ('UPCA') and the Rules of Procedure of the UPC ('RoP'), the following provisions of the JC may be (partially) relevant for the enforcement of a decision emanating from the UPC ('UPC Decision'):

- Title I 'Preliminary rules', setting out the general rules for all enforcement procedures, including provisions relating to (i) the attachment judge ('*juge des saisies*' or '*beslagrechter*'), who has sole jurisdiction to hear any dispute relating to an enforcement procedure (Articles 1395–1396 JC), (ii) the provisional enforceability of a decision (Articles 1397–1402 JC), (iii) the attachment of property (Articles 1403–1407bis JC), and (iii) property that cannot be attached (Articles 1408–1412quinquies JC).
- Title II 'Conservatory seizures' ('*Saisies Conservatoires*' or '*Bewarend beslag*'), first setting out the general provisions common to all types of conservatory seizures (Articles 1413–1421 JC), and then considering each type of conservatory seizure separately (Articles 1422–1493 JC).
- Title III 'Forced enforcement' ('*Exécutions forcées*' or '*Gedwongen tenuitvoerlegging*'), first setting out the general provisions common to all types of enforcement measures (Articles 1494–1498 JC), and then considering each type of enforcement measure separately (Articles 1499–1675 JC).

For the sake of good order, we note that this chapter is exclusively devoted to the examination of the rules prescribed by Belgian law for the enforcement, in Belgium, of court decisions, and therefore does not examine the few specific provisions in this regard provided for by the UPCA and/or the RoP (unless relevant to underline the application (or not) of a Belgian rule).

§3.02 OVERVIEW OF THE AUTHORITIES EXECUTING ENFORCEMENT IN BELGIUM

In Belgium, any court decision, including a UPC Decision, is enforced through a bailiff and, if necessary, an attachment judge ('*juge des saisies*' or '*beslagrechter*'):

- The bailiff is authorised to carry out all acts necessary for the execution of the measures ordered under the terms of the court decision. Thus, if such measures have been ordered, the bailiff may, subject to compliance with the legal conditions laid down for this purpose, demand and receive payment of the damages, costs and/or procedural indemnity awarded to the successful party (the 'Creditor'), as well as, where applicable, the penalty payments which the court decision would have attached to one and/or other of the measures ordered.

  The territorial jurisdiction of a bailiff is limited. Bailiffs may only act (i.e. serve a judgment and/or perform an act for the execution of the measures ordered) in the judicial district in which they have been appointed.[1] If different acts need to be carried out in different judicial districts (e.g. service of a judgment in one district and an execution act such as a seizure in another), several bailiffs will need to be involved. However, this does not prevent the claimant from using a single bailiff of their choice. The bailiff in question will prepare the act to be performed and the claimant's file and, for the actual execution of the considered act, will call in a territorially competent bailiff.

  The Creditor can call on a bailiff directly, without necessarily going through a lawyer. If the Creditor decides to act through a representative (whether a lawyer or not), the latter must be duly authorised to act in the name and on behalf of the Creditor. In this respect, we note that in Belgium, a lawyer benefits from a 'mandate *ad litem*' by virtue of which they are presumed to have a general mandate from their client for all legal proceedings and all acts relating thereto without having to prove any power of attorney, except where the law requires a 'special mandate' (Article 440 JC).[2] Under this mandate *ad litem*, at the stage of enforcing a decision, a

1. The list of bailiffs appointed in each judicial district can be consulted online on the National Chamber of Bailiffs' website (https://www.huissiersdejustice.be/bailiff – consulted on 6 June 2023).
2. For the sake of good order, we note that foreign lawyers may only practise in Belgium and benefit from the rules applicable to Belgian lawyers, including the principle of the mandate *ad litem* referred to above, if they are duly registered on the lists held by each Belgian Bar that identify foreign lawyers authorised to practise in Belgium. A foreign lawyer who is not registered on one of these lists could thus instruct a bailiff to enforce a UPC Decision in Belgium, but they would then in principle have to provide the bailiff with a power of attorney from their client.

lawyer may instruct a bailiff to have the decision served and/or to execute the decision without having to prove any special power of attorney from their client.

Lastly, the way in which the bailiff can be called upon to enforce a decision (with a view to serving it first - see §3.03[B] - and/or taking effective enforcement measures at a later stage - see §3.04) is relatively informal: the bailiff may be instructed simply by email, or even by telephone (generally followed by a written exchange to confirm the instructions).

- The attachment judge is a specialised judge of the court of first instance. They have a specific mandate and exclusive jurisdiction to hear disputes on the legality or regularity of measures taken to enforce court decisions (see in particular Articles 569, 5°, 1395, 1396 and 1498 JC). However, they are not competent to rule on the merits of the dispute and/or on the merits of the decision whose enforcement is sought and, consequently, they cannot take any measure likely to modify the decision in question (in this respect, see in particular Article 1489 JC).

  Unless the law provides otherwise, the territorial jurisdiction of the attachment judge is determined by the place where the disputed measure(s) (conservatory or 'forced' enforcement - see §3.04[A] and §3.04[B]) is (are) carried out (Article 633, §1, JC). This rule of territorial jurisdiction is of public policy and is justified in particular by the need to centralise proceedings affecting the same property so that the supervision of the attachment judge can be exercised effectively, and respect for any concurrent rights over the same property can be ensured by publicity. Determining the place of (conservatory or execution) seizure does not generally give rise to difficulties for tangible movables and immovables: it is the place where they are physically located. If the assets to be seized are located in more than one judicial district, the various claims may be brought before one and the same judge by a single action before the attachment judge in whose jurisdiction part of the assets to be seized are located. In matters of garnishment (*'saisie-arrêt'* or *'beslag onder derden'*), Article 633, §1, indent 2, JC specifies that the competent judge is that of the domicile of the defendant (the 'Debtor') or, if located abroad or unknown, of the place where the seizure must be carried out.

  The language of the proceedings carried out before the attachment judge will be determined by the linguistic region (French, Dutch or German-speaking) in which their judicial district is located.[3] If the proceedings are to be brought in the Brussels district, the Belgian law of 15 June 1935 concerning the use of languages in judicial matters[4] specifies that the writ initiating the proceedings must be drawn up in French if the defendant is domiciled in the French language region; in Dutch, if the defendant is domiciled in the Dutch language region; in French or in Dutch, at the choice of the claimant,

3. English is not an official language of Belgium. Proceedings cannot therefore be conducted in English, but interpreters may assist parties who do not speak one of the official languages (at the latter's expense).
4. Belgian Official Gazette, 22 June 1935.

if the defendant is domiciled in a commune of the Brussels conurbation or has no known domicile in Belgium. The proceedings will in principle be conducted in the language used for the introductory writ, unless the defendant requests *in limine litis* that the proceedings be conducted in the other language (a request that the judge will rule on before anything else at the introductory hearing and is subject to formal requirements, including the presentation a specific mandate granted to the intervening lawyer in view thereof).

§3.03 GENERAL REQUIREMENTS FOR ENFORCEMENT

[A] Preliminary Remarks

A court decision can be carried out spontaneously/voluntarily by the Debtor as soon as the decision is made. In such a case, the enforcement procedure discussed in this chapter may *a priori* seem to lose some of its relevance since, by definition, the decision in question will in fact have already been enforced.

The measures to be observed prior to the (forced) enforcement of a decision and, more specifically, the service of the decision to be enforced by a bailiff (see the second condition set out in §3.03[B] below) remain, however, of interest even in the case of voluntary compliance as soon as the decision has been delivered, since in Belgium, the service of the decision entails the following effects:

- Service is an essential prerequisite for the payment of the penalty payment which the UPC may have imposed in accordance with its decision. In this respect, Article 1385bis, §3, JC stipulates that no penalty payment can be incurred before the notification of the decision that has declared it, and the Belgian Court of Cassation has recalled that the judge cannot in any case exempt the Creditor of the penalty payments from proceeding with the notification of the decision that has ordered the penalty payments before being able to claim payment.[5]
- The service of the decision sets in motion the legal time limit within which appeal or opposition must be lodged, both against the Creditor (at whose request the decision is served) and against the Debtor (on whom the decision is served), which is useful if the Debtor, although having voluntarily executed the decision, has not expressly and formally waived the right to appeal or oppose this decision. However, this is only of interest for decisions handed down by the Belgian courts since the time limits within which the remedies provided for in the UPCA must be exercised run from the time the decision is served on the parties by the UPC's registry (Rule 6.1.a RoP), and not from the time of any act (such as service by a bailiff as provided for in Belgian law) to be performed in accordance with the national rules of the Member State in which the decision has to be enforced.

5. Cass., 22 June 1989, *Pas.* 1989, I, p.1168.

[B] The General Rules that Must be Observed Before Enforcement

In Belgium, as is apparently the case under the UPCA, a final or preliminary decision made after an adversarial debate is, unless otherwise provided for by law or unless the judge decides otherwise (*ex officio* or at the request of one of the parties), provisionally enforceable as soon as it is delivered, regardless of any appeal (Article 1397 JC).[6]

However, the following conditions must be met before the decision may *actually* be enforced:

- Article 1386 JC stipulates first of all that a decision can only be enforced on production of the 'expedition' (an official, complete and true copy of the decision) or the 'minute' (the original of the decision) 'bearing the enforcement formula' provided for in Article 1 of the Royal Decree of 21 July 2013.[7]

  In the case of a UPC Decision (which, pursuant to Article 71a of Regulation 1215/2012 of 12 December 2012 on jurisdiction and the recognition and enforcement of decisions in civil and commercial matters, is assimilated to a national decision of the Member State in which it is to be enforced), it is reasonable to assume that an official, complete and true copy of the UPC Decision to which the order for its enforcement has been appended in accordance with Article 82.1 UPCA satisfies this first condition.

- Next, Article 1495 JC (read in conjunction with Article 32, 1°, JC) stipulates that (i) the decision to be enforced (bearing the enforcement formula prescribed by the first condition described above) must necessarily be served on the defendant by way of a bailiff's writ, (ii) if necessary accompanied by a translation of the decision to be served in French, Dutch or German, depending on the linguistic region in which it is to be served.[8]

  To fully understand this condition, the following clarifications must be made:

  (i) Since 2020, bailiffs can decide whether to serve their writ (in this case, a UPC Decision) by 'traditional' means (i.e. in person or at the defendant's domicile – Articles 33 to 35 JC) or by electronic means (Articles 32quater/1 and 32quater/2 JC). In practice, the bailiffs seem most often (if not, until now, exclusively) to favour service by traditional means to the defendant itself (in the case of a legal entity: to the organ or agent who is entitled, by law, by the articles of association or by regular delegation, to represent the legal entity in court) or to the defendant's domicile or

6. For the sake of completeness, we note that Article 1398 JC states that 'the provisional execution of the judgment is only at the risk of the party pursuing it' (approximate translation). Thus, if the decision of the court of first instance is annulled on appeal, things will have to be put back in their original state. The Creditor who enforced the first decision will have to reimburse the sums paid to them and may be ordered to pay damages if the Debtor against whom the first decision was enforced can show that they have suffered damage as a result of the provisional enforcement of the first decision.
7. *Belgian Official* Gazette, 21 July 2013.
8. Where necessary, the translation in question does not have to be certified.

residence (in the case of a legal entity: to its registered or administrative office). Electronic service presupposes that an 'electronic judicial address' has first been assigned to the defendant by a competent authority, failing which service may be made to an 'elected electronic judicial address', subject to the defendant's express prior consent to be served in this way for each considered service. To date, from the information available, it appears that an electronic judicial address does not yet exist and that the only way of serving judgments electronically is therefore by means of an elected electronic judicial address.

(ii) The linguistic region in which a judgment is to be served is generally determined by the domicile or residence of the defendant on whom the judgment is to be served (and therefore, as indicated above, by the registered or administrative office in case of a legal entity). As regards the language into which the judgment may have to be translated, Article 38 of the Law concerning the use of languages in judicial matters states that:
  - any judgment that must be served in the French-speaking region must, if it is not already written in French, be accompanied by a French translation;
  - any judgment that must be served in the Dutch-speaking region must, if it is not already written in Dutch, be accompanied by a Dutch translation;
  - any judgment to be served in the German-speaking region must, if it is not already written in German, be accompanied by a German translation;
  - any judgment that is to be served in a municipality in the bilingual Brussels-Capital region must, if it is not already in French or Dutch, be accompanied by a French or Dutch translation.

  The above-mentioned Article 38 then specifies that the foregoing rules may be waived if the party to whom service is to be made has chosen or accepted for the proceedings the language in which the judgment is drawn up. It is therefore reasonable to think that this derogation could also apply in the case of a UPC Decision handed down at the end of proceedings in which the defendant participated and accepted the language.

In the light of the above, it seems clear that, in the case of a UPC Decision, service by the UPC registry in accordance with Rule 6.1.a RoP is not sufficient and that an additional service by a bailiff must take place in order to be able to enforce the decision in Belgium.

- Finally, although this is not strictly speaking a rule to be observed prior to the enforcement of a court decision, we note that no act of enforcement, including the service of the decision, may take place between 9 pm and 6 am, or on a Saturday, Sunday or public holiday, unless expressly authorised by the judge for reasons of imperative necessity (Article 1387 JC).

In addition to the above, we note that Belgian law does not make the enforceability of a decision conditional on the posting of a bond and/or the provision of a guarantee, unless the judge has expressly ordered it. Thus, the enforcement of a UPC decision will only be conditional upon the posting of a bond or the provision of a guarantee if the UPC has expressly ordered it in accordance with Article 82.2 UPCA and Rule 352 RoP.

Finally, and for the sake of completeness, we note that, when the parties are represented by a lawyer, although this is not strictly speaking a legal requirement to be complied with before a court order can be enforced, the Code of Ethics of Lawyers (both from the Dutch-speaking and the French-speaking bar associations) requires the Creditor's counsel to inform the counsel of the opposing party (i.e. the Debtor) of any service or enforcement measure of a court decision, before or at the latest at the time of the envisaged act. A lawyer who does not comply with this obligation to inform the other party beforehand is not only likely to be held liable, but may also be obliged to bear the costs of the service and/or enforcement measure carried out without prior warning.

[C] People Entitled to Request Enforcement

Service of a decision for enforcement is made at the request of the party with an interest in the proposed enforcement.

While it is self-evident that the Creditor has an interest in the enforcement of the UPC Decision in its favour, it is not unreasonable to assume that if the UPC has provided for the application of a penalty payment in its favour (which is possible under the UPCA rules, whereas in Belgium, penalty payments are in principle only decided in favour of one of the parties to the proceedings), in the event of non-compliance with its decision in accordance with Article 82.4 UPCA and Rule 354.3 RoP, it can also be considered as an interested party that can request service of the decision for enforcement and, more specifically in this case, payment of the periodic penalty payments due to it.

As indicated in §3.02, a party with an interest in the enforcement of a UPC Decision does not necessarily have to be represented by a lawyer (Belgian or foreign). They may decide to act alone and directly contact a bailiff to request enforcement of the considered decision, or to do so through a lawyer (foreign or Belgian).

§3.04 OVERVIEW OF PROCEEDINGS

[A] Preliminary Remarks

If the Debtor does not voluntarily comply with a court decision – either directly after it has been given or after it has been served (see §3.03[A]) – the Creditor may obtain enforcement through a bailiff and, if necessary, the attachment judge (see §3.02).

Enforcement is usually used to recover the amounts awarded in the court decision (e.g. damages or procedural indemnity), but it can also be pursued to obtain the performance or abstention from a certain act provided for in the decision, where appropriate, through the recovery of penalty payments specifically provided for to ensure the performance or abstention from the act in question.

As indicated in §3.03[B], before requesting the performance of any enforcement measure, the Creditor must have the decision against the Debtor served by a bailiff. It is only once this first formality has been completed that the Creditor will be able to effectively activate the enforcement measures provided for by the JC in the absence of voluntary compliance by the Debtor. In this respect, a distinction can be made according to the nature of the enforcement measure envisaged (conservatory seizure and so-called 'forced' enforcement) and according to the type of goods seized (movable or immovable). The process to be followed to enforce a court decision, including the different phases of this process, can be illustrated (in a very simplified way) as shown in Figure 1.

For the sake of completeness, we note that in addition to the 'normal' (more common) seizures of (movable or immovable) goods, there are also special rules for the seizure of ships and boats (Articles 1467–1480 and 1545–1559 JC), distress (*'saisie-gagerie'* or *'Pandbeslag'* – Article 1461 JC), revendication seizure (*'saisie-revendication'* or *'Beslag tot terugvordering'* – Articles 1462–1466 JC) and seizure of fruit hanging by the root or the seizure of a stumpage tree (Articles 1529–1538 JC). However, this chapter will not examine these special rules, and will be devoted exclusively to 'normal' seizure measures.

[B] Conservatory Seizures

[1] Purpose and Interest of a Conservatory Seizure

The purpose of a conservatory seizure is to freeze the Debtor's assets – and, in so doing, prevent them from being able to freely dispose of the assets constituting their personal patrimony – for as long as it takes the Creditor to obtain 'sufficient title' to act.

In this case, given the starting point on which this chapter is based (i.e. the UPC has given a decision and this decision is provisionally enforceable – see §3.03[B]), the conservatory seizure is especially of interest in the case of a preliminary decision (i.e. the judge has not yet given a decision on the merits), or if an appeal against the decision (on the merits) is still possible, and the Creditor does not wish to take the risk of (forced) enforcement before being sure of the final and definitive outcome of the proceedings (see footnote 6 – any provisional enforcement is at the Creditor's risk).

[2] Conditions and Procedure for Recourse to the Mechanism of Conservatory Seizure

According to Article 1413 JC, the Creditor may only resort to conservatory seizure 'in cases requiring promptness', i.e. in cases where the Debtor's attitude or financial situation gives rise to a reasonable suspicion that failure to take such a conservatory measure will jeopardise the future recovery of the claim, which would undeniably be prejudicial to the Creditor.

Article 1415 JC then specifies the qualities that the claim for the protection of which the conservatory seizure is sought must have, namely that it must be certain (i.e. not conditional), due and liquid (i.e. its amount must be determined or determinable). The nature and amount of the claim, on the other hand, are irrelevant. In the present case, given that the considered claim is based on a court decision, it is reasonable to assume that these three conditions will necessarily be met, if not at the time when the decision is handed down, at least at the time of its enforcement

Figure 1. Enforcement of court decision

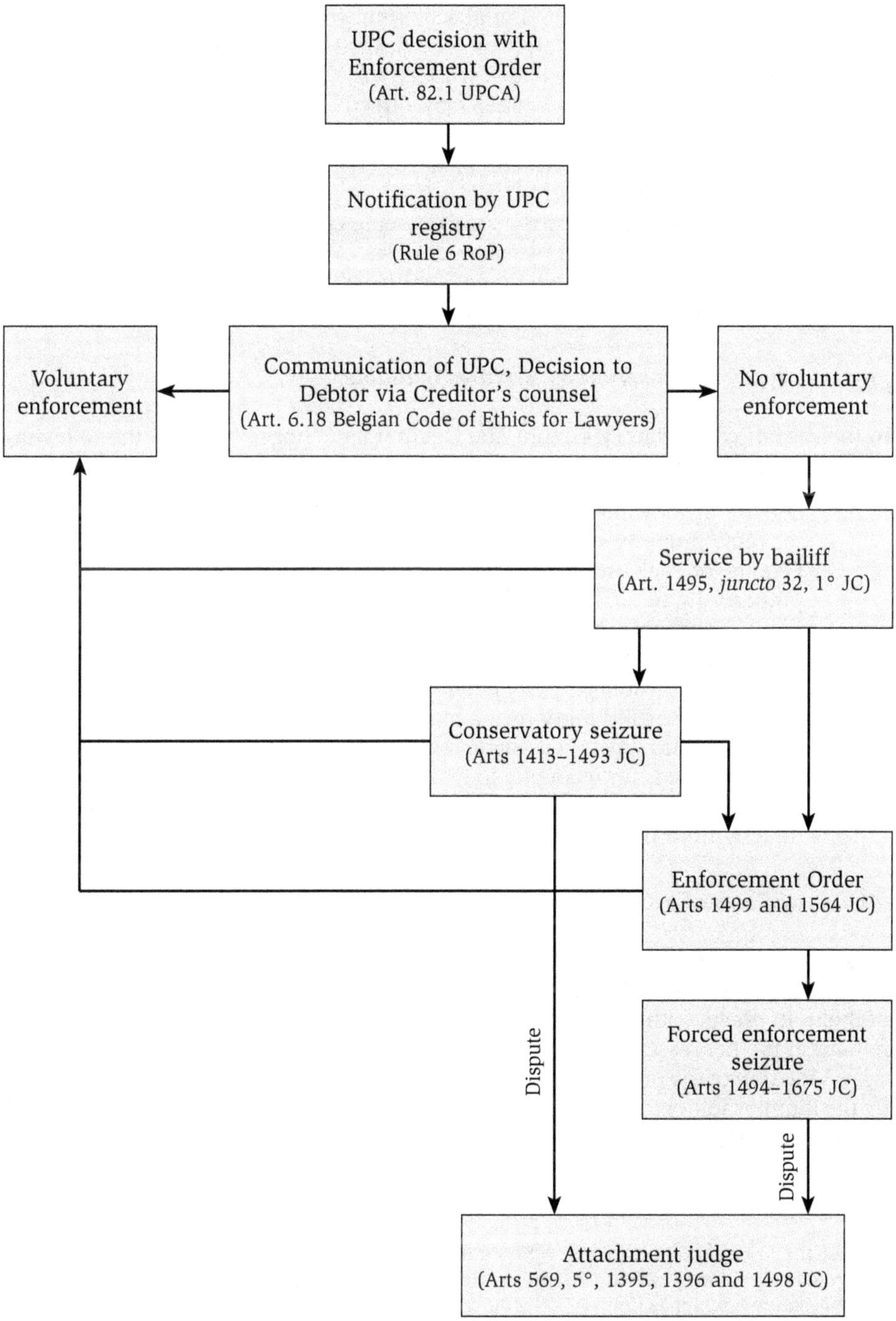

(for example, the UPC may have imposed penalty payments, but the exact amount will have to be calculated at the time of the considered seizure).

Where, as is the case in the initial scenario used as a basis for the drafting of this chapter, the claim whose protection is envisaged is enshrined in a court decision (which is provisionally enforceable - see §3.03[B]), the 'promptness' condition is considered to be met and the Creditor may directly mandate a bailiff to carry out a conservatory seizure on the basis of the decision that has been made without additional authorisation (see Article 1414 JC, which provides that any decision constitutes an enforceable title).

Finally, we note that the conservatory seizure can be converted into (and often precedes) a forced enforcement measure (Articles 1489–1493 JC), simply by serving the enforcement order (*'commandment'* or *'bevel'*) prescribed before effectively carrying out any forced enforcement measure (see footnote 11).

[3] Types of Conservatory Seizure Available

In the case of conservatory seizure, the Creditor can choose between the following three types of measure:[9]

- Seizure of movable goods (Articles 1422–1428 JC): this concerns tangible movable property owned by the Debtor (furniture, vehicles, etc.).
- Seizure of real estate (Articles 1429–1444 JC): this concerns real estate property by nature or by destination owned by the Debtor, as well as the right of usufruct, emphyteusis and surface area of which they are the holder.
- Garnishment (Articles 1445–1460 JC): this is used to attach money and/or intangible movable property (shares, securities, etc.) belonging to the Debtor and held by a third party (e.g. a bank), as well as claims that the Debtor has against a third party (e.g. income owed by their employer). Garnishment is typically used, for example, to seize sums deposited by the Debtor in their bank account directly from the bank or to seize (part of) the Debtor's salary directly from their employer.

[4] Effects of a Conservatory Seizure

As soon as the goods are seized, the Debtor loses the right to dispose of them freely (i.e. to alienate or encumber them), without, however, being effectively dispossessed of them. In practice, there is therefore no change in the factual situation (the goods remain in the possession of the Debtor), but the legal situation is different.

Violation of the prohibition on the Debtor to dispose of their assets is sanctioned by the inopposability to the Creditor (as well as to other creditors who subsequently join the seizure) of acts performed by the Debtor.

9. For the sake of completeness, we note that there are other types of conservatory seizure that are specific to certain situations. However, we do not discuss them in the context of this chapter, which is limited to the most common types of conservatory seizure discussed above.

[5] Duration of Validity of a Conservatory Seizure

The period of validity of a conservatory seizure is three years (excluding possible causes of suspension). In the case of seizure of movable goods and garnishment, the three-year period runs from the date of the bailiff's writ/notification (Articles 1425 and 1458 JC). In the case of seizure of immovable property, the three-year period starts to run from the date of the recording of the seizure in the registers of the mortgage registry (Article 1436 JC).

This period may be extended if there are good reasons for doing so (Articles 1426, 1459 and 1437 JC).

[C] (Forced) Enforcement Seizure

[1] Purpose and Interest of a (Forced) Enforcement Seizure

The (forced) enforcement measures provided for by the Belgian legislator are in a way the corollary of the right to an effective remedy and access to an independent and impartial court, which is enshrined at both the European and Belgian levels. This fundamental right would indeed be particularly illusory if no guarantee could be given that the court decision obtained could effectively take effect when the Debtor does not spontaneously comply with the obligations incumbent upon them under the terms of the considered decision.

[2] Conditions and Procedure for Recourse to the Mechanism of (Forced) Enforcement Seizure

The use of coercive enforcement measures requires first of all an enforceable title for a claim that is certain, liquid and due (Article 1494 JC). As stated in §3.04[B][2], it is reasonable to assume that a UPC decision constitutes an enforceable title within the meaning of Belgian law.

Before taking any steps towards (forced) enforcement, the UPC decision must be served on the Debtor by a bailiff (Article 1495 JC). Any (forced) enforcement measure must also be preceded by an 'enforcement order', which may be served to the Debtor at the same time as the decision or afterwards, but must in any event be served before the planned enforcement seizure is actually carried out (see §3.04[C][3]).[10] This is not only the first act for the actual enforcement of the decision, but also the last warning for the Debtor, who thus has a last chance to avoid the envisaged seizure measures.

Within three working days of the service of the above-mentioned enforcement order, the bailiff must send a notice to the central file of seizure notices ('*fichier central des avis de saisie*' or '*Centraal bestand van berichten van beslag*') in order to allow persons who are legally entitled to do so to take note of the state of enforcement

10. As indicated in §3.04[B][2] *in fine*, the service of the enforcement order alone will transform the conservatory seizure into a forced enforcement seizure, thus dispensing the Creditor from having to renew the procedural formalities already completed at the conservatory stage.

proceedings against the Debtor, as well as the state of indebtedness of the Debtor and the debt-relief processes in which they are involved (Articles 1389bis/1 and 1390, §1, JC).

The goods can only be effectively seized – through the bailiff mandated by the Creditor – at the end of the waiting period referred to in the enforcement order and, of course, in the absence of voluntary execution by the Debtor within that period. If a seizure is actually carried out, then the bailiff will also have to send a notice in this respect to the central file of seizure notices.

[3] Types of (Forced) Enforcement Seizure Available

At the enforcement stage, the Creditor mainly has the choice between the following three types of seizures:[11]

- Seizure of movable property (Articles 1499–1528 JC): this concerns movable property of which the Debtor is the owner and can only be effectively carried out at least one day after the service of the enforcement order referred to in the previous Section (Article 1499 JC).
- Seizure of real estate (Articles 1560–1626 JC): this concerns real estate property owned by the Debtor and can only be effectively carried out at the earliest fifteen days and at the latest six months after the service of the enforcement order referred to in the previous Section, failing which the enforcement order ceases to have effect as of right (Articles 1566 and 1567 JC). The bailiff's writ reporting the enforcement seizure must be recorded in the register of mortgages kept by the competent administration of the place where the seized property is located within fifteen days, failing which the seizure will be considered null and void (Article 1569, §1, JC). The recording of the writ is valid for a period of three years, at the end of which, unless renewed, the seizure automatically ceases to have any effect if the seized property has not been sold (Article 1569, §2, JC).
- Garnishment (Articles 1539–1544 JC – see §3.04[B][3]).

[4] Effects of a (Forced) Enforcement Seizure

The purpose of a forced enforcement seizure is to effectively seize the Debtor's property (and not only to 'freeze' it as in the case of a conservatory seizure) with a view to selling it to enable the Creditor to pay off the amount of their claim from the price of the sale thus made. As in the case of a conservatory seizure, the Debtor loses the right to dispose of their property as soon as it is seized (as from the recording of the seizure or of the enforcement order in the case of a seizure on real estate property – Article 1577 JC). Violation of this prohibition is sanctioned by the inopposability to the Creditor of the acts performed by the Debtor.

---

11. For the sake of completeness, we note that there are other types of enforcement seizure measures specific to certain situations. However, we do not discuss them in the context of this chapter, which is limited to the most common types of enforcement seizures discussed above.

In the case of a seizure of movable goods, the seized goods will be sold at the earliest one month after service of the copy of the report drawn up by the bailiff at the end of the seizure. This period is intended to give the Debtor a last chance to prevent the sale of their goods by voluntarily complying with the decision.

In the case of a seizure of real estate, the Creditor must submit a request to the attachment judge within one month of the recording of the seizure for the appointment of a notary to proceed with the sale of the seized property. The procedures for the sale of the property are laid down by law (Articles 1582 et seq. JC).

The bailiff must draw up a proposal for the distribution of the proceeds of the sale between the various creditors within fifteen days of the sale or seizure of the Debtor's money (Articles 1627 et seq. JC). For this purpose, the bailiff will take into account the order of priority of creditors provided for by law (Articles 1639–1654 JC).

[5] Duration of Validity of a (Forced) Enforcement Seizure

In the absence of specific legal provisions, the period of validity of a forced enforcement seizure of movable goods is ten years, which corresponds to the period of validity of the decision to be enforced (see §3.04[D]).

The enforcement order served prior to the execution of a seizure of real estate property must be followed by a writ of effective seizure within six months (unless possible renewal in the event of suspension of the effects of the enforcement order), failing which it will cease to have any effect (Article 1567 JC). The writ of seizure must be recorded within fifteen days, on pain of nullity, after which the recording will be valid for three years, unless renewed (Article 1569 JC).

[D] Time Limits to Enforce a UPC Decision

In a way, each court decision gives rise to a new action that the Creditor can enforce. This new action is time-barred after ten years, irrespective of the length of the limitation period for the initial claim on which the considered decision is based (Article 2262bis of the Belgian Civil Code). The starting point of this ten-year period is the date of the decision to be enforced.

This basic period of ten years can be extended if causes of suspension or interruption arise. In practice, however, the Creditor must begin performance within the first ten-year period in order to be able to obtain the extension.

§3.05 COSTS

The costs to be borne by a Creditor wishing to enforce a court decision generally consist of the costs of the bailiff (both for the service of the decision to be enforced and for any subsequent act aimed at the effective enforcement thereof) and the costs of the Creditor's counsel who, if necessary, assists them in the steps to be taken (in particular with the bailiff) with a view to the envisaged enforcement.

Only the costs related to the bailiff's intervention are considered as 'enforcement costs' within the meaning of Article 1024 JC and, as such, will in principle be borne by the Debtor against whom enforcement is pursued (and who will therefore have to reimburse these costs to the Creditor if the Creditor has already advanced them).[12]

In accordance with Article 1 of the Royal Decree of 30 November 1976 fixing the tariff of acts performed by baillifs in civil and commercial matters as well as that of certain allowances, the acts performed by bailiffs in the exercise of their functions are remunerated as follows:

- by 'graduated rights' ('*droits gradués*' or '*gegradueerde rechten*'), for the determination of which the acts of the bailiffs are classified in ten classes, according to the amount at stake and which, in the case in point, generally corresponds to the amount of the sentence (Articles 6–8);
- by 'proportional rights' ('*droits proportionnels*' or '*evenredige rechten*'), which correspond to a percentage of the amount at stake depending on the act in question (public sale, distribution by contribution of funds, etc.) (Articles 9–11);
- by 'vacations' ('*vacations*' or '*vacaties*'), allocated in addition to the graduated rights and corresponding to a predetermined amount per hour spent on the performance of the corresponding act, including in particular for the performance of all conservatory and enforceable seizures (Article 12);
- by 'fixed rights' ('*droits fixes*' or '*vaste rechten*'), corresponding to predetermined amounts attributed to the performance of certain specified acts, possibly performed in view of or in addition to acts for which graduated or proportional rights will also be due (Article 13).

Where the acts envisaged are to be performed, at the request of the party and with the authorisation of a judge, on a Saturday, a Sunday, a public holiday, or outside the legal hours (i.e. from 9 pm to 6 am), the rights and the vacations are doubled.

Bailiffs are also entitled to reimbursement of their costs and expenses (copies and extracts of documents drawn up by the bailiffs, translations made by the bailiffs, advances made by the bailiffs to obtain the documents necessary for the performance of certain acts, the costs of removing furniture for an execution sale, etc.) and to travel allowances.

The amounts indicated in the Royal Decree above are adapted annually and can be consulted on the National Chamber of Bailiffs' website.[13]

Bailiffs are ethically bound to apply the legal tariff and may not apply higher tariffs. They are also obliged to clearly identify in their acts the amount of the rights and fees corresponding to the acts performed as well as the details of all related costs, including reimbursement of their expenses (see in particular Article 43, 6°, JC).

12. As indicated in §3.03[B] *in fine*, the costs of the service and/or enforcement that would have been carried out without giving prior notification to the Debtor might be charged to the Creditor's counsel who would not have respected their ethical obligations in this respect.
13. See https://www.huissiersdejustice.be/lhuissier-de-justice/lhuissier-de-justice-son-cout (consulted on 4 May 2023).

§3.06 COUNTERMEASURES ON ENFORCEMENT

The Debtor who is the subject of enforcement measures adopted on the basis of a court decision may refer to the attachment judge any disputes they may have concerning the legality and/or regularity of the measures in question (Articles 1395, 1396, 1420 and 1498 JC). As indicated in §3.02, it should be borne in mind that the attachment judge is in no way competent to hear any disputes that the Debtor may have regarding the decision on the basis of which the enforcement measures in question were taken; any disputes in this respect have to be brought before the judge specifically competent for this purpose, taking into account any appeal or opposition procedures that may still be available. Nor is the attachment judge competent to grant facilities and/or delays in payment if such facilities and/or delays have not been expressly provided for in the decision to be enforced (Article 1333 JC).

With regard to the rules on territorial jurisdiction and the language of proceedings before the attachment judge, we refer to §3.02.

Among the arguments that can be put forward to challenge the enforcement measures directed against them, the Debtor can, among other things, invoke the specific rules of non-seizability prescribed regarding certain movable goods and certain (parts of) revenues of which the Debtor cannot be deprived (see in particular Article 1408, §3, JC). The main purpose of the unseizability of these movables and (parts of) revenues – specifically identified in Articles 1408 to 1410 JC – is to ensure that the Debtor can meet their minimum private vital needs, as well as those of their family, and, where applicable, that they can continue to exercise their professional activity.

The JC does not provide for any specific time limit within which the Debtor must formulate and/or refer their objections to the attachment judge, except in specific cases, such as, in particular, in the event of objections relating to the unseizability of certain movable goods and/or (part of) revenues (in which case the Debtor must, under penalty of forfeiture, have their observations recorded by the bailiff either at the time of the attachment or within five days of service of the first attachment document – Article 1408, §3, JC), or in the case of an enforcement garnishment (where the law prescribes a period of fifteen days to refer the matter to the attachment judge from the time the Debtor is notified of the garnishment made – Article 1541 JC).

Finally, we note that the introduction of an action (by way of a writ of summons) before the attachment judge does not in principle have a suspensive effect (see §3.03[B] on the provisional enforceability of a court decision, which is at the Creditor's risk).

Even though this is not strictly speaking a countermeasure, the Debtor against whom a conservatory seizure is directed in execution of a court decision against which an opposition or an appeal has been lodged may (generally through the intermediary of a bailiff) release the assets to which it relates or prevent the seizure from taking place by depositing the amount of the claim in principal (plus interest and costs) with the *'Caisse des Dépôts et Consignations'*/*'Deposito- en Consignatiekas'* or in the hands of an approved or appointed receiver pending the processing of the pending opposition or appeal (Article 1404 JC).

The advantage of such a 'cantonment' is twofold:

- It allows the Debtor to avoid the seizure of their property or, in the case where enforcement has already been initiated, leads to the stop and lifting of the seizure.
- It protects the Debtor against the Creditor's possible insolvency, in case the initial decision is overturned following an appeal or opposition.

Cantonment is not an absolute right. It is only possible if the judge who made the decision to be enforced has not prohibited it (Article 1406 JC), and it is in any event prohibited when 'it concerns a claim of a maintenance nature' (Article 1404 JC).

§3.07 PARTICULARITIES WITH RESPECT TO SPECIFIC ORDERS

The orders that can be ordered under the UPCA all already exist as such or in an equivalent or at least similar form in Belgium:

- permanent injunctions (Article 63 UPCA);
- order to produce evidence (Article 59 UPCA);
- order to preserve evidence and to inspect premises (Article 60 UPCA);
- freezing orders (Article 61 UPCA);
- preliminary injunctions (Article 62(1) UPCA);
- seizure or delivery up of infringing products (Article 62.3 UPCA);
- conservatory seizure of movable and immovable property (Article 62.3 UPCA);
- recalling from the channels of commerce (Article 64.2.b UPCA);
- depriving the product of its infringing property, Art. 64.2.c UPCA);
- removing from the channels of commerce (Article 64.2.d UPCA);
- destruction (Article 64.2.e UPCA) ;
- communication of information (Article 67 UPCA).

The rules and measures discussed in the previous Sections of this chapter are in principle applicable irrespective of the order to be enforced, subject of course to the fact that the nature and/or the subject matter of the order may influence the choice of the enforcement measure considered.

As indicated in §3.03[B], whatever the order envisaged, any enforcement measure will necessarily have to be preceded by the service of the decision to be enforced by a bailiff, if necessary together with (or followed by) an enforcement order before the court decision in question may actually be executed.

The enforcement measures that can be adopted and executed after the service of the court decision (and, where applicable, of an enforcement order) also generally require a bailiff's intervention. In some cases, the bailiff will possibly be accompanied or assisted by others depending on the specific order to be executed. In this respect, the following measures come to mind in particular:

- An order to preserve evidence or to inspect premises: in Belgium, measures to preserve evidence and/or to inspect premises are often carried out through an expert specifically appointed for this purpose. In the absence of any specification in this respect, it is not impossible that a bailiff alone can carry out the measure in question, but their role will then be strictly limited to observing and recording the facts as expressly referred to in the order to be enforced (whereas an expert is generally given more leeway in assessing the best way to carry out the mission entrusted to them).

- An order to deprive a good of its infringing properties: the removal of the infringing characteristics is in principle carried out by the Debtor or by a third party appointed for this purpose, preferably under a bailiff's supervision.
- A destruction order: the actual destruction of the goods is in principle carried out by the Debtor or by a third party appointed for this purpose, preferably under a bailiff's supervision.

If they consider it useful or necessary, the bailiff may call upon (and be assisted by) the police in carrying out the tasks entrusted to them to enforce a court decision.

Finally, whatever the order envisaged, the attachment judge alone is competent to hear all disputes relating to the measures adopted with a view to its enforcement (see §3.02).

Chapter 4

Bulgaria

Dimitar Batakliev

---

§4.01 SOURCES OF LAW FOR ENFORCEMENT

The Agreement on a Unified Patent Court ('UPC Agreement') is a treaty within the meaning of the Vienna Convention on the Law of Treaties. According to the Bulgarian Constitution, such treaties, when ratified by the Parliament, promulgated and in force for the Republic of Bulgaria, become part of the national law and prevail over the internal legislation in case of conflict. Accordingly, any provisions of the UPC Agreement on the enforcement of Unified Patent Court ('UPC') decisions are situated above the enforcement provisions of national legislation in the order of priority of the sources of law.

The national sources of law governing enforcement of judicial decisions include the Code of Civil Procedure, the Code of International Private Law, and the Code of Tax Insurance Procedure.

The Code of Civil Procedure contains the main set of rules for the enforcement of claims of private nature, recognised by judicial decisions of national and European Union ('EU') courts, the initiation, suspension and finalisation of enforcement and the various enforcement measures available. Claims of a private nature include those arising from intellectual property ('IP') rights, property rights, contractual relations, and so on.

The Code of Civil Procedure also contains rules on the enforcement of measures of a preliminary character imposed by the courts during judicial proceedings such as provisional and protective measures to prevent disposal of assets via a so-called protective procedure.

Measures of preserving evidence and for preventing the entry of infringing products in the channels of commerce as given in Articles 7 and 9(1) of the Enforcement Directive have been introduced in the national legislation for the first time during its transposition specifically in IP legislation. Such measures are prescribed only in the copyright, trademark and design laws and are absent from the patent legislation and carried out in accordance with the protective procedure prescribed in the Code of Civil Procedure. Therefore, Articles 7 and 9(1) of the Enforcement Directive have not been clearly transposed with respect to enforcement of patents. Nevertheless, in the context of patent infringement, such measures apply by analogy.

The Code of International Private Law provides for a procedure for the authorisation of enforcement of decisions of foreign non-EU courts.

The Code of Tax Insurance Procedure contains a set of rules for the enforcement of public debts, including the initiation, suspension and finalisation of enforcement and the various enforcement measures available. Claims of a public nature include penalty payments to courts imposed by a judicial decision or order.

In addition, certain rights and obligations of the bailiffs related to the enforcement procedure are contained in the Law on the Judiciary and the Law on Private Bailiffs.

The national sources of law do not contain specific rules on the enforcement of UPC decisions and orders. The absence of such rules in the Code of Civil Procedure does not preclude the enforceability of UPC decisions. Their enforceability follows directly from Article 82(1) UPCA. However, the absence of national rules creates uncertainty as to some aspects of the enforcement procedure to be followed by the national enforcement authorities.

§4.02 OVERVIEW OF AUTHORITIES EXECUTING ENFORCEMENT IN BULGARIA

The authorities executing enforcement in Bulgaria are the bailiffs. There are three types of bailiffs under the Bulgarian legislation depending on their status and the types of claims they enforce.

State bailiffs and private bailiffs generally enforce claims of a private nature in accordance with the enforcement procedure provided in the Code of Civil Procedure. However, state bodies can entrust them with the enforcement of public debts.

The status of private bailiffs is regulated by the Law on Private Bailiffs. They are private persons entrusted with public functions. Private bailiffs can generally enforce private rights. They can enforce public debts only if so entrusted by state authorities, which includes the courts. A private bailiff can act on the territory of the provincial court of his seat, which covers the territorial jurisdiction of several district courts.

The status of state bailiffs is regulated by the Law on the Judiciary. They are public officials appointed by the Minister of Justice. State bailiffs can enforce claims of a private nature but can also be entrusted by the judiciary to collect its public debts. There must be state bailiffs at each district court – the lowest-level courts in the hierarchy of the judiciary. In district courts without a state bailiff, his functions are exercised by a district judge designated by the president of that court. A state bailiff can act only within the district of the respective court he belongs to. He has a narrower territorial competence compared to a private bailiff who can act on the territory of a provincial court, which covers the territorial jurisdiction of several district courts.

Public bailiffs have the authority to enforce public debts in accordance with the enforcement procedure provided in the Code of Tax Insurance Procedure. There are public bailiffs at each territorial directorate of the National Revenue Agency who can act on the territory of competence of the respective directorate.

§4.03 GENERAL REQUIREMENTS FOR ENFORCEMENT

There are two general requirements for the initiation of enforcement proceedings:

- an enforcement title; and
- an application by the holder of the enforcement title or his successor in title.

To initiate enforcement proceedings in Bulgaria, the party seeking enforcement must normally obtain an enforcement title. In the case of enforcement of orders for provisional and protective measures the enforcement title is in the form of a protective order. In the case of enforcement of a final decision, the enforcement title is in the form of a writ of execution.

The protective order and the writ of execution are judicial acts certifying the right to seek enforcement and authorising enforcement by the enforcement authorities. Therefore, a bailiff cannot carry out enforcement measures in the absence of a protective order or a writ of execution issued by a court. A national court's enforceable decision or order are grounds for issuing a protective order or a writ of execution. Protective orders and writs of execution are issued by the courts. Different courts are competent to issue protective orders or writs of execution depending on the type of the enforceable act.

The Code of Civil Procedure expressly voids the requirement for a protective order or a writ of execution with respect to decisions or orders issued by a court of another Member State of the EU, which are directly enforceable under Regulation (EU) No. 1215/2012. It is sufficient for the applicant to provide the bailiff with a copy of the judgment and a certificate issued pursuant to Article 53 of the Regulation. Therefore, decisions or orders of a court of another Member State are privileged compared to decisions or orders of a national court in that their enforcement does not depend on the issuance of an enforcement title.

UPC is a functional part of the judicial systems of the Contracting Member States as provided in Article 21 UPCA and confirmed by Article 71a of Regulation (EU) No. 1215/2012. It follows that its decisions and orders are enforceable in each Contracting Member State as the decisions of the national courts without being subject to procedures for authorisation of enforcement by national courts. As in the case of decisions and orders of the national courts, however, the requirement for enforcement title will also apply to decisions and orders of the UPC. The order for enforcement of a decision, which is to be appended to the decisions of the UPC pursuant to Article 82(1) clause 2 UPCA, has the role of an enforcement title required by the national law. It is a substitute for the protective order and the writ of execution regulated in the Code of Civil Proceedings. Therefore, a bailiff should not require a protective order or a writ of execution to carry out enforcement measures prescribed in an order for enforcement of the UPC. The bailiff should act on the basis of the order for enforcement.

To avoid uncertainty, the Code of Civil Procedure must be amended to accommodate the direct enforceability of the decisions and orders of the UPC.

§4.04 OVERVIEW OF PROCEEDINGS

[A] Enforcement of Final Decisions and Orders

According to the provisions of the Code of Civil Procedure, enforcement proceedings can be initiated by the holder of an enforcement title by filing an application with a private or state bailiff. It must be accompanied by the enforcement title itself – the order of the UPC.

In the case of decisions and orders of the UPC subject to the additional enforceability requirements of Rule 118.8 of the Rules of Procedure of the Unified Patent Court ('RoP UPC'), the enforcement authority must be satisfied that an enforcement notice and a certified translation of the order, if applicable, has been served on the defendant by the Registry.

Enforcement proceedings concerning fines, fees, and other sums payable to a court can be initiated upon application by the respective court. The UPC would be able to request enforcement of penalty payments ordered by it. As a functional part of the judicial system of Bulgaria, the UPC should be able to entrust the enforcement of penalty payments to a public bailiff, as well as to a private or a state bailiff.

The application can be filed on paper or electronically. A qualified electronic signature is accepted. The use of a locally qualified attorney is not mandatory but is in fact inevitable.

The language of proceedings is Bulgarian. It cannot be expected that the authorities understand and communicate in English.

In the case of enforcement of damages or other payments, the application must indicate the enforcement measures to be carried out by the bailiff, such as the property against which the enforcement is to be directed. If necessary, the applicant can authorise the bailiff to determine the enforcement measures after researching the property of the debtor.

If the application meets the formal requirements, the bailiff sends a notice for voluntary performance to the debtor. The time limit for voluntary performance is two weeks. During this period, the bailiff shall not take any enforcement measures.

Where appropriate, the notice of voluntary performance shall contain information on blocking of assets and seizure of property aiming at preservation and securing of assets on which the entitled person may later levy execution.

In the absence of voluntary performance, the bailiff can proceed with carrying out the enforcement measures provided by the law.

Generally, the enforcement measures taken by the bailiffs are divided into measures for enforcement of claims of pecuniary and non-pecuniary nature. Claims of a pecuniary nature such as claims on damages are enforced by bailiffs in a procedure consisting of steps to freeze and monetise the property of the debtor. The enforcement of claims of a non-pecuniary nature is subdivided into 1) procedures for enforcement of obligations for delivery up of property which takes place by forceful transfer of possession to the claimant; and 2) procedures for enforcement obligations to act or refrain from certain acts which prescribe imposition of penalties when the obligations are breached.

Figure 1.

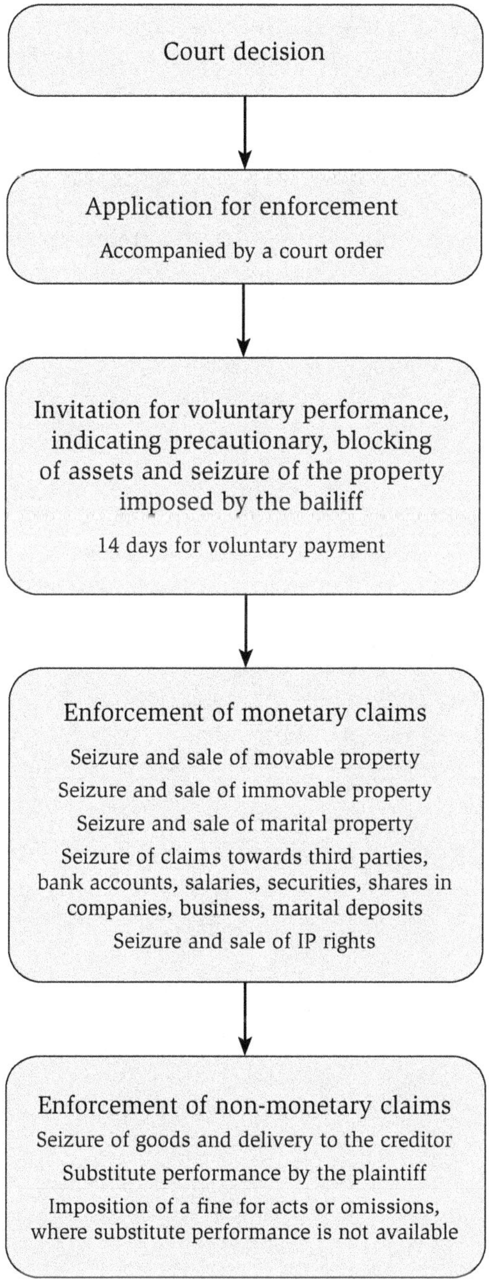
Court decision
Application for enforcement
Accompanied by a court order
Invitation for voluntary performance, indicating precautionary, blocking of assets and seizure of the property imposed by the bailiff
14 days for voluntary payment
Enforcement of monetary claims
Seizure and sale of movable property
Seizure and sale of immovable property
Seizure and sale of marital property
Seizure of claims towards third parties, bank accounts, salaries, securities, shares in companies, business, marital deposits
Seizure and sale of IP rights
Enforcement of non-monetary claims
Seizure of goods and delivery to the creditor
Substitute performance by the plaintiff
Imposition of a fine for acts or omissions, where substitute performance is not available

[B] Enforcement of Provisional and Protective Measures

Enforcement of provisional and protective measures can be initiated by the plaintiff by filing an application with the enforcement authority accompanied by a protective order.

Seizure of movable or immovable property is carried out by a bailiff who notifies the defendant of the imposed measures. Seizure of infringing devices and the sealing of premises is also carried out by a bailiff in a similar way.

Preliminary injunctions are notified by the court to the defendant or the intermediary whose services have been used to infringe a patent.

Figure 2.

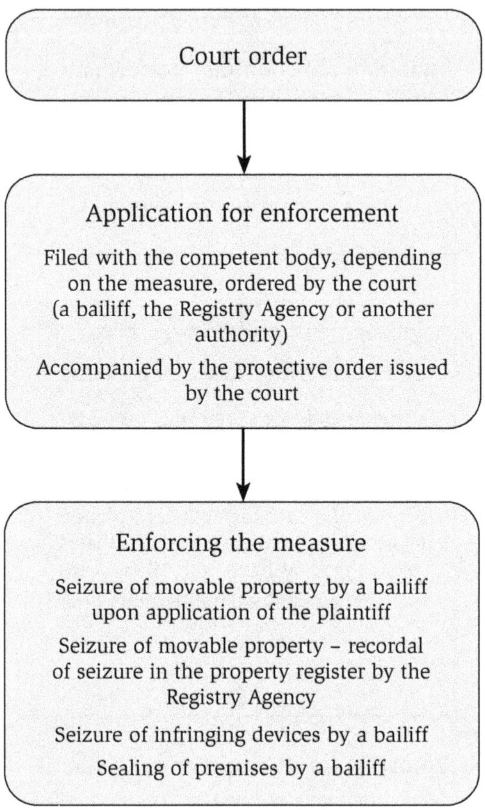

§4.05 COSTS

The costs of enforcement shall be for the account of the debtor. They include bailiff fees, attorney costs, remuneration for expert witnesses and keeping of goods in custody. They can be collected by the bailiff together with the enforcement of monetary claims of the creditor.

The enforcement fees of the bailiff are payable in advance by the enforcement applicant. If not paid by the applicant, the bailiff collects them from the debtor. The legislation provides upper limits of the collectable bailiff fees for small-size debts (currently up to BGN 2,340 (approx. EUR 1,200)). Any fees exceeding the limit shall be for the account of the applicant. The limits are as follows:

Debt size	Limit of fees collectable from the debtor
Up to 10% of the minimum wage	30% of the minimum wage
10–20% of the minimum wage	40% of the minimum wage
20–50% of the minimum wage	50% of the minimum wage
50–100% of the minimum wage	70% of the minimum wage
100–200% of the minimum wage	80% of the minimum wage
200–300% of the minimum wage	90% of the minimum wage

The above limits do not apply to debts exceeding triple the amount of the minimum wage for the country which are fully recoverable.

§4.06 COUNTERMEASURES ON ENFORCEMENT

The party against whom enforcement is sought can appeal the following acts of a bailiff:

- orders imposing fines;
- acts of enforcement directed against unseizable property;
- acts of seizure of movable or immovable property resulting from failure to duly notify the party of the enforcement;
- refusal to re-evaluate property when the initial violation was contested;
- the designation of a third party as a keeper of seized goods in violation of the corresponding rules;
- refusal by the bailiff to suspend, terminate or finalise the enforcement proceedings;
- calculations of the enforcement costs.

Appeals are filed with the provincial court where the enforcement takes place. The time limit to appeal is two weeks from the appealed act, if the party was present or was summoned, or from the date of notifying the act if it took place in absentia.

Appeals are filed via the bailiff who shall notify the other party and allow it to respond in writing within three days. The bailiff then forwards the enforcement case file to the court.

The court shall issue a decision within one month. The decision is final. It shall be based on the materials on file and the evidence provided by the parties. There are no oral hearings unless questioning of witnesses and experts is necessary.

The filing of appeal has no automatic suspensive effect, but the court has discretion to suspend the enforcement proceedings.

The party against whom enforcement is sought can also challenge the substantive grounds for enforcement, i.e., the existence of an enforceable right.

§4.07 PARTICULARITIES WITH RESPECT TO SPECIFIC ORDERS

[A] Permanent Injunctions, Article 63 UPCA

The enforcement of an obligation to refrain from certain actions or to tolerate actions aims at compelling the infringer to comply with the injunction.

Under national legislation, obligations for inaction are enforced by the bailiff by imposing a fine. The bailiff establishes non-compliance with the injunction personally or through witnesses. For every case of established non-compliance, the bailiff shall impose a fine. The bailiff establishes non-compliance at the request of the right holder by drawing up a protocol establishing the breach of the injunction. There is no upper limit of the number of fines imposed. Each fine has a limit of BGN 400 (about EUR 200). By determining the size of the fine, the bailiff shall take into account the economic status of the debtor, its behaviour during the enforcement proceedings, the duration of the breach, and so on.

However, the UPCA contains provisions displacing national law with respect to the enforcement of permanent injunctions. Article 63(2) and Article 82(4) UPCA provide that the UPC may impose a recurring penalty payment payable to the court in the case of non-compliance with the injunction order. Thus, permanent injunctions are enforced by the UPC itself through the penalty payments imposed by the court.

The penalties imposed by the court can be enforced in Bulgaria via the national procedure for enforcement of public debts. Having the status of a national court, the UPC should be able to entrust the enforcement of penalty payments to a public bailiff, as well as to a private or a state bailiff.

[B] An Order to Produce Evidence, Article 59 UPCA

Bulgarian national legislation provides for evidential disadvantages for a party that does not comply with an order to produce documents or objects in its possession. According to the Code of Civil Procedure, at the reasoned request of a party the court can order the adverse party to present a document or object lying in its possession. The court can deem proven any fact for which a party has failed to produce evidence in breach of the order. If a document or object is in possession of a third party, the failure to comply with an order of the court to produce evidence can be sanctioned by penalty.

Similar provisions can be found in the copyright, trademark and design laws aiming to transpose Article 6 of the Enforcement Directive. However, these provisions do not specify any means of enforcement. Therefore, the corresponding rules of the Code of Civil Procedure would apply.

The Rules of Procedure of the Unified Patent Court prescribe similar consequences for the failure to comply with an order to produce evidence. According to Rule 190.7 RoP UPC, if a party fails to comply with an order to produce evidence, the court shall take such failure into account when deciding on the issue in question. The rule thus provides for the possibility of evidential disadvantages during the evaluation of evidence.

According to Rule 190.4b RoP UPC, an order to produce evidence shall specify any sanction which may be imposed if the evidence is not produced according to the order. The Rule is not specific about the possible sanction. If the sanction takes the form of a recurring pecuniary penalty as pursuant to Article 82(4) UPCA, it would be the UPC acting as the enforcement authority of its order.

Consequently, no provisions of national law would apply to the enforcement of an order to produce evidence.

[C] An Order to Preserve Evidence and to Inspect Premises, Article 60 UPCA

The Bulgarian Code of Civil Procedure does not provide for measures for preserving evidence. It provides for a procedure for taking evidence by a court before an action is brought or at a stage of the proceedings on the merits preceding the stage of the taking of evidence. The conditions to admit the taking of evidence are either the risk of loss of a piece of evidence or the risk of complicated collection. Such provisional taking of evidence is possible only at the request of the applicant. The law requires notifying the other party, which has the right to be heard.

The described provisional taking of evidence takes place in accordance with the principle of immediacy, i.e., before a court. The court may allow any legally prescribed means of evidence at this stage, which includes inspection of objects or premises, production of documents, hearing of witnesses or expert opinions, or hearing of parties.

The described national procedure differs from the procedure under Article 60 UPCA in that it is a procedure for the advance taking of evidence by a court, not just for the preservation evidence to be subsequently produced before a court. The Bulgarian Code of Civil Procedure lacks an equivalent procedure.

Measures for preserving evidence as in Article 7 of the Enforcement Directive have been introduced in the national legislation during its transposition specifically in IP legislation. Such measures are prescribed only in the copyright, trademark and design laws and are absent from the patent legislation. Therefore, Article 7 of the Enforcement Directive has not been clearly transposed with respect to patent-related proceedings. In the context of patent infringement, such measures apply only by analogy.

The copyright, trademark and design laws provide for the same procedure of imposing measures for preserving evidence and provisional measures. Carrying out such measures has been entrusted to the bailiffs. In general, the bailiffs do not take part in the process of collecting evidence - their role is in the process of enforcement of rights. However, IP legislation has extended their functions to the process related to collecting evidence.

According to Rule 196.4 RoP UPC, the order to preserve evidence shall specify a person who shall carry out the measure to preserve evidence. According to Rule 196.5 RoP UPC, where appropriate and allowed under applicable national law, the person may be a bailiff or assisted by a bailiff. Bulgarian national law authorises a bailiff to carry out physical seizure of infringing products and materials, and implements and documents by application of the plaintiff accompanied by a protective order issued by a court. Therefore, a bailiff should be able to carry out or assist with the enforcement of an order to preserve evidence issued by the UPC.

Description is regulated in the Code of Civil Procedure as part of the procedure for seizure of property aiming to prevent dealing with assets. It is carried out by a bailiff by producing a protocol indicating the enforcement title, location, detailed description of the object, its value, any objections by the parties and any claiming of rights by third parties. Similarly, description ordered by the UPC can be carried out by a bailiff by preparing a detailed record of the object. The UPC can appoint an expert to draw up the description if special knowledge is required.

Physical seizure of infringing products is specifically envisaged as a means of preserving evidence by the copyright, trademark and design legislation to be carried out by a bailiff. By analogy, this applies to patent cases. The seized objects are removed from the possession of the defendant and placed in the custody of the applicant who cannot use them except for evidential purposes. The measure must be imposed within three days from receipt of the application. The plaintiff is allowed to attend and assist during the seizure. The seizure is performed by drawing up a protocol with detailed description of the seized objects and issuing an order for placement of them in the custody of the plaintiff.

National law prescribes the inspection of premises as a means of taking evidence personally by the members of the court with or without the participation of witnesses or experts. In practice, inspection is frequently conducted by experts as part of the process of producing an expert opinion ordered by the court. In case of resistance, the court may impose a penalty. There are no specific rules on inspection of premises as a means of preserving evidence. However, the Code of Civil Procedure prescribes that for enforcement purposes a bailiff can open the debtor's buildings and search his belongings, home and other premises. State institutions, municipalities, organisations and citizens are obliged to cooperate with the bailiff. The police authorities shall, on request, assist the bailiff when the performance of his functions is being obstructed. A bailiff can also impose a fine on a party creating obstructions. Therefore, a bailiff can perform or assist with inspection of premises as means of preserving evidence ordered by the UPC.

[D] Freezing Orders, Article 61 UPCA

Bulgarian national law does not regulate freezing orders as means of securing a monetary claim as prescribed in Article 61 UPCA. Instead, a precautionary seizure of movable and immovable property with *in rem* effect is available.

A freezing order under the UPCA creates an obligation for the respondent not to remove from its jurisdiction any assets or not to deal in any assets, which is in essence an obligation for inaction. According to the Code of Civil Procedure, such obligations for inaction can be enforced by penalties imposed by the bailiff. However, Article 82(4) UPCA enables the UPC itself to enforce a similar order by imposing recurring penalty payments. As the UPCA provisions prevail over national law, the national procedure would not apply.

[E] Preliminary Injunction, Article 62(1) UPCA

Preliminary injunctions are enforced just as final injunctions. The UPC is competent to impose a penalty in case of non-compliance.

[F] Seizure or Delivery up of Infringing Products, Article 62(3) UPCA

Seizure of products suspected of infringement as a provisional measure is prescribed in the national copyright, trademark and design laws. By analogy it applies also to patent infringement proceedings. The procedure for carrying out such seizure does not differ from the seizure as a measure for preserving evidence.

The seizure is performed by drawing up a protocol with detailed description of the seized objects and issuing an order for placement of them in the custody of the plaintiff.

Delivery up of infringing products requires transfer of control over the infringing product by the addressee to the court or to a person appointed by it. National legislation does not expressly regulate a similar measure. However, its proximity to the seizure means that a bailiff can assist by being appointed by the court for delivery up. Once the bailiff receives control of the product, he shall draw up a protocol and appoint a custodian as in the seizure procedure.

In relation to premises, where infringement takes place, the legislation prescribes the possibility for sealing such premises.

[G] Precautionary Seizure of Movable and Immovable Property, Article 62(3) UPCA

The precautionary seizure of movable and immovable property aiming to prevent potential disposal of assets by the defendant is regulated by the Code of Civil Proceedings. Under Bulgarian legislation such measures have *in rem* effect. The respondent is not only prohibited from disposing of the property but any such dealings made in breach of the prohibition have no effect vis-à-vis the applicant.

The seizure of movable property is carried out by a bailiff. The procedure is the same as in seizure of products as a measure to preserve evidence and seizure of infringing products as a measure to prevent entry into the channels of commerce. The seizure ordered by the court is performed by the bailiff immediately upon receiving the applicant's request by notifying the respondent. The bailiff performs a description of the seized property, evaluates it and places it in custody.

The evaluation of movable property is performed by the bailiff. The bailiff can appoint an expert valuator at the request of one of the parties or *ex officio* if special qualifications are required. It is mandatory to appoint an expert valuator for certain objects such as motor vehicles, ships, and aircraft.

Seized property can be placed in the custody of the debtor who can use it in a manner which does not reduce its value. If the debtor refuses to keep the object in custody or for certain reasons the bailiff decides it must not be in the custody of the debtor, it can be placed in the custody of the applicant or a custodian appointed by the bailiff. The custodian shall keep the object with all due care and give account of the income received from it and the costs for keeping it in custody. If the custodian does not fulfil his duties, the bailiff can change him.

The expert valuator and the custodian, if other than the applicant or the respondent, are entitled to remuneration determined by the bailiff. It must be paid by the applicant in advance. Other expenses for transportation and preservation of the object are also for the account of the applicant.

Seizure of immovable property is notified by the court to the registrar of immovable property, which enters it in the corresponding register. The Registry Agency then notifies the debtor of the recordal of the seizure.

[H] Recalling from the Channels of Commerce, Article 64(2) lit (b) UPCA

The copyright, trademark and design laws provide a coercive measure of seizing infringing products, whether from a particular location or from the channels of commerce. This measure can apply also to patent infringement proceedings. Seizure can be enforced by a bailiff who can physically seize infringing devices. On the other hand, seizure from the channels of commerce entails an obligation for the infringer to retrieve the infringing products from the channels of commerce, which is in essence an obligation to undertake certain acts by requesting possessors to deliver up the infringing devices. The Code of Civil Procedures provides that, at the request of the plaintiff, obligations to act can be enforced by a bailiff by imposing a penalty. However, the UPCA provides for an enforcement mechanism by which the UPC itself imposes a recurring penalty payment under Article 82(4) UPCA. The enforcement mechanism provided under the UPCA would displace the national enforcement procedure.

[I] Depriving the Product of Its Infringing Property, Article 64(2) lit (c) UPCA

Depriving a product of its infringing property as a measure is also not regulated in the national law. The considerations that apply to the measure from the foregoing section would apply here as well. This order can be enforced by the UPC by imposing a penalty as prescribed in Article 82(4) UPCA.

[J] Removing from the Channels of Commerce, Article 64(2) lit (d) UPCA

The same considerations as for recalling from the channels of commerce under Item h) apply. This order is enforced by the UPC by imposing a penalty as prescribed in Article 82(4) UPCA.

[K] Destruction, Article 64(2) lit (e) UPCA

The Bulgarian copyright, trademark and design laws provide for a coercive measure of destruction of infringing products, materials and implements. This order can be enforced by a bailiff by imposing a penalty on the infringer if he does not comply or ordering substitute performance by the plaintiff at the expense of the infringer.

In the procedure before the UPC, the power to order substitute performance lies in the UPC itself (Article 64(3) UPCA). In case the plaintiff is not in possession of the products to be destroyed, he can seek the assistance of a bailiff to perform physical seizure and transfer the possession to the plaintiff.

Alternatively, the order for destruction can be enforced by the UPC by imposing a penalty under Article 82(4) UPCA.

[L] Communication of Information, Article 67 UPCA

The Bulgarian copyright, trademark and design laws authorise the court to order the defendant to communicate certain information to the plaintiff. It is regulated in the context of ongoing proceedings. The information is collected by hearing the defendant as a means of taking evidence. The courts can penalise a party that fails to comply.

In the UPCA, the order to communicate information can be issued in the final judgment. This order is enforceable by the UPC by imposing a penalty under Article 82(4) UPCA.

Chapter 5

Denmark

Nicolaj Bording and Victor Fasmer Henum

§5.01 SOURCES OF LAW FOR ENFORCEMENT

[A] Introduction

The Danish Act on a Unified Patent Court etc. (the 'UPC Act') (in Danish: Lov nr. 511 af 2. juni 2014 om en fælles patentdomstol mv.) provides the legal basis for Denmark's ratification of the bilateral Agreement on a Unified Patent Court of 19 February 2013 ('UPCA').

Section 1 of the UPC Act establishes that the UPCA applies in Denmark.

[B] Section 2 of the UPC Act

The general rule under Danish law is that decisions and orders rendered by a court of a foreign country do not have binding effect and cannot be enforced in Denmark.[1]

To ensure conformity with Articles 35 and 82 of the UPCA, Section 2 of the UPC Act establishes that settlements, decisions and orders under the UPCA are recognised in Denmark and can be enforced with the assistance of the Danish Enforcement Court in the same way and in accordance with the same rules that apply to the enforcement of settlements, decisions and orders rendered by a Danish court. Thus, Section 2 of the UPC Act reflects the obligations on the Contracting Member States as laid down in Article 82 of the UPCA.

Section 2(1) of the UPC Act provides that requests for enforcement of settlements, decisions or orders under the UPCA must be submitted to the Danish

1. Accordingly, any recognition and enforcement of such decisions in Denmark will require that special legal basis have been provided. An example of such special legal basis would be The Brussels 1 Regulation (recast), to which Denmark is a party.

Enforcement Court. The provision further stipulates that such requests are in writing.

Section 2(2) of the UPC Act stipulates that the enforcement of settlements, decisions or orders under the UPCA follows the regulation of the Danish Administration of Justice Act. The preparatory works to the provision specifies that enforcement of UPC settlements, decisions and orders will, inter alia, be governed by the chapters included in Part 4 of the Third Book of the Administration of Justice Act which concern enforcement of monetary claims, claims other than monetary claims and forced sale by order of the court.

Under Danish enforcement law, the primary requirement that must be fulfilled before enforcement of monetary claims and claims other than monetary claims can be carried out is that the creditor has a sufficient legal basis for enforcement, cf. Section 478(1) of the Danish Administration of Justice Act (see §5.02[C] below). With the implementation of Section 2 of the UPC Act, Denmark has ensured that court settlements, decisions and orders of the UPC constitute sufficient legal basis in accordance with Section 478(1).

As Section 2(2) of the UPC Act provides that enforcement of settlements, decisions and orders from the UPC is regulated by the general provisions in the Administration of Justice Act, the enforcement procedure, including the requirements that must be met before a decision, settlement or order of the UPC can be enforced in Denmark, will be identical with the procedure in relation to enforcement of settlements, decisions and orders rendered by a national Danish court. This implies, inter alia, that a request for enforcement of a decision of the UPC must comply with the general principles stipulated in Section 488 of the Administration of Justice Act.

As the Administration of Justice Act already contains provisions allowing the Enforcement Court to grant the enforcement of, for example, a decision on the condition that the judgment creditor provides security or an equivalent assurance to ensure compensation for any possible damage suffered on the part of the judgment debtor, the Danish legislator has found that there is no need to implement specific rules in Denmark establishing that settlements, decisions and orders of the UPC may be enforced on the condition that the judgment creditor provides economic security or an equivalent assurance as otherwise stipulated in Article 82(2) of the UPCA.

Also, in order to ensure compliance with Article 82(4) of the UPCA, Section 2(3) of the UPC Act has been implemented stating that 'If a party does not comply with the terms of an order of the Unified Patent Court, the Enforcement Court can impose penalty fines on that party to be paid to the Unified Patent Court. The individual penalty fine must be proportionate to the importance of the order to be enforced and does not limit that party's right to claim damages or security.' Accordingly, the provision establishes that the Enforcement Court has the authority to impose periodic penalty fines on a party, if the party fails to comply with the conditions of an order of the UPC. Payment of such penalty fines should be paid (by the responsible party) directly to the UPC. This is a deviation from basic principles in Danish law as penalty fines imposed on a party by the court are usually paid to the Government Treasury.

Apart from Section 2 of the UPC Act, no other specific rules have been implemented in Denmark regulating the enforcement of settlements, decisions or orders from the UPC. Accordingly, any enforcement of settlements, decisions or orders from the UPC is regulated by the existing provisions in the Danish Administration of Justice Act, in particular the Chapters of the Act which concern enforcement of monetary claims and claims other than monetary, and will be dealt with in the same way as enforcement of settlements, decisions and orders from national Danish courts.

§5.02 OVERVIEW OF AUTHORITIES EXECUTING ENFORCEMENT IN DENMARK

[A] The Entities Involved in Enforcement

The general courts of Denmark are made up of 24 district courts, the Registration Court, the Maritime and Commercial High Court, the two High Courts (Eastern and Western High Courts), and the Supreme Court, cf. Section 1 of the Administration of Justice Act. The enforcement of monetary claims and claims other than monetary claims are handled by the Enforcement Court, which organisationally is a separate division of the Danish district courts.

Figure 1. Overview of the general courts of Denmark

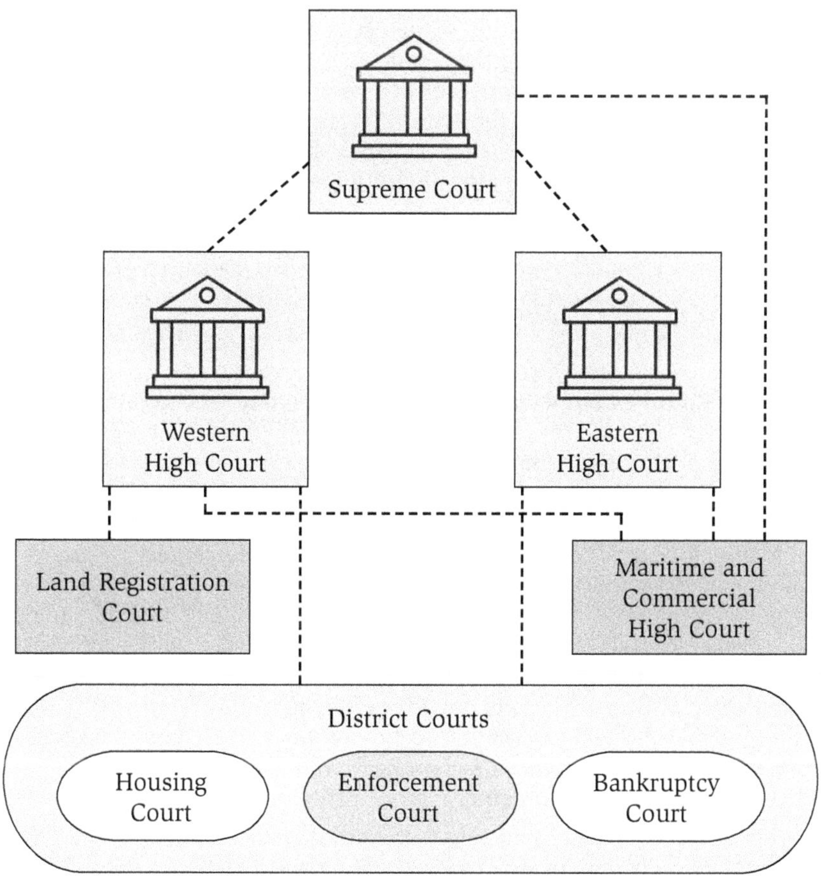

Each district court in Denmark is vested with judicial powers authorising them to handle numerous types of cases such as ordinary civil cases, criminal cases, estate administration cases and enforcement cases. With the aim of being able to efficiently handle these various types of cases, the district courts are divided into different divisions which are each responsible for hearing and deciding cases within the different areas of Danish legislation. One such division is the Enforcement Court.

Typically, the Enforcement Court will be physically located within or near the respective district court to which it organisationally belongs. The district courts are situated in various locations around the country, inter alia, in Copenhagen, Frederiksberg, Aarhus, Odense and Aalborg. Orders of the Enforcement Court are subject to interlocutory appeal and may be appealed to the High Courts. Under specific circumstances, orders of the High Court rendered in interlocutory appeal proceedings may be appealed to the Supreme Court provided that the Danish Appeals Permission Board grants leave to appeal. The requirements for obtaining a leave to appeal to the Supreme Court are rather strict as it is only cases concerning matters of general public importance that may be granted leave to appeal to the Supreme Court.

Appeal of the Enforcement Court's decision does not have suspensive effect unless otherwise provided for in the Administration of Justice Act, either by the court whose order or decision is under appeal or the appellate court, cf. Section 587(1), cf. Section 395 of the Administration of Justice Act.

Accordingly, the general starting point under Danish enforcement law is that an appeal of the Enforcement Court's decisions does not have suspensive effect. It is, however, in the discretion of the Enforcement Court or the appellate court, i.e. the High Court, whether it decides that an appeal should be given suspensive effect. In its assessment of this question, the Court will typically take various factors into account, such as the likelihood that the decision will be overturned in the appeal case and, in particular, the possible consequences associated with both the execution of the claim, but also the possible consequences associated with a postponement of the execution. It is assumed under Danish enforcement law that the courts will not consider giving an appeal suspensive effect unless it is requested by one of the parties.

[B] The Enforcement Court and the Enforcement Proceedings

The Enforcement Court is competent to, inter alia, execute various types of *established* claims, more specifically *monetary claims* and *claims other than monetary claims*, including claims concerning injunctions and orders. The main function of the Enforcement Court is to assist creditors with the enforcement of claims which have already been established for example by a decision or order rendered by a civil court and which have not been voluntarily complied with or fulfilled by the debtor.

The competence of the Enforcement Court is regulated by the Administration of Justice Act, in particular, the provisions included in the Third Book, Part 4, of the Act. Accordingly, unless specifically provided elsewhere, the Enforcement Court must apply the general rules included in that section of the Act when providing assistance with the enforcement of a creditor's claims.

The nature of the enforcement procedure/proceedings differs depending on the type of claim to be enforced. Generally, the rules regulating enforcement proceedings can be found in Chapter 47 of the Administration of Justice Act which regulates enforcement of *monetary claims* and chapter 48 of the Act which regulates the enforcement of *claims other than monetary claims*. Both types of claims are also regulated by the provisions concerning enforcement procedures in general included in Chapters 45–46 of the Act.

The various relevant provisions included in the Administration of Justice Act provide the Enforcement Court with a host of different remedies and measures enabling the Court to assist creditors with the enforcement of their claims. Those remedies and measures include execution, compulsory sale, levy of a security interest on the debtor's assets, and seizure and destruction of infringing goods.

[C] Sufficient Legal Basis for Enforcement

An important requirement for enforcement of a claim which has to be fulfilled in almost all types of enforcement procedures is that the enforcement creditor shall demonstrate a *sufficient legal basis* for enforcement. A common basis for enforcement (which is considered a sufficient legal basis) is decisions or orders rendered by the civil courts. Another type of basis is certain types of legal documents, such as a mortgage or debt instrument signed by the debtor. The underlying idea of this requirement is that any disputes regarding the claim should be settled prior to the initiation of the enforcement proceedings such that the task of the Enforcement Court can be focused on enforcing the already established claim.

It is not the task of the Enforcement Court to decide disputed claims. Disputes concerning, for example, the existence of a claim or the specific scope of the claim must, as a general rule, have been decided by the civil courts before the request for execution is submitted to the Enforcement Court. Therefore, debtors have a rather limited scope of objecting to the correctness of the basis for enforcement during the proceedings before the Enforcement Court. This is, inter alia, reflected in the fact that objections concerning the correctness of a final decision or order constituting the basis of the request for enforcement may not be raised during the enforcement proceedings. However, it is, in all cases, an important task of the Enforcement Court to assess the correct interpretation of the decision forming the basis for the request for enforcement, since the Enforcement Court shall ensure, inter alia, that it is the correct debtor, the correct amount and/or asset that the request for enforcement is directed against.

If a dispute arises between the parties concerning the actual *execution* of the claim in question, the Enforcement Court may under certain circumstances allow presentation of evidence by the parties, but only to a limited extent. Such situations may arise in cases where the parties are in disagreement in relation to exactly what assets of the debtor a security interest may be levied on, or the specific character of the enforcement procedure.

The Enforcement Court is authorised to refuse presentation of evidence which, in the view of the Enforcement Court, falls outside the scope of the proceedings before it. This may be the case if the Enforcement Court finds that the presentation of the necessary evidence in a specific case is of such character and/or scope that it should take place as part of an ordinary civil case.

Apart from the competence to assist with the enforcement of claims already recognised or established by a court decision, order, court settlement or the like, the

Enforcement Court is also authorised to carry out execution without a court order or a similar basis for enforcement in cases concerning, for example, eviction of tenants from tenancies due to failure of payment of rent due. The Enforcement Courts can also assist with enforcement in cases concerning preliminary measures such as arrest of property or the preservation of evidence in the case of infringement of intellectual property rights, cf. section §5.04[D] below.

§5.03 GENERAL REQUIREMENTS FOR ENFORCEMENT

[A] Introduction

Enforcement proceedings are, as mentioned above, dealt with by the Enforcement Court and the proceedings are regulated by the Administration of Justice Act. The relevant parts of the Act establish several requirements which must be observed before the Enforcement Court can assist the creditor with the execution of an established claim.

[B] The Basis for Enforcement

The main criterion that must be met before any enforcement can take place is, as mentioned above, that the creditor can demonstrate that he/she has obtained a sufficient legal basis for the enforcement. This is required both in relation to enforcement of monetary claims and claims other than monetary claims.

Section 478(1) of the Administration of Justice Act stipulates that enforcement may be carried out on the basis of decisions and orders rendered by courts or other authorities provided that relevant legislation has established that their decisions and orders are enforceable. Further, Section 478(2) states that settlements reached under the authorities mentioned in Section 478(1) can also constitute sufficient basis for enforcement. In other words, the provision stipulates that court settlements constitute sufficient basis for enforcement.

As Section 2 of the UPC Act establishes that decisions, orders and settlements under the UPCA are recognised and can be immediately enforced in Denmark, such decisions, orders and settlements will constitute a sufficient legal basis for enforcement under Danish law, cf. Section 478(1)-(2) of the Administration of Justice Act.

Various types of court decisions and orders can be enforced before the Enforcement Court, including decisions establishing, for example:

- monetary claims (e.g. damages for patent infringement);
- injunctions and orders, both permanent and preliminary;
- certain types of declaratory decisions;
- default decisions; and
- decisions concerning the award of legal costs.

It is of course a mandatory requirement for enforcement that the decision, order or settlement is of such nature that it establishes an enforceable claim. Certain declaratory decisions or decisions in which the result is acquittal or dismissal of the case will most often not be enforceable. These decisions are usually only enforceable in relation to the possible legal costs awarded to the winning party. Also, default decisions which have been reopened may not be enforced by the Enforcement Court until the civil court in substantive proceedings has rendered a decision in the (reopened) case.

[C] Proper Forum

Section 487 of the Administration of Justice Act provides that requests for enforcement must be submitted with the proper venue, i.e. the Enforcement Court located in the correct jurisdiction. Typically, requests for enforcement should be submitted with the Enforcement Court located in the jurisdiction of the debtor's domicile or where the debtor has its place of business, cf. Section 487(1) of the Administration of Justice Act. In some cases, it may prove necessary to submit the request with an Enforcement Court located in a jurisdiction where the debtor is (temporarily) staying or has assets located. This latter type of jurisdiction is an alternative to the primary types of jurisdictions mentioned in Section 487(1) and thus only applies if no Enforcement Court is competent under any of the primary types of jurisdictions, cf. Section 487(2) of the Administration of Justice Act.

Upon receipt of the request, the Enforcement Court will examine whether it has been filed before the proper forum. If the court finds that it is not competent in the case because the request has not been submitted with the correct Enforcement Court, it will, in all likelihood, refuse the request for enforcement and inform the creditor of this, cf. Section 489(1) of the Administration of Justice Act.

However, if the Enforcement Court, based on the circumstances prevailing in the specific case, is able to determine what the correct forum is, the court can instead choose to refer the request to that (correct) forum. This is within the Enforcement Court's own discretion.

[D] Written Request for Enforcement

Section 2(1) of the UPC Act stipulates that requests for enforcement of settlements, decisions and orders from the UPC shall be submitted to the Enforcement Court in writing.

Section 488 of the Administration of Justice Act establishes the general requirements applying to all requests for enforcement and states that the request for enforcement must include 'the details necessary for processing the case'.

The basis for enforcement *must* be submitted together with the request. Generally, the creditor should always include the information necessary for the Enforcement Court to decide (i) whether it is the proper venue for the case, and (ii) the information required for the court to schedule the hearing of the case. In practice, this implies that the request must include details required to identify the debtor as well as details required to identify the requesting party, i.e. the creditor. The names of the parties must correspond with the names included in the basis for enforcement. If the basis for enforcement has been assigned to a third party, the requesting party must provide documentation to prove that he/she is the correct creditor, i.e. that he/she is entitled to enforce the claim. It is also advisable that the personal identification number (if one of the parties is a physical person) or the company registration number (if one of the parties is a legal person) is included in the request as this allows the Enforcement Court to search for relevant information on the respective parties in various databases.

All relevant contact details of the debtor, including address, telephone number and email, should also be provided with the request to ensure that the court will be able to serve the request on the debtor. If the request concerns enforcement of a monetary claim, the claimed amount including accrued interest should also be stated in the request for enforcement.

If the creditor is aware that the debtor is represented by an attorney, it is advised that the creditor includes this information in the request and that the request is also sent to the debtor's attorney when bringing the case before the Enforcement Court. There is no requirement under Danish law that the parties are represented by an attorney in enforcement proceedings.

When requesting the Enforcement Court's assistance with enforcement of claims established by a court decision, order or court settlement, the creditor must, as mentioned, also submit copies of the court settlement, decision or order that establishes the claim to be enforced. Such copies should be filed together with the request for enforcement. If the original decision, order or settlement to be enforced is in a foreign language, a certified translation into Danish of the relevant documents must be produced if required by the Enforcement Court. It is in the Enforcement Court's discretion to decide whether it assesses that translations of the submitted documents are necessary.

The language of the enforcement proceedings is Danish. This implies, inter alia, that the formal request for enforcement must be submitted in Danish and that communication with the Enforcement Court during the preparation of the case and the oral hearing will be in Danish. Upon request from a party, the Enforcement Court may allow a party to communicate with the Enforcement Court in a foreign language, including filing written submissions in languages other than Danish for example. However, this requires that the Enforcement Court finds that it has sufficient knowledge of the foreign language to be used and the opposing party does not object to it. Generally, Danish courts' proficiency in English is reasonably good and it is not unusual that the courts allow a party to communicate in English.

Whether the Enforcement Court allows a party to communicate in English, or another foreign language, is entirely in the Enforcement Court's discretion. Thus, a party cannot expect that a request to use a foreign language during the enforcement proceedings is granted.

[E] The Claim Must Be Due

Requests for enforcement cannot be submitted with the Enforcement Court before the execution deadline, i.e. the period by which the debtor shall comply with the order, has expired, cf. Section 486 of the Administration of Justice Act. Court settlements can be enforced when the claim established as part of the settlement is due.

The execution deadline, i.e. the earliest date on which enforcement can be allowed, for decisions is normally fourteen days after the date of the decision, unless it has been appealed before the end of the fourteen-day period. Orders may be executed immediately, cf. Sections 480–481 of the Administration of Justice Act. The deadline for appealing a *decision* is four weeks. If the decision establishing the enforceable claim is appealed more than fourteen days after the date of the decision, but within four weeks of the date of the decision, the Enforcement Court may postpone the enforcement proceedings, cf. Section 502(1)(1) of the Administration of Justice Act. This may be relevant in cases where the Enforcement Court assesses that it will have inappropriate consequences if the enforcement is granted and the decision forming the basis of the enforcement is subsequently overturned during appeal. See also Section 6.2 for further description of Section 502 of the Administration of Justice Act.

Both Sections 480 and 481 of the Administration of Justice Act mention that the term for enforcement may deviate from the general rules if specifically stipulated in the specific decision or order. In light of Rule 354 of the Rules of Procedure of the Unified Patent Court ('Rules of Procedure') which states, inter alia, that decisions and orders of the UPC are enforceable from their date of service, it seems that the date of service will be the relevant date for execution of decisions, orders and settlements from the UPC, although this is currently not clear from the law and it would probably require that the UPC includes a statement to this effect in the decision, order or settlement.

The Rules of Procedure have not (yet) been implemented in Danish law. With Section 1(2) of the UPC Act, the Danish legislator has provided basis for the Minister for Industry, Business and Financial Affairs to decide that the Rules of Procedure should apply in Denmark.

[F] Non-compliance with the Requirements for Requests for Enforcement

If the Enforcement Court finds that the request for enforcement (i) has not been submitted with the correct forum, (ii) does not comply with the requirements stipulated in Section 488, or (iii) that there is not a sufficient basis for enforcement, the court will reject the request and notify the creditor of this, cf. Section 489 of the Administration of Justice Act. Typically, the creditor will then have to correct the deficiencies and submit a new request.

In some cases, the Enforcement Court may also choose to grant the creditor a deadline for remedying any insufficiencies of a submitted request, although the intention is that this exception is only used in situations where the Enforcement Court finds that it is excusable on the part of the creditor that the necessary information and/or documents have not been submitted with the request. Accordingly, the scope of this exception is rather limited. As mentioned above, the Enforcement Court may also refer the request to the correct forum if it is able to determine where that is. Ultimately, it is in the discretion of the Enforcement Court whether it chooses to refer the case or dismiss the request.

[G] Payment of Court Fees

The court fee for requesting enforcement proceedings is DKK 750 and must be paid when initiating proceedings before the Enforcement Court. The regulation of court fees for enforcement proceedings recently underwent a revision. The intention of the revision was, inter alia, to create more clarity in the area. The revision has resulted in an updated regulation according to which creditors now only have to pay a standard fee of DKK 750, irrespective of the value of the claim to be enforced. If the creditor simultaneously requests execution of different types of claims, a separate fee must be paid for each different claim to be enforced. Such a situation may arise if a creditor requests enforcement of a decision establishing a claim for injunction (i.e. a claim other than a monetary claim) as well as enforcement of the legal costs awarded by the same decision (i.e. a monetary claim). In such a scenario, the creditor must pay DKK 1,500 in court fees.

For a general description of the framework concerning costs incurred as a result of enforcement proceedings and possible reimbursement of such costs, see §5.05 below.

[H] The Creditor's Liability for Damages and Compensation for Loss of Reputation or Suffering

Section 505 of the Administration of Justice Act provides that the creditor is liable on a strict liability basis for any (economic) damages suffered by the debtor as a result of the enforcement proceedings if it ultimately turns out that the enforced claim does not exist. Such claim can arise in cases where the creditor has enforced a claim which is based on a patent which is subsequently invalidated by a final court decision or by a final decision from the relevant patent authorities. This strict liability also applies if measures for enforcement have been taken by the Enforcement Court in situations where the relevant requirements for such measures have not been fulfilled and this can be attributed to the creditor, for example because the creditor has provided the Enforcement Court with incorrect or incomplete information concerning the existence or scope of the claim to be enforced.

A claim against the creditor can also include compensation for loss of reputation or suffering on the part of the debtor. The latter may for instance be relevant to claims in cases where the debtor has been detained by the police in connection with the enforcement proceedings.

Claims for damages and/or compensation for loss of reputation or suffering must be raised before the Enforcement Court or the general civil courts no more than *three months* after the date where the debtor was able to raise the claim. A decision by the Enforcement Court under Section 505 is subject to interlocutory appeal. This means that the decision can be appealed to the High Court by one of the parties within four weeks of the date of the decision.

In cases where a substantive presentation of evidence is necessary to determine the possible liability for damages or the proper scope of the debtor's claim, the Enforcement Court may defer the claim to a legal action before the general courts.

[I] Who is Entitled to Request the Enforcement?

Although it is not explicitly stated in the Administration of Justice Act, the general starting point is that it is only the creditor or his/her successor in title who is entitled to request enforcement. This means that, in relation to decisions and orders, it is the winning party, i.e. the party obtaining a legal claim by the decision (judgment creditor), who is entitled to enforce the decision. Usually, it can easily be inferred by or is explicitly mentioned in the conclusion of the decision which of the parties of the case is entitled to enforce the obligations established with the decision.

It is unsettled under Danish law as to whether the Enforcement Court would allow enforcement if requested directly by the UPC. The preparatory works of the UPC Act have not considered the question. However, if a decision or order explicitly mentions that it may be enforced by the UPC, it cannot be ruled out that the Enforcement Court would find that the UPC is entitled to enforce such decision.

§5.04 OVERVIEW OF PROCEEDINGS

As mentioned above in §5.02[B], there are various kinds of enforcement proceedings and they depend on the nature of the enforceable claim. The nature of the proceedings differs depending on the type of claim to be enforced and, in broad terms, the Administration of Justice Act divides enforceable claims into monetary claims and claims other than monetary claims. Because the latter type of claims may be of various nature, the proceedings concerning each different kind of claim will vary. This is reflected in the presentation below. However, since monetary claims and claims other than monetary claims are both regulated by the general provisions in Chapters 45–46 of the Administration of Justice Act, most of the general requirements mentioned in the overview of proceedings concerning monetary claims also apply in proceedings regarding claims other than monetary claims.

[A] General Overview of Enforcement Proceedings – in Cases Concerning Monetary Claims

[1] Submission of the Request for Enforcement

Enforcement proceedings are initiated with the creditor's submission of a request for enforcement to the competent Enforcement Court. The request is typically submitted by letter, secure e-mail or Digital Post. There is no formal requirement under Danish law that the request for enforcement must be signed by the creditor or his/her attorney. It is sufficient that the name of the party and its attorney, if that party is represented by one, is included in the request. It is, as mentioned, not a requirement that a party must be represented by an attorney in enforcement proceedings.

Once the court fee has been paid, the Enforcement Court examines the request in its entirety to assess whether it fulfils the relevant requirements stipulated in the Administration of Justice Act, in particular that it has been submitted at the proper venue and that the creditor has provided sufficient documentation of the basis for enforcement, such as a copy of the court settlement, decision or order establishing the claim for which enforcement is sought.

The Enforcement Court will also examine *ex officio* whether the claim is enforceable. Thus, the Court will examine, inter alia, if the claim is due and that it has not lapsed due to the creditor's passivity or because it has exceeded the statute of limitations. The general period of limitations is ten years if the existence and scope of the claim has been established by a court decision or court order, or by a court settlement.

It is generally assumed that it would require special circumstances before a claim will be considered to have lapsed due to the creditor's passivity. Outside of situations where the claim is unenforceable due to the statute of limitations, the debtor would have to prove that the creditor has acted in such a way that the debtor has been justified in assuming that the claim has been abandoned by the creditor. The evidential threshold in order to succeed in a claim for a creditor's possible loss of rights due to passivity is generally assumed to be rather high.

[2] Summoning the Parties to the Enforcement Hearing

Once the Enforcement Court has established that the request satisfies the formal requirements provided in the Administration of Justice Act, including that the claim is enforceable and has been submitted at the proper venue, the court will summon the parties to an enforcement hearing where the request will be tried, cf. Section 491 of the Act.

The average case processing time varies depending on where the enforcement proceedings are brought and the caseload of the specific Enforcement Court. The type of claim and thus the nature of the enforcement proceedings required will also affect the average processing time. In basic proceedings concerning enforcement of monetary claims, the hearing will often be scheduled within five to six weeks from the date of submission of the request. In proceedings concerning claims other than monetary claims, the average processing time varies, and the processing time of such proceedings is approximately two to four months, depending on the type of claim and the type of enforcement proceeding required.

Once the hearing has been scheduled, the Enforcement Court will notify the parties thereof. In the summons sent to the creditor, the Enforcement Court will indicate whether the creditor (or his/her representative) shall participate in person or whether the creditor can participate over the phone.

The Enforcement Court also ensures that the summons, including the creditor's request for enforcement with appurtenant documents, is served on the debtor. In cases where the Court suspects that the prospects of obtaining coverage for the claim would be significantly weakened if the debtor is notified in advance, the Enforcement Court may decide not to notify the debtor of the proceedings and the date and time of the hearing. In these situations, the Enforcement Court may choose to execute the creditor's claim (*ex parte*) on the condition that the creditor provides security to ensure compensation for any possible damages suffered on the part of the debtor, cf. Section 493(2) of the Administration of Justice Act.

Typically, the hearing will take place at the Enforcement Court's premises, however, the hearing can also be held outside of the Enforcement Court's premises, such as at the debtor's address or place of business, if deemed necessary. In some cases, the hearing can also take place outside normal office hours.

The creditor or his/her representative must participate in the hearing (either in person or over the phone) except if the value of the claim is less than DKK 2,500, cf. Section 492(2) of the Administration of Justice Act. In cases where the creditor or his/her representative is obligated to participate, the Enforcement Court will dismiss the proceedings, cf. Section 492 of the Administration of Justice Act, if the creditor does not participate in the hearing. If the debtor does not participate in the hearing after the summons has been served on him, the Enforcement Court may order that the debtor is taken into custody by the police until the debtor can appear at the hearing.

The enforcement hearing may be held and enforcement carried out even if the debtor does not appear or cannot be reached. In such situations, a security interest may only be levied on certain types of the debtor's assets, for example the debtor's real estate. The Enforcement Court may also decide to postpone the proceedings if the debtor has not appeared at the hearing and the Enforcement Court finds that it is prudent for the further processing of the case that the debtor participates.

[3] The Enforcement Hearing

At the enforcement hearing, the Enforcement Court will usually open the hearing by assessing and calculating the claim indicated in the creditor's request. The claim will typically consist of the principal claim established in the basis for enforcement, such as the decision or order to be enforced, with possible interest accrued. Before execution is carried out, the Enforcement Court will invite the debtor to voluntarily fulfil the creditor's claim.

As the primary method of enforcement used in relation to monetary claims is to levy execution on the debtor's assets to the extent that it covers the creditor's claim (unless payment is made), the main focus of the enforcement hearing - in these types of proceedings - is to clarify whether the debtor owns any assets and, in the affirmative, on which of these a security interest can be levied. Security interests may be levied on cash, movable and immovable property, claims and other assets of the debtor as long as they hold economic value. The levy on the debtor's assets will remain until the debtor has fully satisfied the creditor's claim. The legal effect of a security interest levied on the debtor's asset(s) is that (i) it establishes a charge in favour of the creditor, and (ii) provides the creditor with a right to request that the asset is sold at foreclosure (forced sale by the Enforcement Court), for example if the debtor does not comply with an agreed payment scheme.

Apart from levying security interest(s) on the debtor's asset(s), an arrangement for payment of the debt is typically also made during the hearing. The creditor cannot dismiss payment of the claim by instalments, cf. Section 496(2) of the Administration of Justice Act. If the debtor does not meet the requirements in the agreed payment arrangement, the creditor can subsequently request the Enforcement Court to assist with a forced sale of the assets on which a security interest has been levied. Conversely, as long as the debtor fulfils the requirements in the payment arrangement, forced sale of the assets cannot take place.

During the hearing, the debtor shall provide the information necessary for the Enforcement Court to complete the execution of the creditor's claim, cf. Section 497 of the Administration of Justice Act. This includes, inter alia, an obligation on the debtor to provide information concerning his/her own as well as his/her household's financial situation. If the debtor does not comply with the obligation, the Enforcement Court may decide by order that the debtor should be taken into custody by the police until the debtor is willing to fulfil his/her obligation. Such custody cannot exceed a total period of six months. The debtor may be held liable under the Danish Criminal Code for providing incorrect information to the Enforcement Court.

If proven necessary to carry out the enforcement of the claim at issue, the Enforcement Court may also search the debtor's premises or his/her person, cf. Section 498 of the Administration of Justice Act. If the debtor does not comply with or opposes such search(es), the Enforcement Court is authorised to use the necessary force to carry out the search, including requesting assistance from the police.

[4] Objections Raised during the Enforcement Hearing

Generally, the scope for presenting evidence during enforcement proceedings is limited. In cases concerning enforcement of a claim established by a decision or order, Section 501(2) of the Administration of Justice Act stipulates that the debtor may not raise objections against the correctness of the decision or order during the enforcement proceedings. This implies that the Enforcement Court cannot review the factual and legal assessment that the civil court carried out in the decision or order for which enforcement is sought by the creditor. This means, inter alia, that the Enforcement Court will not review or entertain any objections against the claim raised by the debtor. The debtor would instead have to raise his/her objections during regular court proceedings, such as by appealing the decision which is being enforced (provided that the deadline for appeal has not lapsed) or by requesting the general court to reopen the case. In other words, it is not a task of the Enforcement Court to review and verify the correctness of the decision or order which is sought enforced.

However, some objections against the claim may be raised by the debtor during the enforcement proceedings, for example that the claim can no longer be enforced because the debtor has already fulfilled his/her obligations under the claim. Hence, it is an important obligation on the part of the Enforcement Court to assess whether the claim still exists, including to what extent (scope of the claim) it can still be enforced. The Enforcement Court must therefore always assess whether the debtor has already fulfilled his/her obligations, for example by payment of the debt owed, or whether the claim has lapsed due to passivity or statute of limitations. The debtor may also raise objections in relation to which of the debtor's assets the Enforcement Court can levy a security interest on.

In relation to these types of objections, the Enforcement Court may allow the parties to present evidence in support of their respective arguments.

[5] The Enforcement Court's Decision

After the hearing, the Enforcement Court will send copies of its decision to the respective parties. If the Enforcement Court grants the request for enforcement by ordering a levy of a security interest on the debtor's asset(s), such security interest can, depending on what kind of asset the security interest is levied on, be registered in public registers by the Enforcement Court, i.e. in the land charges register (if security interest is levied on the debtor's real estate) or the motor vehicles securities register (if security interest is levied on the debtor's motor vehicle(s)).

In relation to the costs associated with enforcement proceedings, the general principle is that each party, during the preparation of the case, shall pay the costs associated with any procedural steps taken or requested by that party. At the conclusion of the proceedings, the Enforcement Court will decide whether any of the parties should be awarded legal costs. Unless otherwise agreed between the parties, the unsuccessful party must compensate the opposing party for the costs incurred as a result of the proceedings. This implies that the debtor must pay the court fee

Figure 2. Flowchart of the proceedings before the Enforcement Court

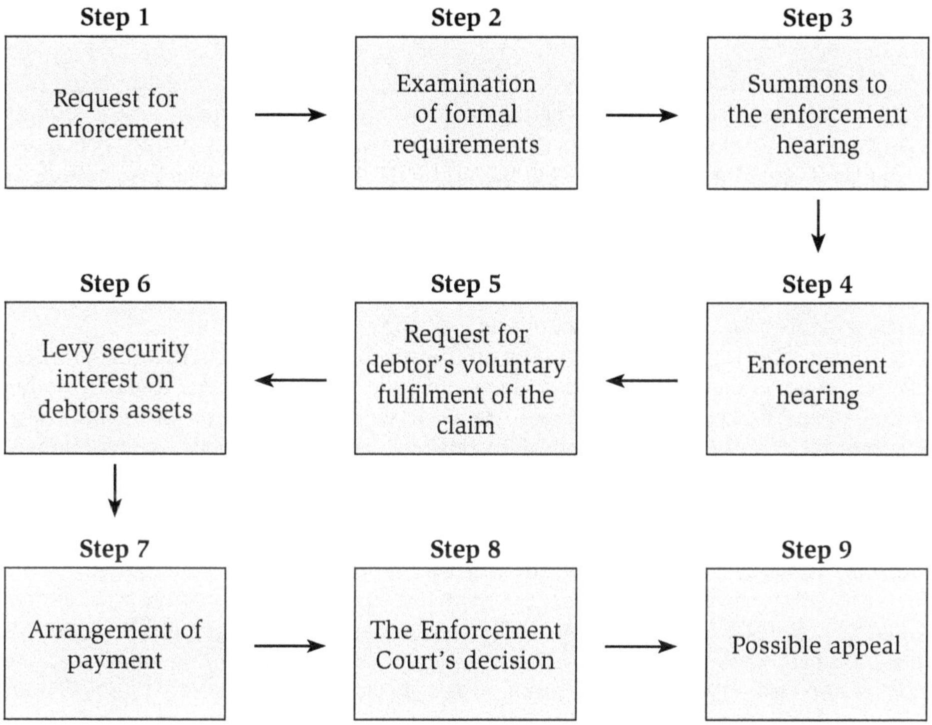

and (some of) the creditor's possible legal fees associated with the enforcement proceedings if the request for enforcement is granted. The debtor may also be ordered to pay other *necessary* costs incurred by the creditor as a result of the proceedings, such as expenses for locksmiths, or transport of the court officer (if the hearing/ proceedings are carried out at the debtor's address or place of business), cf. Section 503 of the Administration of Justice Act.

Decisions of the Enforcement Court are subject to interlocutory appeal and may be appealed to the High Court (having jurisdiction over decisions from the Enforcement Court in question, depending on its physical location in Denmark). The deadline for appeal of the Enforcement Court's decision is four weeks. Decisions concerning security interests having a value of a maximum of DKK 20,000 cannot, as a general rule, be appealed. In special circumstances, the Appeals Permission Board may grant leave for appeal for such decisions concerning small claims. Requests for leave for appeal must be submitted with the Board within four weeks of the Enforcement Court's decision.

As mentioned above in §5.02[A], the general rule under Danish enforcement law is that appeal of the Enforcement Court's decisions in cases concerning enforcement of monetary claims and claims other than monetary claims do not have suspensive effect.

[B] General Overview of Enforcement Proceedings – in Cases Concerning Claims other than Monetary Claims

Enforcement proceedings in cases concerning enforcement of claims other than monetary claims are – to a wide extent – regulated by the same rules and principles as proceedings concerning enforcement of monetary claims. The general overview and the different stages of the proceedings in cases concerning enforcement of claims other than monetary claims thus correspond with the various stages of proceedings concerning monetary claims which are outlined in more detail above.

The description of the regulation on, inter alia, proper venue for the proceedings, the requirements for requesting enforcement, the debtor's access to raise objections to the basis for enforcement etc., similarly applies to proceedings concerning enforcement of claims other than monetary claims.

Accordingly, this section focuses on the specific provisions regulating enforcement of claims other than monetary claims. In addition to the general rules regulating enforcement proceedings (Chapters 45–46 of the Administration of Justice Act), Chapter 48 of the Administration of Justice Act specifically regulates enforcement of claims other than monetary claims. These types of claims concern, inter alia, injunctions or orders, i.e. claims ordering the debtor to carry out an act or refrain from (continuing) to carry out an act. The relevant provisions in this context are Sections 528, 529 and 532 of the Administration of Justice Act.

As is the case with enforcement of monetary claims, it is an absolute requirement that the creditor demonstrates a sufficient legal basis for enforcement, in order for the Enforcement Court to be able to assist with the execution of the claim at issue.

Chapter 48 of the Administration of Justice Act regulates enforcement of, inter alia, *permanent* injunctions and orders. Enforcement of orders concerning *preliminary injunctions* and orders is covered by the regulation in Chapter 57 of the Administration of Justice Act. However, in relation to enforcement of *preliminary orders*, Chapter 48 applies correspondingly, cf. Section 642(2) of the Administration of Justice Act. Therefore, preliminary orders may be enforced under Chapters 48 or 57, whereas orders concerning preliminary injunctions may only be enforced in accordance with the provisions included in Chapter 57 of the Administration of Justice Act.

If the debtor has been ordered to perform multiple or successive tasks/actions or if an injunction can be violated by multiple or successive actions, Section 534 provides that the Enforcement Court can assist the creditor with enforcing his/her claim(s) every time the debtor violates the order or injunction.

[1] Enforcement of Orders Deciding that the Debtor Must Complete or Carry out a Specified Task or Act

Section 529 of the Administration of Justice Act establishes that if the debtor has been ordered to complete a task or carry out an act, the Enforcement Court may allow the creditor to have this task or act carried out by a third party if the debtor has not complied with the order within the date of execution. It is possible to levy a security interest on the debtor's assets to cover the creditor's expenses incurred in relation to the execution of the order. The amount for which a security interest is sought levied must be approved by the Enforcement Court and enforcement of the amount is regulated by the provisions governing enforcement of monetary claims.

If a decision of the UPC has established, for example, that the debtor's infringing products must be removed from the channels of commerce and then be destroyed, the creditor may invoke Section 529 of the Danish Administration of Justice Act and request the assistance of the Enforcement Court in case the debtor has not complied with his/her obligations under the decision. In practice, the decision is enforced by the Enforcement Court granting the proprietor the right to let a third party carry out the task or actions which the debtor has not voluntarily carried out. If the effective enforcement of the decision in question requires access to the debtor's facilities/ premises, the Enforcement Court can search the debtor's premises and use the force necessary, including the assistance of the police, to enforce the creditor's claim, cf. Section 498 of the Administration of Justice Act.

Section 528 of the Administration of Justice Act provides the basis for the Enforcement Court's assistance in relation to enforcement of claims ordering that the debtor must *hand over* movable goods to the creditor.

Depending on the wording of the decision, i.e. the scope of the claim and thus the obligations established by the decision on the part of the debtor, it may prove relevant for the creditor to invoke Section 528 in combination with Section 529 of the Administration of Justice Act. This could be relevant in situations where the decision establishes an obligation on the debtor to hand over subject matter in his/her possession to the creditor, for example all infringing products which are in the possession of the debtor and which are subject to a decision for recall and destruction.

As mentioned above, the Enforcement Court can decide that expenses incurred by the creditor in relation to the enforcement of his/her claim under Section 529 shall be reimbursed by the debtor. Such claims are enforced in accordance with the regulation regarding enforcement of monetary claims. This implies that the Enforcement Court can levy a security interest on the debtor's assets to cover the expenses incurred by the creditor in connection with the enforcement of his/her claim. These expenses will typically consist of the costs associated with the creditor having to employ a third party to carry out the tasks or acts which the debtor has failed to perform and other expenses necessary for the effective enforcement of the claim.

[2] Enforcement of Claims Concerning Permanent Injunctions

Decisions concerning permanent injunctions are enforced under Section 532 of the Administration of Justice Act. The provision provides that if the debtor is prohibited from performing an act, the Enforcement Court must, to the extent possible, prevent the debtor from performing acts which violate the decision. The provision further establishes that the Enforcement Court can destroy anything that has been carried out or produced in violation of the creditor's established rights under the decision. If the debtor violates the injunction more than once, the provision applies and can be invoked every time the debtor violates the decision, cf. Section 534 of the Administration of Justice Act.

[3] Alternative to Enforcement of Claims other than Monetary Claims

Section 533 of the Administration of Justice Act provides that the creditor may (voluntarily) raise a claim for damages instead of invoking the provisions in Sections 528–532 concerning enforcement of claims other than monetary claims. The provision reflects the fact that the creditor is not obligated to receive specific performance of his/her claim, but that the creditor has a liberty of choice in relation to whether he/she prefers to convert his/her claim into a monetary claim rather than to receive specific performance.

Section 533 also applies in situations where enforcement under Sections 528–532 cannot be carried out. In both types of situations, the Enforcement Court must ensure that the damages are calculated in a manner ensuring that the creditor does not suffer any financial loss. The claim for damages is calculated based on the general principles applicable for calculating damages claims under Danish law. In some cases, the Enforcement Court may use expert assistance to undertake this assessment.

A (converted) claim for damages is immediately enforceable under the provisions regulating enforcement of monetary claims.

[C] Enforcement of Preliminary Injunctions and Orders

Enforcement of orders regarding preliminary injunctions and orders are separately regulated by the provisions in Chapter 57 of the Administration of Justice Act, cf. Section 424 (included in Chapter 40) of the Administration of Justice Act, which provides that assistance to maintain or enforce a preliminary injunction or order is provided by the Enforcement Court in accordance with the provisions of Chapter 57.

The central provision of this Chapter is Section 641 which reads:

> 1) If a preliminary injunction or order has been granted under Chapter 40, the Enforcement Court will on request assist the person having obtained the preliminary injunction or order (the applicant) in upholding the injunction or order, including by preventing the injunction from being violated, by ensuring that the order is complied with or by destroying what has been done in violation of the preliminary injunction or order.
>
> (2) The Enforcement Court may seize movable property if it is or has been used in violation of the preliminary injunction or order or if there are particular reasons to believe that it will be used for such purpose.
>
> (3) The seized property is stored at the applicant's expense by the Enforcement Court or any person so authorised by the Enforcement Court.
>
> (4) The Enforcement Court may make a seizure order subject to the applicant providing security for the costs mentioned in subsection (3). In addition, the seizure order may be made subject to an increase in any security required by the Court under Section 415.
>
> (5) If the Enforcement Court issues a seizure order, the Enforcement Court must inform the court having granted the preliminary injunction or order about the order.

The rules on enforcement of preliminary injunctions and orders are very similar to the rules of enforcement of permanent injunctions and orders in Chapter 48 of the Administration of Justice Act, reference is made to §5.04[B].

The Enforcement Court's assistance in relation to enforcement of preliminary injunctions and orders may consist of, inter alia, use of force to ensure that the injunction and/or order is complied with by the debtor, seizure and storage of movable property that is or has been used in breach of the injunction/order and the possible destruction of such infringing property.

The Enforcement Court's assistance with the enforcement of the preliminary injunction and/or order will therefore in many cases be in the form of physical actions necessary for preventing that the injunction is violated or ensuring that the order is complied with. If necessary, in order to effectively enforce the preliminary injunction and/or preliminary order, the Enforcement Court may use the required force and obtain assistance from the police, cf. Section 642(2), cf. Section 498(2) of the Administration of Justice Act.

Naturally, the assistance which the Enforcement Court can provide to ensure the effective enforcement of the preliminary injunction and/or preliminary order must have sufficient basis in the already granted preliminary injunction and order. In other words, the Enforcement Court can only use measures and remedies necessary to prevent or carry out the tasks which are covered by the preliminary injunction or order, and these measures and remedies may only be directed at the preliminary enjoined individuals and/or entities or the individual and/or entities against which the preliminary order is directed.

[1] Enforcement Proceedings Concerning Preliminary Injunctions and Orders

Section 642 of the Administration of Justice Act mentions that a request for enforcement under Section 641 should be submitted at the proper venue, cf. Section 487 of the Administration of Justice Act. This will, as mentioned above, typically be the jurisdiction in which the debtor has his/her domicile or his/her place of business. A copy of the decision establishing the preliminary injunction and/or order must be submitted together with the request for enforcement.

Section 642 also makes reference to many of the rules regulating enforcement proceedings in general (in Chapter 45) and mentions that those rules apply similarly to proceedings concerning enforcement of decisions regarding preliminary injunctions and orders. Accordingly, reference is made to the relevant section above (§5.04[A]) where the various steps in proceedings concerning enforcement of monetary claims, including the requirements that apply in such proceedings, are described in further detail.

The request for enforcement must comply with the general criteria applicable for a writ of summons submitted in regular civil proceedings, cf. Section 642(2), cf. Section 348 of the Administration of Justice Act. This implies that the request must include, inter alia, a detailed summary of the factual and legal circumstances which the request is based upon. The requirements applicable for requests for enforcement of *preliminary* injunctions and orders are therefore more stringent than the requirements stipulated in Section 488 of the Administration of Justice Act (which applies to enforcement of monetary claims and claims other than monetary claims, which, inter alia, includes enforcement of *permanent* injunctions and orders).

If the request for enforcement does not comply with the criteria stipulated in Section 348 and therefore is unsuited to serve as a basis for further processing of the request for enforcement, the Enforcement Court will dismiss the action and notify the creditor of this fact. However, depending on the specific circumstances in the case, the Enforcement Court may decide to grant the creditor a deadline to remedy the deficiencies of the request for enforcement, cf. Section 349, cf. Section 642(2) of the Administration of Justice Act.

[2] Costs and Access to Appeal

Section 643 of the Administration of Justice Act provides that the Enforcement Court decides the issue of legal costs associated with the Enforcement Court's hearing of the case. The decision on legal costs follows the general rules in Chapter 30 of the Administration of Justice Act, which stipulates that the unsuccessful party to the proceedings must, as a general rule, reimburse the costs incurred by the successful party as a result of the proceedings.

The decisions of the Enforcement Court may be appealed under the general provisions of Chapter 53 of the Administration of Justice Act regulating the access to appeal decisions of the Enforcement Court, cf. Section 644 of the Administration of Justice Act. The provision further determines that an interlocutory appeal does not have suspensive effect.

The reference to Chapter 53 of the Administration of Justice Act implies that decisions of the Enforcement Court may be appealed to the High Court within four weeks of the Enforcement Court's decision in the case. Orders concerning legal costs of a maximum of DKK 20,000 cannot be appealed, but the Appeals Permission Board may, in special circumstances, grant a leave for appeal.

[D] Enforcement Proceedings Concerning Preservation of Evidence in the Case of Infringement of Intellectual Property Rights, etc.

It is not entirely clear how an order from the UPC regarding preservation of evidence and inspection of the debtor's premises will be enforced under Danish law. It seems reasonable to think that such orders from the UPC will be treated and enforced in accordance with the procedure for enforcement of claims other than monetary claims. This would imply that the enforcement process for enforcing an order for preservation of evidence by the UPC will be governed by the rules in Chapter 48 of the Administration of Justice Act, see §5.04[B] above. However, in practice, it would seem reasonable to assume that the Enforcement Court, when executing an order from the UPC to preserve evidence and to inspect the debtor's premises, will proceed in a manner similar to the manner applied when the Enforcement Court has decided, in accordance with national Danish rules on the preservation of evidence, that evidence must be preserved. The rules and the general process for enforcing such decisions are therefore described in more detail below.

Under the Danish Administration of Justice Act, the Enforcement Court can grant a search of the debtor's premises if it is rendered likely that an infringement of intellectual property rights has occurred or will occur and there is reason to believe that evidence for the infringement and the extent of the infringement can be found in the premises which are searched. The search is performed with the Enforcement Court's assistance and with the aim of preserving evidence of any existing or contemplated infringements, including the possible extent of such infringements. The enforcement proceedings in these types of cases are independently regulated in Chapter 57a of the Administration of Justice Act.

Searches in these types of proceedings can cover any material considered to be of possible importance in relation to determining whether and to what extent infringements occur or have occurred. This includes, inter alia, subject matter intended for sale, machines and other manufacturing equipment, accounting material, invoices, marketing material and other documents as well as information stored on computer systems and other electronic storage mediums, cf. Section 653(b) of the Administration of Justice Act.

Based on the information provided in the request for enforcement (in the relevant scenario for this book, i.e. in the operative part of the UPC decision ordering the preservation of evidence), the Enforcement Court may appoint an expert as proposed by the applicant - for example an information technology expert in the investigation of information technology systems. In most cases, search and seizure investigations are conducted without prior notification of the debtor as the purpose of the investigation would be defeated if the debtor was notified and had time to destroy or modify possible evidence.

If required to ensure the effective enforcement of the order on preservation of evidence, the Enforcement Court may use necessary force in order to gain access to the debtor's premises. By request, the police will provide assistance to the Enforcement Court in these types of cases.

The creditor must initially pay the costs of expert assistance, storage of seized items, and so on, as well as other expenses pertaining to the search, including expenses for a locksmith. Depending on the complexity of the case, these costs will typically amount to DKK 25,000–75,000.

The investigation itself may typically be completed in two to eight weeks, depending on the complexity of the matter and on the workload in the judicial district where the application is filed. However, additional months of review time should be expected, including to draft and finalise the evidence report.

§5.05 COSTS

The Enforcement Court decides on the question of costs associated with the enforcement proceedings, cf. Section 503 of the Administration of Justice Act.

Several of the general principles regarding the determination and award of legal costs in regular civil cases apply similarly to enforcement proceedings. One of these principles is that the unsuccessful party should, as a main rule, compensate the costs which the successful party has incurred as a result of the proceedings, cf. Chapter 30 of the Administration of Justice Act. The costs awarded will typically cover the expenses for court fees, fees for possible legal representation and other costs necessary for the enforcement proceedings, such as expenses for locksmith and transportation of the court officer (in enforcement proceedings carried out on the debtor's premises).

According to Section 503, the successful party can only expect to have his/her costs for the enforcement proceedings compensated if the Enforcement Court finds that these are reasonable, in light of the nature of the dispute and the extent of the work associated with the proceedings. Only well-founded and reasonable costs are awarded to the successful parties. Accordingly, the Enforcement Court may decide that the successful party should not be awarded costs for the proceedings if the party has caused superfluous procedural steps and/or unnecessary meetings.

In *simple proceedings* concerning enforcement of monetary claims where the debtor has not raised objections against the basis for enforcement or the completion of the proceedings in general, and where the Enforcement Court ultimately grants the enforcement of the claim in question, the total costs awarded to the successful party, i.e. the creditor, will typically consist of the standard 'hearing fees' (in Danish: *mødesalær*) and the court fee which the creditor has paid at the time of submission of the request for enforcement.

The hearing fees are awarded based on a standard fee scale which provides guidance to the Enforcement Court's assessment of legal costs to be awarded to the successful party. The calculation of the hearing fees is determined by the value of the enforceable claim, excluding the court fee, and will only be awarded to parties who have been represented by an attorney at the hearing. The Enforcement Court can of course also order the creditor to pay legal costs to the debtor if the request for enforcement is not granted because the basis for enforcement is insufficient or because the debtor has already fulfilled the claim.

According to the High Court's guiding rates for fees to be awarded in proceedings concerning enforcement of monetary claims, the successful party can expect to be awarded hearing fees in the range of DKK 800–2,700 depending on the value of the enforceable claim. If the value of the claim is less than DKK 2,500, the Enforcement Court will typically not award any hearing fees. The rates included in the fee scale indicate an average standard amount. The character and extent of a specific case may lead to an increase or a reduction in the awarded hearing costs.

In more *complex proceedings* such as cases concerning, inter alia, the preservation of evidence, enforcement of a preliminary injunction or order or cases where a substantive presentation of evidence may be required, the award of legal costs will typically be based on the fee scale applicable for determining legal costs in regular civil cases. The amount awarded in these types of proceedings is normally calculated based on the value of the claim, the extent, complexity and result of the case.

Typically, the Enforcement Court will award legal costs within a range of 50–100% of the amounts listed in the High Courts' scale for fees in regular civil proceedings. As an example, if the value of the enforceable claim is DKK 230,000, the successful party will, depending on the complexity and scope of the case, be awarded between DKK 6,500–43,000 in legal costs. An award of the full rate, i.e. DKK 43,000 in this scenario, is assumed to occur rarely and would require, at least, that the work carried out by the successful party's attorney corresponds with the amount of work necessary for preparing a regular civil action.

The Enforcement Court's decisions concerning costs can be independently appealed to the High Court provided that the costs awarded by the decision exceed an amount of DKK 20,000, cf. Section 584(a) of the Administration of Justice Act.

§5.06 COUNTERMEASURES ON ENFORCEMENT

[A] Appeal of the Enforcement Court's Decisions

Decisions of the Enforcement Court are subject to interlocutory appeal. It follows from Section 584 of the Administration of Justice Act that decisions rendered by an Enforcement Court can, unless otherwise provided by law, be appealed to the High Court having jurisdiction over decisions from the Enforcement Court in question. An appeal must be submitted within four weeks of the conclusion of the enforcement proceedings, cf. Section 586 of the Administration of Justice Act. Appeal of the Enforcement Court's decision will, as a general rule, not have suspensive effect, cf. §5.02[A] above.

However, decisions concerning execution of monetary claims having a value of a maximum of DKK 20,000 cannot be appealed, cf. Section 584(2) of the Administration of Justice Act. If the case concerns matters of general public importance, the Appeals Permission Board may, upon application from one of the parties, grant leave to appeal to the competent High Court. An application for leave to appeal must be submitted within four weeks after the Enforcement Court's decision, cf. Section 584(3) of the Administration of Justice Act.

[B] Possible Postponement of the Enforcement Proceedings

As mentioned above, Section 501(2) of the Administration of Justice Act provides that objections against decisions and orders for which enforcement is sought may not be raised during enforcement procedures. However, Section 502(1) of the Administration of Justice Act stipulates that the Enforcement Court may decide to postpone the enforcement proceedings if (i) the decision for which enforcement is sought has been appealed after the execution date, (ii) if a legal matter, the determination of which will influence the outcome of the enforcement proceedings, is being considered by a court or administrative authority, or (iii) special circumstances apply.

Section 502(2) further determines that if, when taking the creditor's possibility of achieving full satisfaction of his/her claim into consideration, it would be problematic to stay the proceedings, the Enforcement Court may instead order levy of a security interest on the condition that the creditor provides the necessary security, or order that it shall not be possible to proceed with a forced sale of assets on which a security interest has been levied until a particular decision has been made or a specific deadline has expired. Such deadline may be subject to extension.

[C] The Enforcement Court's Possible Liability for Wrongful Decisions

The Enforcement Court is liable for damages on a strict liability basis if the court orders that the debtor should be arrested for non-appearance or that the debtor should be detained for not providing the information required to carry out the enforcement proceedings, if the requirements for rendering these decisions were not fulfilled. A claim against the Enforcement Court may also cover compensation for loss of reputation or suffering on the part of the debtor.

The Enforcement Court will only be held liable for damages suffered by the debtor if the formal criteria for the orders were not fulfilled. This could be the case, for example if the Enforcement Court has ordered that the debtor should be arrested for non-appearance at an enforcement hearing which was based on a claim that had already been paid or otherwise fulfilled and this was something the Enforcement Court should have realised.

Chapter 6

Germany

Oswin Ridderbusch and Christof Augenstein

§6.01 SOURCES OF LAW FOR ENFORCEMENT

In Germany, the enforcement of decisions and orders of the Unified Patent Court ('UPC') is regulated by Article II Sections 19 and 20 of the Act on International Patent Treaties (*Gesetz über internationale Patentübereinkommen*, 'IntPatÜG').[1] These provisions were newly introduced by the Act on the Adaptation of Patent Law Provisions Due to the European Patent Reform (*Gesetz zur Anpassung patentrechtlicher Vorschriften auf Grund der europäischen Patentreform*) of 20 August 2020,[2] which entered into force on the same day as the Agreement on a Unified Patent Court of 19 February 2013 ('UPC Agreement' or 'UPCA'), i.e. on 1 June 2023.

Article II Section 19(1) second sentence IntPatÜG provides that the German legal provisions relating to the enforcement of domestic court decisions shall apply analogously to the enforcement of decisions and orders of the UPC. The corresponding national law regarding the enforcement of domestic court decisions is laid down in Sections 704 to 959 of the Code of Civil Procedure (*Zivilprozessordnung*, 'ZPO').[3] Particularly relevant for the enforcement of UPC decisions are Section 883 ZPO (relating to the surrender of specific movable objects), Section 887 ZPO (relating to fungible acts), Section 888 ZPO (relating to non-fungible acts), and Section 890 ZPO (relating to the enforcement of tolerance and injunction).

1. The complete text of the Act on International Patent Treaties ('IntPatÜG') can be found online at: https://www.gesetze-im-internet.de/intpat_bkg/.
2. The Act on the Adaptation of Patent Law Provisions Due to the European Patent Reform can be found online at: http://www.bgbl.de/xaver/bgbl/start.xav?startbk = Bundesanzeiger_BGBl&jumpTo = bgbl121s3914.pdf.
3. The complete text of the Code of Civil Procedure ('ZPO') can be found online at: https://www.gesetze-im-internet.de/zpo/. A non-binding English translation is provided by the German authorities at: https://www.gesetze-im-internet.de/englisch_zpo/.

Moreover, according to Article II Section 20(1) IntPatÜG, the provisions of the German Act on the Recovery of Judicial Fines (*Justizbeitreibungs*gesetz)[4] shall apply analogously to the recovery of periodic penalty payments ordered by the UPC. Article II Section 20(1) still refers to the Regulation of Judicial Fines (*Justizbeitreibungsordnung*) but what is meant is the Act. It has been renamed.

In accordance with the purpose of the UPC to create a harmonized system for protection of patent rights, the enforcement of the decisions of the Court is also primarily regulated by the UPC Agreement. In line of hierarchy of applicable law (Article 24(1) UPCA) the regulations of the UPCA are applicable with priority. National law only applies if there is no provision in the UPCA.[5] Since the UPCA foresees measures of enforcement for most cases, the scope of application of the national law of the Contracting Member States is very narrow. Basically, it only applies in cases in which a recurring penalty is inappropriate or useless[6] or the UPC might have forgotten to include the threat of recurring penalties.[7]

§6.02 OVERVIEW OF AUTHORITIES EXECUTING ENFORCEMENT IN GERMANY

The Code of Civil Procedure regulates enforcement in a complex system. It foresees not only different provisions with different requirements but also different competent authorities. The possible competent authorities are the bailiff, the enforcement court and the trial court of the first instance.

Which provisions apply and which authority is competent in which case depends in principle on two factors. The first factor is the specific asserted claim. The second factor is what ultimately is to be enforced or, in other words, what is seized or imposed on the debtor (for example movable or immovable assets, receivables, (fungible or non-fungible) acts and omission).

The competent authority for the execution of the enforcement of monetary claims directed against movable assets is the bailiff (Section 808(1) ZPO), i.e., a court-appointed enforcement officer (see Section 753 ZPO). Bailiffs are civil servants but maintain their own independent offices. They act independently when enforcing court decisions and can be directly entrusted by the enforcement creditor (i.e., the party that seeks enforcement). While bailiffs are subject to the supervision of a local court, they are not under the direct management of the respective court (see Section 2 of the Bailiffs Code (*Gerichtsvollzieherordnung*, 'GVO')). There are more than 4,000 bailiffs in Germany.

If the enforcement of monetary claims is directed against claims that the debtor has against a third person, the enforcement court is the competent authority. The enforcement court is also competent for claims against other property rights. The enforcement court is the local court (*Amtsgericht*) in whose district the enforcement debtor (i.e., the party against which a decision or order is enforced) has its residence

4. The complete text of the Act on the Recovery of Judicial Fines ('JBeitrG') can be found online at: https://www.gesetze-im-internet.de/jbeitro/.
5. Tilman GRUR Int. 2016, 409, 417.
6. Augenstein/Kather GRUR 2021, 127, 128.
7. Nieder, GRUR 2017, 38, 39.

or seat or, if the debtor has no residence or seat in Germany, the local court in whose district the enforcement is carried out (see Sections 828(1), (2) and 764(1), (2) ZPO). Within the court, the judicial officer is responsible (see Section 20(1) no. 17 of the Act on Senior Judicial Officers (*Rechtspflegergesetz*, 'RPflG')).

For enforcement measures directed against immovable assets (e.g. real estate), the competent authority for the registration of a security mortgage in the land register (*Grundbuch*) is the land registry (*Grundbuchamt*) at the local court where the corresponding land registry is located (see Section 867(1) ZPO and Section 1 of the Land Registry Code (*Grundbuchordnung*, 'GBO')). For foreclosure and receivership (forced administration), the competent authority is the local court in whose district the property in question is located (see Section 869 ZPO and Section 1(1) of the Act of Foreclosure and Receivership (*Gesetz über die Zwangsversteigerung und die Zwangsverwaltung*, 'ZVG')).

The enforcement of claims other than monetary claims, namely fungible or non-fungible claims or injunctive relief, is governed by Sections 883 et seq. ZPO. If the creditor seeks enforcement of a claim for surrender of movable or immovable property, the bailiff is competent (Sections 883(1) and 885(1) ZPO).

If the creditor seeks enforcement of fungible acts (which can be performed by a third party) or non-fungible acts (which cannot be done by a third party, but only by the debtor), the competent authority for the enforcement is the trial court of first instance (Sections 887(1) and 888(1) ZPO). The trial court of first instance is also competent for the enforcement of injunctions (Section 890(1) ZPO).

Theoretically, in the original meaning of the wording, the UPC is the competent trial court of first instance. But the German legislator has assigned the competence to the regional court (*Landgericht*).

In Article II Section 19(3) sentence 1 IntPatÜG, the German legislator has determined that in cases of enforcement according to Sections 887, 888 and 890 ZPO, instead of the trial court of first instance the regional court in whose district the debtor is domiciled or has its registered office or, in the absence of a residence or registered office in Germany, in whose district the enforcement takes place shall have jurisdiction. According to Article II Section 19(3) sentence 2 IntPatÜG, the provision of Section 143(2) of the German Patent Act (*Patentgesetz*, 'PatG') also applies here, i.e. only one of the regional courts which are designated for patent litigation can be the competent court.

According to Section 143(1) PatG, in the case of German national court decisions, the trial court of first instance in patent disputes is a regional court. Under Section 143(2) PatG, the governments of the Federal States are authorized to assign patent litigation for the districts of several regional courts to one of them. All governments have made use of this possibility. The competence for patent litigation in all German districts has been concentrated on only twelve regional courts, namely the regional courts of Berlin, Braunschweig, Düsseldorf, Erfurt, Frankfurt am Main, Hamburg, Leipzig, Magdeburg, Mannheim, Munich I, Nuremberg-Fürth, and Saarbrücken. Among these twelve courts, the regional courts of Düsseldorf, Hamburg, Mannheim, and Munich I are most frequently seized.

In proceedings before the regional courts, parties must be represented by a lawyer (not a patent attorney) admitted to practise in Germany (see Section 78(1) ZPO). The requirement of being represented by a lawyer also applies to the application of enforcement and the request for appeals in the enforcement proceedings, if the regional court has jurisdiction.

It must be appreciated, however, that the provision of Article II Section 19(3) IntPatÜG can be effective only insofar as it does not curtail the UPC's own competence and, therefore, can only extend to areas in which the UPC itself does not have jurisdiction.

Since the UPC Agreement contains a comprehensive system of enforcement provisions which take precedence over corresponding national law (see Articles 82(3) and 24(1) UPCA),[8] and since the UPC constitutes a common court of the Contracting Member States, which forms part of their judicial system (see Articles 1 and 21 UPCA), the UPC can directly act as an enforcement court in Germany. It can thus be expected that most enforcement measures will be executed by the UPC itself, except for specific measures that require the involvement of a German national court (e.g., making changes to the German land register which is maintained by the local courts) and specific measures that are not prescribed in the UPC Agreement (such as the ordering of coercive detention or coercive punitive detention).

Under Article II Section 20(2) IntPatÜG, the German Federal Office of Justice (*Bundesamt für Justiz*) has been given the authority to collect periodic penalty payments ordered by the UPC (for further details see below under §6.07[A]).

§6.03 GENERAL REQUIREMENTS FOR ENFORCEMENT

Under German national law, the enforcement creditor (i.e., the party that seeks enforcement) generally requires according to Section 750 ZPO an enforcement title (see Sections 704 and 794 ZPO), an enforcement clause (see Section 725 ZPO) and the service of the judgment on the debtor (see Sections 750(1) and 166 ZPO).[9]

8. Note that Article 82(3) UPCA provides that '[w]ithout prejudice to this Agreement and the Statute', enforcement procedures shall be governed by the law of the Contracting Member State where the enforcement takes place. This may be understood as meaning that the national law of the respective Contracting Member State where enforcement takes place shall be applied only insofar as it does not contravene the provisions of the UPC Agreement and the Statute of the UPC. Based on this interpretation, and in accordance with the legal hierarchy reflected in Article 24(1) UPCA, the enforcement provisions of the UPC Agreement should prevail over corresponding national law. The German government draft bill (*Regierungsentwurf*) for the Act on the Adaptation of Patent Law Provisions Due to the European Patent Reform (*Gesetz zur Anpassung patentrechtlicher Vorschriften auf Grund der europäischen Patentreform*) also confirms the precedence of enforcement provisions in the UPC Agreement over corresponding national law (see page 29, first paragraph of the government draft bill, which is accessible online at: https://www.bmj.de/SharedDocs/Gesetzgebungsverfahren/Dokumente/RegE_Anpassung_patentrechtlicher_Vorschriften.pdf).
9. German Federal Court of Justice (FCJ), decision of 21 November 2013 – docket-no.: V ZB 109/13 = NJW-RR 2014, 400 marg. 8.

[A] Enforcement Title

The enforcement title is the document in which the existence of the enforceable claim has been established by the competent body. The enforcement title determines the type and scope of the claim to be enforced, as well as the creditor and the debtor, so that the competent enforcement authority does not have to verify the claim. According to German law there are many types of enforcement title. The most important title is a court's final judgment (see Section 704 ZPO). Other possible enforcement titles are determined in Section 794(1) ZPO (e.g. enforcement order or court settlement). A decision or order of the UPC which, according to Article 82(1) UPCA and Rule 354(1) of the Rules of Procedure of the Unified Patent Court ('RoP UPC'), is directly enforceable in each Contracting Member State, is the enforcement title.

[B] Enforceable Copy with Enforcement Clause (*Klausel*)

For the enforcement of decisions issued by German civil courts, the creditor further requires an enforceable copy of the corresponding decision (see Sections 724 et seq. ZPO), containing an enforcement clause (*Klausel*, see Section 725 ZPO). The enforcement clause is an official notice reading, for example, 'The above copy is issued to the plaintiff for the purpose of enforcement', which is affixed to the copy of the decision by the respective court. In principle, the clerk of the court's office is competent for issuing the enforcement clause. The clause is necessary because the original of the decision remains with the court.

In the case of decisions and orders of the UPC, however, Article II Section 19(1) first sentence IntPatÜG provides that such decisions and orders can be enforced in Germany without the need for an enforcement clause. In the corresponding preparatory materials, the German government explained that an enforcement clause was not necessary because Article 82(1) second sentence UPCA already provides that the UPC shall append an order for enforcement to its decisions.[10]

[C] Service of Decision

Moreover, the enforcement title must have been served on the debtor. The enforcement title must be served prior to the commencement of the execution or at the latest simultaneously with the enforcement (see Sections 750(1) and 166 ZPO). This is in accordance with Rule 354(1) RoP UPC, which provides that decisions and orders of

10. See the government draft bill (*Regierungsentwurf*) for the Act on the Adaptation of Patent Law Provisions Due to the European Patent Reform (*Gesetz zur Anpassung patentrechtlicher Vorschriften auf Grund der europäischen Patentreform*), which explains in connection with the new provision of Article II Section 19(1) IntPatÜG (in English translation):

> A separate clause under German enforcement law is not required. This is because the second sentence of Article 82(1) of the [UPC] Agreement provides that the order for enforcement of a decision shall be attached to the decision of the Unified Patent Court.

The government draft bill is accessible online at: https://www.bmj.de/SharedDocs/Gesetzgebungsverfahren/Dokumente/RegE_Anpassung_patentrechtlicher_Vorschriften.pdf.

the UPC shall be directly enforceable 'from their date of service' in each Contracting Member State.

In this regard, it should be noted that the enforcement title, i.e. the enforceable decision or order of the UPC, must be written in German or must have been translated into German by an authorized translator in order to allow enforcement in Germany (see Article II Section 19(2) IntPatÜG and likewise Rule 118(8) RoP UPC). In the case of an enforceable decision, only the appended order for enforcement should need to be translated into German but not the complete decision. Pursuant to Article II Section 19(2) IntPatÜG, this translation requirement likewise applies to any other documents evidencing that the conditions for enforcement, such as the provision of a security (if ordered by the UPC), have been fulfilled. In practice, however, it should normally suffice to provide a certified translation of the order for enforcement. The costs for any such translations must be borne by the creditor (see Article II Section 19(2) third sentence IntPatÜG).

In addition to the general requirements, other special requirements must be met. There must be no obstacles to enforcement and the general procedural requirements must be met as well.

[D] Issue of an Enforcement Clause

In principle, the clerk who is competent to issue the enforcement clause examines whether the title can be enforced. If he issues the clause, the enforcement authority is bound to this action. However, there are few cases in which the enforcement authority itself must check before enforcing whether the title can be enforced. German procedural law provides three cases. The first case is when the title is suspended, i.e. when the title is dependent on the occurrence of a certain calendar day (see Section 751(1) ZPO). If the title can only be enforced against the creditor's provision of security, the enforcement body must check whether the security has been provided (see Section 751(2) ZPO). If the title is directed to a contemporaneous performance, the competent body must verify whether the performance to be rendered contemporaneously has been offered or whether this is exceptionally dispensable. Pursuant to Section 756 ZPO, this duty of verification applies in the case of enforcement by the bailiff, and pursuant to Section 765 ZPO also if the enforcement court is the competent enforcement body.

[E] Obstacles for Enforcement

If there are procedural obstacles, the enforcement body shall refrain from, suspend, limit or cancel the enforcement. The obstacles to enforcement are primarily governed by Section 775 ZPO. The competent authority must respect the obstacles *ex officio*, but is not obliged to conduct an *ex officio* investigation regarding the existence of such obstacles. Rather, the party invoking the impediment must bring it to the attention of the enforcement body and present the respective decisions or documents.[11] Obstacles to enforcement may exist if the enforceable copy shows that the judgment

11. BeckOKZPO/Preuß, 47th edition (01.12.2022), § 775 marg. 30.

or provisional enforceability has been revoked or that enforcement has been declared inadmissible (Section 775 no. 1 ZPO). Enforcement shall also be suspended if it is clear from the enforceable copy that enforcement has been suspended on a provisional basis (Section 775 no. 2 ZPO).

Finally, the competent enforcement body examines whether the general procedural requirements are met. There are, inter alia, the capacity to sue and to be sued, the capability of a party to participate, and the interest of bringing proceedings.

§6.04 OVERVIEW OF PROCEEDINGS

The course of enforcement proceedings depends on the specific enforcement measure sought by the enforcement creditor. The execution of the corresponding enforcement measure has to be applied for at the competent authority, as set out in §6.02 above. The appointed enforcement authority shall examine *ex officio* whether the above-mentioned conditions (§6.03) are met.

The bailiff who enforces a monetary claim directed against movable assets seizes the movable property by taking possession of the property and thus removing it from the debtor's power of disposal (Section 808(1) ZPO). After seizure the item is to be exploited by the bailiff (see Sections 814 et seq. ZPO). The item shall be disposed of in accordance with Sections 814 et seq. ZPO. Seized money is to be surrendered to the creditor, seized items are to be sold at public auction.

If the enforcement of a monetary claim is directed against a claim, the creditor must sufficiently specify the claim to be seized in its request for enforcement. The competent enforcement court only checks whether the claim could exist, but not whether it actually exists. It then issues an attachment order. The order contains the pronouncement that the specifically designated claim is seized, a prohibition on the third-party debtor to pay to the enforcement debtor and a command to the debtor to refrain from any disposal of the claim. This is regulated in Section 829 ZPO.

There are three different enforcement measures when enforcing monetary claims directed against immovable assets (real estate). First, the creditor can apply to the competent land registry for the registration of compulsory mortgage (see Sections 866, 867 ZPO). Further measures may include an order for foreclosure or receivership of the property by the competent local court (Section 866 ZPO). The foreclosure and receivership are regulated in the ZVG.

In the case of enforcement of a fungible act, the trial court of first instance authorizes the creditor to have the act performed at the debtor's expense (see Section 887 ZPO). In the case of non-fungible acts, enforcement shall be effected by the trial court, at the creditor's request, requiring the debtor to perform the act by way of a penalty payment or coercive detention (Section 888 ZPO).

Enforcement for the surrender of movable property is carried out in such a way that the bailiff takes the relevant property away from the debtor and hands it over to the creditor (Sections 883, 884 ZPO). If the claim is for the surrender of immovable property (real estate), the bailiff shall remove the debtor from possession and give possession to the creditor (Section 885 ZPO).

For the enforcement of fungible and non-fungible acts as well as injunctions, the German law also provides a penalty payment – but not a recurring penalty payment as the UPCA – and provides for the possibility of coercive detention (see Section

890(1) ZPO) if a penalty payment has already been imposed on the enforcement debtor but the debtor cannot pay or the penalty payment is not effective. But since the enforcement of fungible acts and injunctions is in the competence of the UPC (see Articles 62(1), 63(2) and 82(4) UPCA), the corresponding German national law should be applied only insofar as there is no regulation in the UPC Agreement (see also §6.07[A] below). It is possible that besides the ordering of recurring penalty payments, the imposition of coercive detention or coercive punitive detention according to German law constitutes an additional potential enforcement measure, which is further discussed in §6.07[A] and [H] below.

Collecting of the recurring penalty payment, which is likely to be the most important enforcement measure of the UPC, has been entrusted to the Federal Office of Justice (*Bundesamt für Justiz*) under Article II Section 20(2) IntPatÜG. Further details are discussed in §6.07[A] below.

The enforcement of legally established claims and enforceable titles is subject to a limitation period of thirty years (see Section 197(1) of the German Civil Code (*Bürgerliches Gesetzbuch*, 'BGB')).

§6.05 COSTS

In accordance with Section 788 ZPO, the costs for enforcement shall be borne by the debtor (against whom enforcement is sought). However, this applies only to the extent that these costs were necessary, i.e., insofar as the enforcement creditor was entitled to consider them as objectively necessary for the enforcement of its claim at the time when the corresponding costs were incurred.

The enforcement costs must be advanced by the creditor but can be recovered from the debtor concurrently with the enforcement claim (see Section 788(1) ZPO). If several debtors have been sentenced as joint debtors, they are also liable for the enforcement costs as joint debtors (see Section 788(1) ZPO).

The recoverable enforcement costs include the costs of execution and service of the decision (see Section 788(1) ZPO), the costs of preparation (including costs for ascertaining the debtor's whereabouts and for obtaining the necessary documents), and the costs of execution (including lawyer's fees as well as bailiff's fees or costs of the execution court).

The fees of the bailiff are defined by lump sums which are set out in the fee schedule annexed to the Act on Costs of Bailiffs (*Gesetz über Kosten der Gerichtsvollzieher*)[12] and rarely exceed EUR 100.

The recoverable lawyer's fees are limited to a lump sum which is calculated on the basis of the value in dispute (relating to the corresponding enforcement measure) which is set at the discretion of the competent court. Based on the value of the dispute, Annex II to the Act on the Remuneration of Lawyers (*Rechtsanwaltsvergütungsgesetz*, 'RVG') defines a standard fee.[13] For most enforcement measures, the Remuneration

12. The Act on Costs of Bailiffs is accessible online at: https://www.gesetze-im-internet.de/gvkostg/.
13. The complete text of the Act on the Remuneration of Lawyers can be found online at: https://www.gesetze-im-internet.de/rvg/. A non-binding English translation is provided by the German authorities at: https://www.gesetze-im-internet.de/englisch_rvg/.

Schedule (Annex I to the RVG) defines a procedural fee amounting to a rate of 0.3 of the standard fee (fee code 3309), which covers the entire enforcement process. Only in case the lawyer participates in a court hearing or a hearing to provide information on financial status or to record an affidavit, an additional hearing fee amounting to a rate of 0.3 (fee code 3310) is due. In the case of enforcement against real estate, slightly higher lawyer's fees are incurred for enforced auction and receivership, i.e., a procedural fee of 0.4 (fee code 3311) and a hearing fee of 0.4 (fee code 3312). Generally, the own lawyer's fees are normally calculated on an hourly basis and, thus, depend strongly on the complexity of the precise measure.

Conversely, other costs are not recoverable, such as costs of foreign enforcement measures in the enforcement of foreign titles and costs of special appeal proceedings having no origin in the enforcement.

§6.06 COUNTERMEASURES ON ENFORCEMENT

Insofar as the UPC directly conducts the enforcement of its decisions and orders in Germany (see Article 82 UPCA) any countermeasures on enforcement must be sought before the UPC itself, not before the German national courts and authorities.[14] It follows that countermeasures provided under German national law can only be used against enforcement measures taken by German national authorities.

Under German law, the enforcement debtor (i.e., the party against which enforcement is sought) can assert substantive objections regarding the enforcement claim as such by filing an action opposing the enforcement (*Vollstreckungsabwehrklage* or *Vollstreckungsgegenklage*; see Section 767(1) ZPO). The aim of the action opposing the enforcement is to have the enforcement from the title declared inadmissible as a whole and not only individual measures.

Such an action must normally be filed with the trial court of first instance (see Section 767(1) ZPO). In the case of decisions and orders of the UPC, however, Article II Section 19(3) IntPatÜG provides that the trial court (which would be the UPC itself) shall be replaced by the German regional court in whose district the debtor has its residence or seat or, in the absence of a residence or seat in Germany, in whose district the enforcement takes place (see §6.02 above).

The action is justified if, for substantive reasons, the creditor's claim can no longer be enforced. This may be the case, for example, if the debtor fulfils the titled claim or subsequent impossibility of fulfilment occurs. Objections asserted in a corresponding action opposing enforcement can only be based on grounds that arose after the closure of the oral hearing at the UPC that gave rise to the decision to be enforced (see Section 767(2) ZPO). Conversely, the debtor cannot rely on objections that could already have been raised in the oral hearing at the UPC. This limitation, however, does not apply to actions against enforcement under a court settlement agreed before the UPC (see Article II Section 19(4) IntPatÜG).

When filing an action opposing enforcement, the debtor must assert all objections available at that time, or else risks forfeiting the right to assert such objections in a later action (see Section 767(3) ZPO).

14. BeckOK PatR/Augenstein, 27. Ed. 15.01.2023, EPGÜ Art. 82 marg. 48.

As a further defence against enforcement, the debtor can raise objections against the enforcement from the formally valid enforcement title, i.e. the corresponding UPC order, by means of an action opposing the enforcement title (*Titelgegenklage*), which is acknowledged in German case law in analogy to Section 767 ZPO. This action is admissible according to the Federal Court of Justice in cases in which a title is invalid for formal reasons without this being apparent from the content of the title.[15] Meanwhile, the action is also admissible if the ineffectiveness can be inferred from the title for formal reasons (e.g. recognizably indefinite title).[16] It is also admissible if the title itself is invalid for substantive reasons (e.g. invalid declaration of submission in property development contracts).[17] Such an action has to be filed at the same regional court that would be competent for an action opposing enforcement under Section 767 ZPO.

Moreover, the debtor can also raise formal objections against the manner in which enforcement is executed by filing a formal complaint which is referred to as an 'enforcement reminder' (*Vollstreckungserinnerung*; see Section 766(1) ZPO). For example, the debtor may file a reminder in case of deficiencies regarding a security deposit made by the creditor or in order to object to the seizure of an object exempted from attachment. The subject of the 'enforcement reminder' may be the entire conduct of the bailiff and his measures during the enforcement or the enforcement measures of the enforcement court, but the latter being only those orders issued without hearing the person concerned. If, on the other hand, the person concerned is heard, it is a decision of the court. The person concerned can only take action by filing an immediate appeal. The 'enforcement reminder' is not admissible against any enforcement measure of the trial court of first instance. The enforcement reminder could also be admissible if a bailiff refuses to enforce an order of the UPC or to perform a specific enforcement action. This could become relevant, for example, if a bailiff did not recognize an enforceable order issued by the UPC.

Such a reminder must be filed with the competent execution court, i.e., the German local court in whose district the enforcement is to be (or has been) executed (see Sections 766(1) and 764(2) ZPO). The execution court may order that the enforcement be temporarily stayed, with or without the provision of a security, or that it is to be continued only against the provision of a security (see Sections 766(1) and 732(2) ZPO).

A decision of the execution court after an oral hearing which cannot be subject of an 'enforcement reminder' may be appealed by filing an 'immediate appeal' (*sofortige Beschwerde*, Section 793 ZPO). It is also admissible against decisions of the trial court even if it is issued without an oral hearing. Such an immediate appeal has to be filed within an inextensible period of two weeks from the service of the decision with either the execution court or the competent appellate court (see Section 569(1) ZPO).

---

15. Federal Court of Justice, Judgment of 18.11.1993 – docket-no.: IX ZR 244/92 = NJW 1994, 460 (461 f.).
16. Higher Regional Court Koblenz, Judgment of 02.05.2002 – docket-no.: 5 U 245/01 = NJW-RR 2002, 1509 (1510).
17. Federal Court of Justice, Judgment of 27.09.2001 – docket-no.: VII ZR 388/00 = NJW 2002, 138 ff.

After filing, the court that issued the contested decision may remedy the appeal. If it refrains from doing so, the immediate appeal will be decided by the appellate court (see Section 72(1) of the Courts Constitution Act (*Gerichtsverfassungsgesetz*, 'GVG')). If the appellate court grants leave for appeal, a further appeal may be filed before the Federal Court of Justice (see Section 574 ZPO).

A third party affected by enforcement measures against the debtor may also defend itself by filing an action (*Drittwiderspruchsklage*) with the court in whose district the enforcement takes place (see Section 771 ZPO). The purpose of the action is to declare the execution on the specific object inadmissible. The action is justified if the third party has a right that would prevent the sale of the object.

If a judgment that has been provisionally declared enforceable is revoked, the creditor is obligated under Section 717 ZPO to compensate the debtor for the damage that the debtor has suffered as a result of the pre-enforcement or averting of the enforcement. In Germany, it is accepted that if a patent is revoked (or limited) after the enforcement of a final decision based on that patent, the enforcement debtor may claim the restitution of damage payments previously made to the enforcement creditor based on the general legal provisions on unjust enrichment (see Sections 812 et seq. BGB, which may be relied upon by analogous application of Sections 580 no. 6 and 717(3) ZPO).

The UPCA provides similar provisions for compensation in case a decision is subsequently revoked or varied on appeal (Article 82(2) UPCA and Rule 354(2) first and second sentence RoP UPC). Conversely, however, the UPC Agreement does not explicitly foresee any compensation in the case that a *final* decision or order is enforced but the corresponding patent is later revoked or amended in a different action. In such a case, it is merely foreseen that the UPC may order, upon the request of the enforcement debtor, that the respective decision or order ceases to be enforceable (Rule 354(2) third sentence RoP UPC), in which case any ongoing enforcement activities by German national authorities must also be terminated (see Sections 775 no. 1 and 776 ZPO). If, however, the UPC Agreement is interpreted as not having regulated the possibility of claiming restitution under such circumstances in the first place, it could be argued that the corresponding national law should be applicable.

§6.07 PARTICULARITIES WITH RESPECT TO SPECIFIC ORDERS

All of the specific orders addressed in the following can be imposed by the UPC and enforced by the threat and order of recurring penalty payments in accordance with Article 82(4) UPCA. The following examples present respective cases where German law applies.

[A] Permanent Injunctions, Article 63 UPCA

Permanent injunctions are enforced primarily by the threat and imposition of recurring penalty payments by the UPC (see Articles 63(2) and 82(4) UPCA as well as Rule 354(3), (4) RoP UPC), so there should be no room for the application of German national law on the ordering of penalty payments.

The actual collection of penalty payments, however, is governed by national law. In Germany, the Federal Office of Justice (*Bundesamt für Justiz*) has been given the authority to collect recurring penalty payments ordered by the UPC (see Article II Section 20(2) IntPatÜG). The Federal Office of Justice can act *ex officio* on the basis of a corresponding order from the UPC, without any need for the involvement of a German national court.

As established in Article II Section 20(1) IntPatÜG, such collection is conducted in accordance with the Act on the Recovery of Judicial Fines (*Justizbeitreibungsgesetz*, 'JBeitrG'). For the collection of penalty payments, the Act on the Recovery of Judicial Fines mainly refers to the Code of Civil Procedure (see Section 6(1) no. 1 JBeitrG), whereby the creditor is replaced by the executing authority (*Vollstreckungsbehörde*; see Section 6(2) JBeitrG) and the bailiff is replaced by the judicial enforcement officer (*Vollziehungsbeamter* or *Vollstreckungsbeamter*; see Section 6(3) JBeitrG). The Federal Office of Justice as the executing authority can thus employ all execution measures provided in the Code of Civil Procedure.

A permanent injunction according to German national enforcement law is enforced pursuant to Section 890 ZPO. The provision also provides a penalty payment - but not a recurring penalty payment - and it additionally provides for the possibility of coercive detention (see Section 890(1) ZPO). A coercive detention can be ordered if a penalty payment has already been imposed on the enforcement debtor but the debtor cannot pay or the penalty payment is not effective. Arguably, since there are no corresponding provisions in the UPC Agreement (which would take precedence over national law), it follows that the respective German national law should apply in accordance with Article 82(3) UPCA. Consequently, coercive detention should, in principle, be available as a further enforcement measure if the recurring penalty payment turns out not to be effective.

Coercive detention must be applied for at, and be ordered by, the trial court of first instance, which would normally be the UPC. According to Article II Section 19(3) IntPatÜG, the competent court for the imposition of coercive detention should be a regional court which is competent for patent litigation and in whose district the debtor has its residence or seat or, in the absence of a residence or seat in Germany, in whose district the enforcement takes place (see above in §6.02). Since detention is a drastic intervention in the personal rights of the affected individual(s) and since the UPC Agreement does not bestow the competence to order this measure on the UPC, it seems reasonable that detention can only be imposed on the enforcement debtor by a German domestic court as such courts are more experienced with ordering this measure, and there is, of course, respective case law.

A prerequisite for ordering coercive detention is that a penalty payment has already been imposed on the enforcement debtor and that payment of the penalty payment could not be obtained (see Section 890(1) ZPO). In the case of UPC decisions, the recurring penalty payments ordered by the UPC should replace the penalty payment required in Section 890(1) ZPO. In practice, this means that coercive detention may be imposed if the recurring penalty payments previously ordered by the UPC cannot be collected or have proven to be ineffective, i.e., if it is evident that the imposition of yet further penalty payments could not reasonably be expected to induce the enforcement debtor to comply with the injunction to be enforced. However, a sentence of coercive detention by the competent regional court must be preceded by a corresponding warning to be issued by the same court (see Section 890(2) ZPO).

Coercive detention may be ordered for a duration of up to six months for each violation of the respective injunction, but the total period of detention is limited to two years (see Section 890(1) ZPO). If the enforcement debtor is a legal person, such as a company, coercive detention will be executed on the legal representative(s) of the respective company.

In practice, even though the threat of coercive detention is regularly included in cease-and-desist orders issued in German national patent infringement proceedings, it rarely happens that coercive detention is actually imposed on the enforcement debtor in such cases.

[B] An Order to Produce Evidence, Article 59 UPCA

At the request of a party having specified evidence which lies in the control of the opposing party or a third party, the UPC may order the opposing party or the third party to present such evidence, including banking, financial or commercial documents under the control of the opposing party (see Article 59 UPCA).

A corresponding order to produce evidence is enforced in Germany in accordance with the rules on the surrender of movable objects (see Section 883 ZPO), which requires that the object/evidence to be surrendered is sufficiently specified in the enforceable title.

The order is executed by a bailiff who will take the object/evidence away if the debtor does not surrender it voluntarily. The provisions of Section 811 ZPO exempting certain objects from seizure do not apply.

To this end, the bailiff is authorized to search the debtor's residence and any means of storage and have any corresponding doors and locks unlocked and opened (see Section 758 ZPO). While the bailiff can also enter and search the residence of the debtor against the debtor's will, this is only permitted on the basis of a search warrant issued by a judge of the local court in whose district the search is to be performed, unless the procuring of a corresponding search warrant would jeopardize the success of the search (see Section 758a(1) ZPO). In practice, it is advisable to inform the competent judge at the local court about the intended inspection in advance and to hand over any relevant documents as a matter of precaution in order to obtain a search warrant more quickly in case the debtor should refuse entry to his residence.

An inspection order may be enforced by the imposition of recurring penalty payments and, under German national law, by coercive detention (see Section 890(1) ZPO and the corresponding further explanations in §6.07[A] above).

If the evidence to be surrendered cannot be found by the bailiff, the debtor is obliged, upon request by the creditor, to declare in an affidavit that he is not in possession of the corresponding evidence and that he does not know where it is located (see Section 883(2) ZPO). Summoning the debtor to give a corresponding affidavit is within the competence of the bailiff (see Sections 883(2) and 802e ZPO).

Orders to produce evidence and inspect premises are served by a bailiff. As German courts grant such orders regularly without any prior hearing, the debtor is typically taken by surprise. Therefore, the debtor is given two hours to seek legal assistance before the actual inspection is allowed to begin. Generally, a court-appointed expert will inspect the premises together with an attorney-at-law and a patent attorney. The attorneys are bound to confidentiality even in relation to their own client, which means that they are not allowed to inform their client about details of the inspection. Only after the court has identified confidential information in the report of the court-appointed expert does it have to assess whether infringement is likely, or at least has become more likely with the additional evidence the court expert was able to evaluate. If the court believes that there is infringement, the confidential information will be disclosed to prove infringement. Otherwise, the respective passages will be redacted and the plaintiff can only use the redacted version for any future patent litigation proceedings.

[C] An Order to Preserve Evidence and to Inspect Premises, Article 60 UPCA

An order to preserve evidence (see Article 60 UPCA and Rules 192 to 198 RoP UPC) is enforced in Germany according to the rules on the surrender of movable objects (see Section 883 ZPO), so the explanations in §6.07[B] apply accordingly.

The competent bailiff is thus authorized to take the corresponding evidence from the debtor as described (see Section 883(1) ZPO), and the debtor must allow the premises to be entered.

[D] Freezing Orders, Article 61 UPCA

According to Section 929(2) ZPO the enforcement of a freezing order is possible only within one month after the order has been issued and been served on the creditor. According to Section 928 ZPO, the provisions of enforcement apply to the enforcement of a freezing order. A freezing order is enforced pursuant to Section 890(1) ZPO, as set out in detail in §6.07[A] above.

[E] Preliminary Injunction, Article 62(1) UPCA

Preliminary injunctions are enforced in the same way as permanent injunctions (see §6.07[A] and [D] above).

In addition, a corresponding application to the competent enforcement body must be made by the enforcement creditor within one month from the service of the injunction order on the debtor for foreign defendants. For defendants situated in Germany, a preliminary injunction must be separately served by a bailiff on the defendant within that one-month time limit (see Sections 936 and 929(2) ZPO).

If the provision of a security has been ordered by the UPC, the creditor must also provide the security and corresponding proof to the debtor within this same one-month period (see Section 751(2) ZPO).

[F] Seizure or Delivery up of Infringing Products, Article 62(3) UPCA

A corresponding order under Article 62(3) first sentence is enforced in Germany in accordance with the rules on the surrender of movable objects (see Sections 936, 928 and 883 ZPO).

The enforcement requires that the products to be surrendered are sufficiently specified. The physical seizure is effected by a bailiff (see Section 883(1) ZPO). In this regard, the corresponding explanations provided in §6.07[B] above likewise apply.

Furthermore, as set out above (see §6.07[E]), since it is a preliminary measure, the creditor has to apply for the enforcement within one month from the service of the order on the debtor (see Sections 936 and 929 ZPO).

[G] Precautionary Seizure of Movable and Immovable Property, Article 62(3) UPCA

Article 62(3) second sentence UPCA provides that the UPC may order the precautionary seizure of the movable and immovable property of the alleged infringer, including the blocking of bank accounts and other assets of the alleged infringer, if the plaintiff demonstrates circumstances likely to endanger the recovery of damages.

The precautionary seizure of movable property is conducted by a bailiff in accordance with the German national rules on the surrender of movable objects (see Sections 936, 928 and 883 ZPO). In particular, the bailiff either takes possession of the corresponding movable objects or, if they are left in the custody and control of the debtor, attaches them by applying a seal or other visible means (see Section 808 ZPO). The aim of these measures is to provide a security for the enforcement creditor but they do not allow exploitation. However, if the seized objects are eventually used to satisfy the creditor's claims, the bailiff may offer them for sale at a public auction (see Section 814(1) ZPO).

Monetary claims and other property rights of the debtor, including ongoing emoluments, income and bank accounts, may also be attached (see Sections 829, 832, 833 and 833a ZPO). The corresponding attachment is ordered by the enforcement court (see Section 828(1) ZPO), which would be the UPC itself. In this case Article II Section 19(3) IntPatÜG does not delegate jurisdiction to the regional court at the debtor's domicile.

The precautionary seizure of immovable property (real estate) is effected by registering a security mortgage in the German land register (see Sections 866 and 867 ZPO), which cannot be done by the UPC itself. Making a corresponding entry into the land register is within the jurisdiction of the local court that maintains the land register for the respective plot(s) of real estate (see Section 867(1) ZPO and Section 1 GBO). This same local court would also be competent for possible subsequent enforcement measures aimed at satisfying the creditor's claims from the seized real estate, particularly by means of foreclosure or receivership/forced administration (see Section 869 ZPO and Section 1(1) ZVG).

[H] Recalling from the Channels of Commerce, Article 64(2) lit (b) UPCA

The recall of infringing products from the channels of commerce (see Article 64(2)(b) UPCA) is considered as a non-fungible act (which depends exclusively on the will of the debtor and cannot be taken by third parties; see Section 888 ZPO) and, as such, is enforced by the threat and imposition of recurring penalty payments by the UPC.

As a further enforcement measure in relation to non-fungible acts, German national law allows the imposition of coercive detention (see Section 888(1) ZPO), which can be ordered either directly or for the case that coercive penalty payments cannot be obtained. Analogous to the discussion of coercive detention in §6.07[A] above, it may be argued that since there are no corresponding provisions in the UPC Agreement, the subsidiary German national law should apply (see Article 82(3) UPCA), so that coercive punitive detention should also be available for the enforcement of recall claims ordered by the UPC if the (recurring) penalty payment cannot be collected or is ineffective.

The general rules on coercive detention in enforcement proceedings apply analogously (see Section 888(1) third sentence ZPO in conjunction with Sections 802g et seq. ZPO). Thus, a corresponding detention may not be ordered for a period longer than six months, after which the debtor shall be released *ex officio* (see Section 888(1) third sentence ZPO in conjunction with Section 802j(1) ZPO).

According to national law, coercive detention must be applied for at, and is ordered by, the trial court of first instance (see Section 888 ZPO). In this case the German legislator has assigned the jurisdiction to the competent patent litigation chamber of the regional courts in whose district the debtor is domiciled (Article II Section 19(3) IntPatÜG). What has been laid out above about the injunction applies here accordingly (see above §6.07[A]).

[I] Depriving the Product of Its Infringing Property, Article 64(2) lit (c) UPCA

In principle, the UPC also imposes recurring penalty payments if it orders depriving the product of its infringing property as an enforcement measure under Article 82(4) UPCA.

Under German law, the order to deprive an infringing product of its infringing property (see Article 64(2)(c) UPCA) requires a fungible act (see Section 887 ZPO).

If German law applies, the fungible act is enforced in Germany by authorization for substitute performance imposed by the trial court of first instance (see Section 887 ZPO). The creditor, upon request, may thus be authorized by the trial court to have the corresponding act performed by a third party at the cost of the debtor. The creditor may further request that the debtor be ordered to pay in advance the costs that will arise from the performance of the act (see Section 887(2) ZPO). If German law is applicable, the competent court will not be the UPC itself, even though it is the trial court of first instance, but rather the competent regional court (see Article II Section 19(3) IntPatÜG; see §6.07[A]).

While German national law does not foresee penalty payments for the enforcement of fungible acts, the UPC could, in principle, also impose recurring penalty payments as an indirect enforcement measure under Article 82(4) UPCA in such a case.

[J] Removing from the Channels of Commerce, Article 64(2) lit (d) UPCA

The removal of infringing products from the channels of commerce is enforced under German national law as a non-fungible act (see Section 888(1) ZPO). With respect to the corresponding enforcement measures, i.e. the ordering of penalty payments as well as coercive detention, the same considerations as set out in relation to the recall of infringing products from the channels of commerce in §6.07[H] apply.

[K] Destruction, Article 64(2) lit (e) UPCA

The destruction of patent-infringing products ordered by the UPC in accordance with Article 64(2)(e) UPCA is a fungible act, which is enforced in Germany by authorization for substitute performance by the trial court of first instance (see Section 887 ZPO). In this regard, the same considerations as set out in §6.07[I] apply.

[L] Communication of Information, Article 67 UPCA

Ordering an infringer or a third party to communicate information to the plaintiff in accordance with Article 67 UPCA entails a non-fungible act, which is enforced in Germany by the threat and imposition of recurring penalty payments by the UPC. In this regard, the corresponding explanations provided in §6.07[A] above likewise apply.

In addition, coercive punitive detention should also be available under German national law (see Section 888(1) ZPO). In this regard, the corresponding explanations provided in §6.07[H] above likewise apply.

Chapter 7

Finland

Johanna Flythström and Juhani Sinkkonen

§7.01 SOURCES OF LAW FOR ENFORCEMENT

The most important Finnish act governing enforcement of Unified Patent Court ('UPC') decisions and orders in Finland is the Finnish Enforcement Code (705/2007). Direct enforceability of UPC decisions and orders and applicability of national enforcement procedures pursuant to Article 82 of the Agreement on a Unified Patent Court ('UPCA') have been expressly addressed by an amendment of the Enforcement Code.

Section 2, Chapter 1 of the Enforcement Code concerns applicability of the Enforcement Code in cases where its applicability is provided for by other acts, EU legislation, or international treaties binding on Finland, i.e., where the grounds for execution are such that their execution has not been expressly mentioned in the provisions on the scope of application of the Enforcement Code and the list of enforceable grounds for execution. According to Subsection 1, Section 2, Chapter 1 of the Enforcement Code (which is the provision amended to accommodate the enforcement procedures relating to the UPC), the procedure according to the Enforcement Code is to be followed, *inter alia*, in the enforcement of a judgment and other grounds for execution rendered by an international court where an international treaty provides for application of the Enforcement Code. The preparatory works of the amendment mention the UPC as an example of an international court meant by the amended Section 2, Chapter 1 of the Enforcement Code. Thus, where Article 82 UPCA points to application of Finnish enforcement procedures, the applicable rules are primarily the rules laid down in the Enforcement Code.

The Enforcement Code sets forth comprehensive regulation of the enforcement procedure. Chapter 1 of the Enforcement Code covers general provisions on the scope of application of the Enforcement Code and its relation to other legislation, definitions, provisions on the organization, competence, eligibility and disqualification of enforcement authorities, certain general principles the enforcement authorities must follow, as well as provisions on the handling of information to be entered into the register of enforcement matters. Chapter 2 includes provisions on enforceable judgments, decisions, and orders and their enforceability. Chapter 3 lays down general rules applicable in all enforcement whereas Chapters 4 through 8 include specific provisions on enforcement of different types of obligations and decisions such as payment obligations, obligations of assignment, obligations to act, injunctions, and provisional measures. Chapter 9 governs enforcement costs and Chapters 10 and 11 dispute resolution and remedies against erroneous enforcement measures. Chapters 12 and 13 include miscellaneous provisions. The Government Decree on Enforcement Proceedings (1322/2007) complements the Enforcement Code by setting more specific rules on certain aspects of enforcement procedure that relate mostly to enforcement of payment obligations.

Even though the Enforcement Code and the Government Decree cover the entire enforcement procedure, the regulation is not entirely self-contained. In addition to provisions of Chapter 1 of the Enforcement Code, the General Data Protection Regulation (EU) 2016/679 and the Finnish Data Protection Act (1050/2018) apply to the handling of personal data in connection with enforcement, and the Act on Openness of Government Activities (621/1999) contains rules on the parties' and public's access to information concerning enforcement.

Furthermore, the Enforcement Code refers to certain provisions of other acts that are applicable in enforcement proceedings. These provisions include, *inter alia*, provisions on service of documents and on administrative complaints of the Administrative Procedure Act (434/2003), the Act on Electronic Services and Communication in the Public Sector (13/2003), as well as certain provisions of the Language Act (423/2003) and the Act on Conditional Fines (1113/1990).

Enforcement fees are laid down by the Act on Enforcement Fees (34/1995) and the Decree on Enforcement Fees (35/1995).

More detailed rules on internal organization and administration of the enforcement services have been set out in government and ministry decrees and in the Rules of Procedure of the National Enforcement Authority Finland.

§7.02 OVERVIEW OF AUTHORITIES EXECUTING ENFORCEMENT IN FINLAND

The Finnish enforcement system is, according to a long tradition, based on a strict division of competencies between the enforcement authorities and the courts. Courts are not part of enforcement organization and they do not, as a main rule, have any first instance enforcement tasks that belong to enforcement authorities.[1] Pursuant to Section 10, Chapter 1 of the Enforcement Code, courts act as appeal instances in enforcement matters and handle enforcement matters that have been specifically assigned to them. This strict division of competencies is reflected in the so-called principle of non-intervention. According to said principle, the courts may not give enforcement orders unless a provision of law expressly provides the courts with such a competence. The enforcement authorities, respectively, must enforce judgments and other court orders strictly as ordered by the court. Consequently, the enforcement

1. Tuula Linna et al., *Ulosotto-oikeus I: Ulosottomenettely* 24 (3d rev. ed. 2022).

authorities may not interpret or 'fix' the grounds for enforcement.[2] In the event the ground for execution is so ambiguous or incomplete that it cannot be enforced without clarification or there is a clerical mistake, the enforcement officer must refer the applicant seeking enforcement to lodge a complaint about the judgment or request for correction of the clerical mistake before the authority having issued the ground for execution. Some of the few exceptions to the courts' lack of competence to issue enforcement orders concern interim measures under Chapter 7 of the Code of Judicial Proceedings (4/1734) and the Act on Securing of Evidence in Civil Cases Concerning Industrial and Intellectual Property Rights (344/2000). These provisions give the courts certain powers to rule on enforcement matters. These provisions, however, are not applicable to enforcement of UPC decisions and orders.

The enforcement service has recently gone through a reorganization. Currently, the enforcement service is organized through one national enforcement authority, the National Enforcement Authority Finland ('the Authority'). The Authority has nationwide jurisdiction in enforcement matters. The Authority's enforcement tasks are on practical level divided to enforcement units that have different tasks and regional competencies. These include the Basic Enforcement Unit, five regional Extensive Enforcement Units, and the national Special Enforcement Unit. The Authority has sixty-four enforcement offices across Finland. In addition to the enforcement units, the Authority has Central Administration that steers, develops, and supervises the enforcement service.

The Basic Enforcement Unit is tasked with the collection of monetary receivables from natural persons, apart from self-employed persons. The Basic Enforcement Unit has a nationwide area of responsibility and it takes care of its tasks without meeting the customers in person, using electronic means. Thus, in most cases the enforcement of UPC decisions and orders falls outside of the competence of the Basic Enforcement Unit, in which case the matter will be transferred to a competent regional Extensive Enforcement Unit or the national Special Enforcement Unit that enforce all types of obligations and interim measures. The extensive enforcement regions are Southern Finland, Western Finland, the Interior of Finland, Eastern Finland, and Northern Finland.

Under the Enforcement Code, 'enforcement officer' is a general term referring to all civil servants who carry out enforcement duties and exercise independent decision-making power in enforcement matters. Enforcement officers include the Enforcement Inspectors of the Basic Enforcement Unit and Senior Enforcement Inspectors of the Extensive and Special Enforcement Units, the Senior Enforcement Officers serving as their supervisors, and the Chief Enforcement Officers. In Åland, the corresponding titles are Senior Enforcement Inspector and Provincial Senior Enforcement Officer. The Director General and the Deputy Director General, who lead the whole Authority, are also enforcement officers within the meaning of the Enforcement Code.

The decision-making power of Enforcement Inspectors and Senior Enforcement Inspectors is based on the Senior Enforcement Officer's delegation. This delegation power is limited by Section 9, Chapter 1 of the Enforcement Code, according to which more demanding enforcement duties that require special legal competence

2. Tuula Linna, 'Ulosotto-oikeuden yleiset opit – missä ja mitä?', *Lakimies* 16–17 n. 1 (2009).

belong to the exclusive competence of Senior Enforcement Officers. These duties include for example:

- enforcement of grounds for enforcement that may still be subject to appeal;
- withdrawal of enforcement acts in case of revocation of the grounds for enforcement;
- acceptance and use of a security;
- decision to use an external expert in enforcement;
- passing over artificial arrangements executed to avoid enforcement;
- enforcement of an obligation to act;
- enforcement of injunctions;
- sale of certain types of pledged property; and
- decision on self-correction, referral to an enforcement dispute, or stay of enforcement.

Chief Enforcement Officers, the Deputy Director General, and the Director General of the Authority have the same competence as the Senior Enforcement Officers.

§7.03 GENERAL REQUIREMENTS FOR ENFORCEMENT

[A] Grounds for Execution

In order for enforcement to take place, there need to be valid grounds for execution. Namely, the beginning of *lis pendens* of the enforcement proceedings and enforcement under the Finnish Enforcement Code require the existence of enforceable grounds for execution that include an obligation or an order that may be enforced according to the Enforcement Code.

Enforceable UPC decisions and orders with enforceable content are valid grounds for execution pursuant to Subsection 1, Section 2, Chapter 1 of the Enforcement Code. Their enforceability is governed by the UPCA and the Rules of Procedure of the Unified Patent Court ('UPCRoP').

The enforceable content of a ground for execution is defined by Section 1, Chapter 1 of the Enforcement Code. Said provision contains the following list of enforceable private law obligations included in a judgment or other court decision:

- a payment obligation in money or in goods;
- an obligation to surrender real property or specified movable property to another party;
- eviction;
- an obligation to act;
- injunction; and
- an obligation to let another party to do something.

While practice will be developed on the interpretations, such enforceable content may be read to have been included, for example, in the UPCA's:

- order to produce evidence (Article 59 UPCA);
- permanent injunctions (Article 63 UPCA);

- order to recall infringing products from the channels of commerce (Article 64(2)(b) UPCA);
- order to deprive the infringing product of its infringing property (Article 64(2)(c) UPCA);
- order to definitively remove the infringing products from the channels of commerce (Article 64(2)(d) UPCA);
- order to destroy the infringing products and/or the materials and implements concerned (Article 64(2)(e) UPCA);
- order to communicate information (Article 67 UPCA);
- award of damages (Article 68 UPCA), and
- cost order (Article 69 UPCA).

In addition, Subsection, 1 Section 2, Chapter 1 of the Enforcement Code provides that the Enforcement Code is applied to enforcement of provisional measures other than those governed by Chapter 7 of the Code of Judicial Proceedings. Therefore, the UPC's orders on provisional measures under Articles 60, 61, and 62 UPCA include content that is enforceable according to the Enforcement Code to the extent its provisions are not superseded by provisions of the UPC legal framework as provided for by Article 82(1) UPCA.

In contrast to the above enforceable obligations, declaratory decisions such as a declaration of infringement under Article 64(2)(a) UPCA or revocation of a patent according to Article 65 UPCA do not have content that could be enforced according to the procedures provided by the Enforcement Code.

Before enforcement, the enforcement officer must check that the obligation is not statute-barred. In case of doubt, the enforcement officer must hear the parties. Enforcement may not begin if the application is premature, for example, because a time limit that the UPC has set for fulfilling a certain obligation has not yet lapsed.[3] If the grounds for execution order alternative ways to fulfil the obligation, and these have been presented in a hierarchical order, the beginning of the enforcement requires that the applicant seeks enforcement of the primary obligation first.[4]

In addition, enforcement requires that the obligation or order in the grounds of execution is clear enough to be enforced by the enforcement officer. As mentioned above, the enforcement officer does not have competence to interpret the grounds for execution.

Obligations arising out of enforcement proceedings constitute an important exception to the requirement of separate grounds for enforcement issued by a court. Therefore, payment obligations that the enforcement officer has set as part of the enforcement proceedings in accordance with an explicit provision of the Enforcement Code, for example an obligation to pay enforcement costs, are directly enforceable without a separate court order.

3. Tuula Linna et al., *Ulosotto-oikeus I: Ulosottomenettely* 275 (3d rev. ed. 2022)
4. Tuula Linna et al., *Ulosotto-oikeus I: Ulosottomenettely* 282 (3d rev. ed. 2022)

[B] Legitimacy as the Proper Party

In addition to valid grounds of execution, it is required that the applicant has the legitimacy to seek the enforcement. I.e., that the applicant is the proper party to enforce the order. Thus, it is required that the grounds for execution entitle the applicant to what they are seeking to enforce.

It is notable that, according to Rule 354.4 UPCRoP, if it is alleged that a party has failed to comply with the terms of a UPC order, the first instance panel of the division in question may decide to order payment of penalty payments provided for in the order upon the request of the other party or of its own motion. The penalty payments are payable to UPC. Thus, the interesting question arises as to who may seek enforcement of the penalty payment decision in Finland.

While the interpretations and practice of UPC enforcement cases are yet to develop, on the one hand a view may be that in case the penalty payment decision has been given upon request of a party in their favour, such party would have legitimacy as the proper party to seek enforcement of the decision.

Furthermore, another line of argument could also be that the UPC would have legitimacy to apply for enforcement as well. Namely, according to Article 4 UPCA, the UPC has legal personality in Finland. Further, an order to pay a penalty payment establishes a payment obligation towards the UPC which the first instance division in question could be argued to establish without a request from any of the parties. While for the time being the interpretations are speculative, penalty payments ordered of the first instance division's own motion in particular could prove to be unenforceable, in violation of Article 82 UPCA, unless the UPC is recognized as the proper party to seek enforcement as there would be no other party in whose favour the order would be given. Therefore, while the developing practice will tell, the UPC could be recognized as the proper party at least in cases of penalty payments ordered of the Court's own motion.

As to the defendant, enforcement cannot take place against a defendant who has no legitimacy as the proper party. Thus, enforcement may be sought only against the party against whom the grounds for execution have been rendered. Legal succession on the defendant side forms an exception to this rule. In case the grounds for execution name primary and secondary obligors, the enforcement proceedings cannot be commenced if the applicant seeks enforcement against a party other than the primary obligor first.[5]

[C] Other

Under Finnish law, special enforcement of an individual payment obligation is barred by general enforcement. Under the Finnish Bankruptcy Act (120/2004) and the Corporate Debt Restructuring Act (47/1993) enforcement of payment obligations may not take place under the Enforcement Code during insolvency proceedings.

The Enforcement Code has several provisions on securities that must be provided in connection with the enforcement of grounds for execution that have not become final as well as with the enforcement of provisional measures. However,

5. Tuula Linna et al., *Ulosotto-oikeus I: Ulosottomenettely* 285 (3d rev. ed. 2022)

these provisions concern explicitly such grounds for execution that are rendered by Finnish courts and do not extend to other grounds for execution which are enforced in accordance with the Enforcement Code pursuant to its Section 2, Chapter 1. Moreover, Rules 118.8 and 352 UPCRoP contain comprehensive regulation of securities as a condition for enforceability of UPC decisions and orders. Thus, Article 82 UPCA precludes the application of the Enforcement Code's provisions on securities as a condition of enforceability.

In relation to enforcement of UPC decisions and orders that are not final and may still be revoked, it is good to note that the applicant may become liable for damages. According to the Enforcement Code the applicant is liable to compensate all kinds of damage caused to the defendant by enforcement and cancellation or enforcement of grounds for enforcement that are subsequently revoked or varied. The damages are determined by applying the Damages Act (412/1974) *mutatis mutandis*. Pursuant to Rule 354.2 UPCRoP, the UPC is the competent court to decide these damages claims.

§7.04 OVERVIEW OF PROCEEDINGS

Enforcement proceedings start by an application that includes the details listed in Section 2, Chapter 3 of the Enforcement Code. The application may be submitted as signed in writing, by an electronic message, or by using the Authority's electronic application service. Instructions on the filing of the enforcement application are available on the website of the Enforcement Authority in English.[6] Said instructions also include links to the electronic form for filing the application as well as template applications for filing the application via e-mail, post, or personal delivery, both also available in the English language. It is to be noted that while English is generally well-understood and information may be provided in English, the official proceedings may be conducted in the Finnish or Swedish languages.

The enforcement application must include the UPC order to be enforced (as a copy or as an original). In the event it is not possible to attach the order to the electronic application, it can also be delivered to the Authority afterwards. The enforcement officer may request the applicant to present the original order.

In case the applicant uses a representative, a power of attorney may be required. An attorney at law (a member of the Finnish Bar) and licensed legal counsel (Finland) may represent the applicant without presenting a power of attorney unless the enforcement officer requires otherwise. However, they too, like all other representatives, need a specified power of attorney to receive funds or to take possession of property. A foreign applicant that has not given a Finnish address for receiving notices related to enforcement must have a representative domiciled in Finland who is authorized to receive the notices. There are, however, no specific formal qualification requirements for the representative; for example, it is not required that the representative must have been trained as a lawyer.

The enforcing enforcement office (and thereby the enforcement officer) will primarily be determined based on the actual place of business or based on the place of domicile of the defendant in Finland. If the defendant is not domiciled in Finland

6. https://ulosottolaitos.fi/en/index.html.

and does not have a place of business in Finland, the enforcement office is as a main rule determined based on adequacy.

Once the application has been filed, before taking enforcement measures, the enforcement officer verifies that the applicant and the defendant have legitimacy as the proper party, meaning that the applicant has the grounds for execution described above against the defendant. In case the legitimacy as the proper party is not clear, for example if the applicant is different from the claimant in the grounds for execution because of succession in title of the claim after the court proceedings, the enforcement officer will request for evidence on the transfer.[7]

After the application has been received and the defendant has been notified of the enforcement application, under the Enforcement Code, the enforcement must be completed without undue delay. Typically, the Authority will grant the defendant certain time to voluntarily comply with the order. If the order is not complied with, the Authority will proceed to implementing the order via the means available to it under the Enforcement Code.

Once the proceedings are pending, any questions can be addressed to the Authority primarily through their customer service. While English is generally well-understood, the official languages in which service is provided are Finnish and Swedish.

Figure 1.

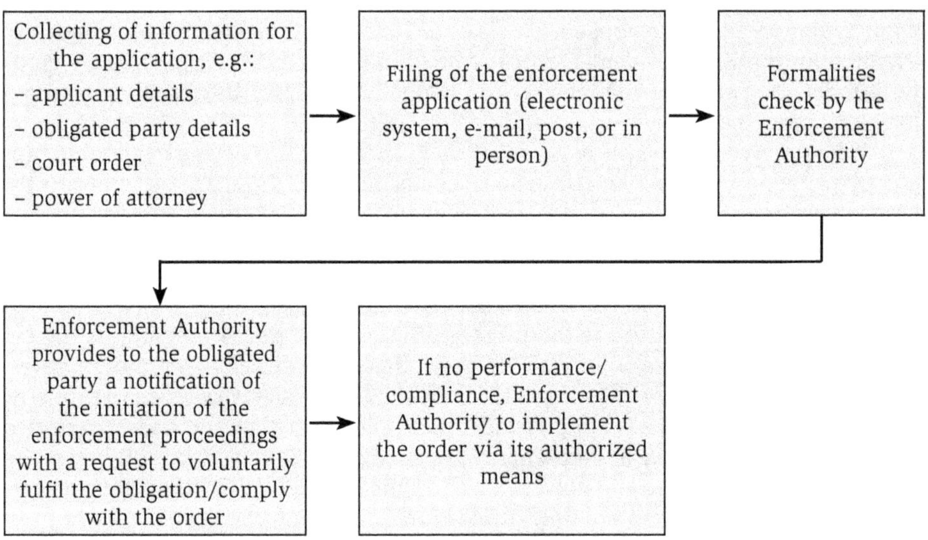

7. Tuula Linna et al., *Ulosotto-oikeus I: Ulosottomenettely* 273–274 281 (3d rev. ed. 2022)

As noted above, as the first step in the enforcement, the Authority may instruct the defendant to voluntarily comply with the obligation ordered by the UPC. If the defendant does not comply voluntarily, the Authority may proceed to forcing the order. In the Finnish system, if the defendant failed to comply with an order, the Authority may in a number of cases order compliance with the threat of a fine.

However, as noted above, in the UPC, the UPC has the competence to set forth recurring penalty payments for deterring non-compliance (e.g., Articles 62 and 63 UPCA). While the competence for such penalty payments vests with the UPC, the Authority should be deemed to have the competence to enforce the collection of such payments (e.g., for permanent injunctions and preliminary injunctions). If the threat of a penalty/fine is not sufficient, the Authority may proceed to the enforcement with the measures appropriate for the order. For example, with respect to permanent injunctions and preliminary injunctions, the Authority may enforce the order, for instance, through preventing the use of equipment or interrupting work, while in matters concerning production or preservation of evidence, the Authority may search the premises to locate relevant evidence. Under Finnish practice certain orders would qualify as precautionary measures (Chapter 7 of the Finnish Code of Judicial Procedure) the enforcement of which under the Finnish system requires the placing of a security (typically as a bank guarantee or as a cash payment to the Authority) by the applicant of the precautionary measure.[8]

The placing of a security is also acknowledged in the UPCA (Article 82 UPCA) by stating that the enforcement of a decision may be subject to the provision of a security. The UPC itself is also competent to order the placement of security (Rule 352 UPCRoP). Thus, in the event where the UPC has ordered the security, the Authority should be deemed to have the competence to enforce the collection of such security also when its placement has been ordered by the UPC.

§7.05 COSTS

Ultimately the defendant of the enforcement proceedings is liable to cover the necessary enforcement costs. These costs include costs the enforcement officer incurs in connection with carrying out the enforcement measures. They may include for example the cost of warehousing distrained or confiscated property or fees of an external expert whose expertise is needed to carry out the enforcement. The applicant bears secondary responsibility for these costs. The enforcement officer collects the costs from the defendant. In case this collection is unsuccessful, or the defendant is not liable to cover the costs, the costs are collected from the applicant. If the applicant needs to pay costs which the defendant is liable to pay, the applicant may collect the costs from the defendant through later enforcement proceedings.[9] This may prove

8. Moreover, under the Finnish system, the applicant must lodge the main action within one month from the decision on precautionary measure (e.g., preliminary injunction) in order for the precautionary measure to remain effective (Chapter 7 of the Finnish Code of Judicial Procedure). In addition to the aforesaid, for example, an order to preserve evidence would under Finnish practice typically require the placement of a security.
9. Tuula Linna et al., *Ulosotto-oikeus I: Ulosottomenettely* 727 (3d rev. ed. 2022).

to be futile if the enforcement officer has already failed to collect the costs from the defendant due to lack of distrainable property.

Under certain circumstances the enforcement officer may ensure recovery of the enforcement costs by demanding either the applicant or the defendant make an advance payment before incurring the costs.

The applicant may be required to make an advance payment to cover all costs of enforcement of different types of obligations and grounds of execution apart from enforcement of a payment obligation. In connection with enforcement of a payment obligation, an advance payment may be required only for the cost of securing distraint, cost of sales, and cost of enforcement of a provisional measure. A natural person is not required to pay an advance if it is likely that the enforcement will result in accrual covering its costs as required by the Enforcement Code's provisions on enforcement of payment obligations. To ensure that the state will not have to bear the enforcement costs, the enforcement officer may order that the enforcement be dropped if the applicant does not pay the required advance.

When enforcing an obligation to act, the enforcement officer may, upon the applicant's request, require the defendant to pay an advance for necessary enforcement costs. This requires that the applicant submits a reliable cost estimate, and that the enforcement officer hears the defendant. Unless the defendant pays the advance voluntarily, the enforcement officer will collect it.

In addition to the enforcement costs, the parties are responsible for enforcement fees. For the enforcement of a payment obligation, the defendant is liable for a scheduled fee and a sales fee and the applicant for a handling fee and an account fee. The scheduled fee and the account fee are relative to the accrual of the enforcement. The scheduled fee varies between EUR 2.50 and EUR 210. The account fee is 1.45 percent of the account up to a maximum of EUR 5,000 per account. For the enforcement of other obligations, the defendant is liable to pay an enforcement fee that is either EUR 110 or EUR 225 depending on the type of the obligation. If the enforcement fee cannot be collected from the defendant, the applicant is liable to pay the fee to the Authority.

The system of the Enforcement Code is based on an ideal that the applicant is required only to submit the application after which the enforcement officer handles the enforcement *ex officio* in accordance with law. It has been considered that neither the applicant nor the defendant would need external assistance for example from an attorney for the enforcement. Consequently, the Enforcement Code does not include general provisions on reimbursement of parties' own costs such as legal fees, and it is not possible to demand the counterparty to pay these costs. This ideal behind the Enforcement Code is unrealistic, and legal assistance may be needed especially in more complex enforcement cases to secure realization of the parties' rights and ability to make the right claim at the right time.

The Enforcement Code's provisions on appeal and enforcement disputes make exceptions to the lack of provisions on parties' own legal costs, although these provisions reflect the above ideal behind the Enforcement Code too.

According to Section 20, Chapter 11 of the Enforcement Code the main rule in appeal proceedings (see §7.06[B] below) is that the parties bear their own legal costs. However, for a special reason the Court may order the party to whom the decision is unfavourable, to cover the successful party's legal costs in full or in part applying, *mutatis mutandis*, the Finnish Code of Civil Procedure's general rules on reimbursement of legal costs. Under these rules the winning party may reimburse reasonable legal costs for necessary actions from the counterparty. In case of a partial victory the parties bear their own costs, or the costs may be divided otherwise based on the result of the proceedings. If a third party is successful in their enforcement appeal, the state may be ordered to reimburse their reasonable legal costs if it would be unreasonable to make them bear their own legal costs. The parties of enforcement procedure may recover their legal costs from the state only if the enforcement officer has made such a clear error that it should have been corrected through self-correction (see §7.06[A] below).

According to Section 18, Chapter 10 of the Enforcement Code, the main rule in enforcement dispute proceedings (see §7.06[C] below) is that the parties bear their own legal costs if the enforcement dispute has been commenced based on a referral. However, for a special reason the court may order the party to whom the decision is unfavourable, to cover the successful party's legal costs in full or in part applying, *mutatis mutandis*, the Finnish Code of Civil Procedure's general rules on reimbursement of legal costs. If the enforcement dispute has been commenced without a referral, the general cost rules applicable to civil disputes apply. The state's responsibility for legal costs follows the above rules applicable to appeal proceedings too.

§7.06 COUNTERMEASURES ON ENFORCEMENT

The Enforcement Code provides for three different remedies against enforcement measures that violate or threaten to violate national or UPC provisions. These include self-correction, appeal, and enforcement dispute procedures. In addition, it is possible to file an administrative complaint. The Enforcement Code provides for the possibility to stay enforcement in connection with self-correction, appeal, and enforcement dispute procedures.

[A] Self-Correction

Both factual and clerical errors in enforcement measures of a decision of the enforcement officer may be corrected through self-correction.

The enforcement officer must correct an enforcement measure or a decision – except for certain measures related to enforcement of payment obligations – if the measure or decision is based on a clearly erroneous or insufficient examination of facts or apparently erroneous application of law. The correction must be made without delay once the error has been noticed. Thus, self-correction may be initiated by simply notifying the enforcement officer of the error and requesting correction. There are no formal requirements for a correction request. In addition, if an appeal has been filed, the enforcement officer may correct the enforcement measure or decision under appeal. Before deciding on a factual correction, the enforcement officer must hear the parties who will be worse off due to the correction unless that is redundant for a particular reason.

A clear clerical error in a decision or other document made during the enforcement procedure must be corrected without delay once the error has been noticed.

Self-correction of both factual and clerical errors may be appealed in accordance with Chapter 11 of the Enforcement Code as explained below.

The enforcement officer may stay the enforcement when considering self-correction.

[B] Appeal

An enforcement measure or a decision of the enforcement officer may be appealed by all concerned parties. It is possible to appeal the assessment of the merits as well as procedural issues. The grounds for an appeal may be either evidentiary or legal. An appeal may not concern an issue subject to enforcement dispute proceedings described below.[10]

The enforcement procedure is a process consisting of a series of measures and decisions which may be subject to separate appeals. However, after the final account has been rendered, only the rendering of account may be subject to an appeal. The scope of appealable measures and decisions is wide. The starting point is that all enforcement measures and decisions are appealable unless the Enforcement Code expressly excludes the possibility to appeal. It is important to note, however, that the grounds for execution, such as an UPC decision, may not be appealed as part of the enforcement. By contrast, events that take place after the grounds for execution have been rendered (*factum superveniens*), such as payment of the debt subject to the grounds of appeal, may be invoked in an enforcement appeal. To be appealable, the enforcement measure or decision must have a legal effect on a party or a third party. These include particularly such measures and decisions by which a certain issue has been finally decided or dismissed as inadmissible. Purely practical and preparatory measures that do not create rights or interfere with sphere of someone's rights are not appealable.[11]

The competent court has the power to examine the correctness of the enforcement measure or a decision more widely than with respect to the facts invoked in the appeal. If the appeal is based on such illegal act or omission that may not lead to reversal of the enforcement measure or decision, for example too slow actions or bad behaviour, the court must refer the appellant to file an administrative complaint as described below.

The concerned parties entitled to appeal include all parties whose private, individual interest is affected by the enforcement measure or decision. The right to appeal is based on existence of a sufficient individual interest in the matter. The right to appeal does not require that the party is a party to the enforcement proceedings. A third party whose private, individual interest is affected, or may be affected, illegally is entitled to file an appeal. Respectively, if the measure or order does not affect the

10. Tuula Linna, *Ulosotto-oikeus III: Erityiset täytäntöönpanon lajit ja oikeussuojakinot* 257–259, 387–388 (2018).
11. Tuula Linna, *Ulosotto-oikeus III: Erityiset täytäntöönpanon lajit ja oikeussuojakinot* 263–265 (2018).

interest of a party to the enforcement proceedings, that party is not entitled to file an appeal merely because they are a party to the enforcement proceedings.[12]

An appeal must be filed with the Authority within three weeks from the proceedings in which the enforcement measure or decision was taken or made if the party had been informed of the proceedings beforehand or was present. Otherwise, the time limit is calculated from the date on which the party got information about the enforcement measure or decision. If the party has a legal excuse to file the appeal within the three-week time limit, or there is another acceptable reason, the enforcement officer may set a new time limit upon request. If they consider that there are no grounds for setting a new time limit, they must refer the question to the competent District Court.

Enforcement matters have been assigned to nine District Courts. The competent District Court is determined by the place of residence, domicile, or centre of administration of the defendant of the enforcement proceedings. In matters concerning real property, the *forum rei sitae* has parallel competence. In case no District Court has competence under the above rules, the competent District Court is determined by the place of the enforcement measure or decision subject to the appeal. The District Court's decision may be appealed to a Court of Appeal subject to a permit granted by the Court of Appeal and further to the Supreme Court subject to a leave to appeal granted by the Supreme Court.

The Court handles an enforcement appeal applying, *mutatis mutandis*, Chapter 8 of the Finnish Code of Judicial Proceedings governing procedure in petition cases. This procedure is simpler than proceedings in a civil case. An enforcement appeal must be handled urgently. A request for a stay of the enforcement must be decided immediately. An interim order to stay may be issued *ex parte*. When considering a stay, the following aspects must be taken into account: the phase of the enforcement, the likelihood of success of the appeal, possible harm caused to the parties by the stay or continuation of the enforcement, and other comparable circumstances. In certain cases, in which the stay could be particularly harmful, the enforcement may be stayed only for a weighty reason or if the applicant places a security that covers possible costs and damage caused by the stay. An appeal does not have a suspensive effect on the enforcement unless the court issues an order to stay the enforcement.

If the court refers the appellant to file for an enforcement dispute as explained below, the appeal is dropped to the extent its subject matter is covered by the referral. The same applies if self-correction explained above makes the appeal redundant entirely or in part.

[C] Enforcement Dispute

An enforcement dispute is commenced by filing an application for a summons with a court. The purpose of an enforcement dispute is to resolve such factual dispute that needs to be resolved before the enforcement procedure may be continued. An enforcement dispute may not concern a purely legal issue or a procedural question. The possibility to commence an enforcement dispute and bring a factual dispute to

12. Tuula Linna, *Ulosotto-oikeus III: Erityiset täytäntöönpanon lajit ja oikeussuojakinot* 268–277 (2018).

a court before the enforcement officer has ruled on the issue is an exception to the main rule. The main rule is that the enforcement officer is competent to resolve all factual, legal, and procedural claims and issues encountered during the enforcement procedure. However, the enforcement officer does not have similar possibilities for taking evidence as civil courts do. Most notably the enforcement officer cannot hear witnesses. Therefore, it may be necessary that such factual disputes the handling of which requires presentation of more complex evidence, are referred to a court that can handle the disputes according to the same rules as normal civil cases.[13]

A dispute arising during enforcement may be handled as an enforcement dispute, for example, if:

(1) the enforcement is contested by claiming that the debt has been paid or become statute-barred, or another bar for the enforcement has occurred after the grounds for enforcement have become final;
(2) a payment or restitution obligation ordered in the enforcement is disputed;
(3) a third party claims that the enforcement violates their rights; or
(4) another similar claim, that must be resolved before the enforcement may continue, is made.

An enforcement dispute may be commenced after the enforcement officer has issued a referral to an enforcement dispute, or without a referral if the prerequisites for commencing an enforcement action are met. These prerequisites are identical to the circumstances under which the enforcement officer issues a referral to an enforcement dispute. The enforcement officer refers a party making an above-mentioned claim to file for an enforcement dispute if the following conditions are met:

(1) there are likely grounds to support the claim;
(2) the claim has made the enforcement matter unclear; and
(3) necessary evidence cannot be taken in the enforcement proceedings.

Furthermore, a court handling an appeal against a decision of an enforcement officer may refer parties to an enforcement dispute if the issue is such that it may be handled as an enforcement dispute, and it is too complex or otherwise unsuitable to be handled according to the procedural rules applicable to enforcement appeals. The parties to the dispute must be heard before issuing the referral but a decision to issue a referral may not be appealed.

The enforcement officer may not issue a referral to file for an enforcement dispute if the enforcement proceedings have gone so far that the final account has been rendered in enforcement of a payment obligation or enforcement of another type of an obligation has become final. In addition, a referral may not be issued if:

(1) the claim has been resolved by an enforcement officer or a court and the decision is final and binding towards the party making the claim;
(2) the party has failed to make the claim in such proceedings in which they should have made it according to law;
(3) the party has received an earlier referral concerning the same claim; or

13. Tuula Linna, *Ulosotto-oikeus III: Erityiset täytäntöönpanon lajit ja oikeussuojakinot* 385 (2018).

(4) an appeal has been filed on the same issue. Correspondingly an appeal may not be based on a claim that the party has invoked in enforcement dispute proceedings.

In addition to the above-mentioned ways to commence an enforcement dispute, a normal civil case may be continued as an enforcement dispute if the above prerequisites for handling the dispute at hand as an enforcement dispute are met. A party to civil proceedings that are pending before a court simultaneously with the enforcement may request that the dispute be handled as an enforcement dispute. This may be advantageous because an enforcement dispute, unlike a normal civil case, has an impact on the enforcement proceedings as explained below.

The party who has received a referral to an enforcement dispute must file the action within four weeks of the service of the referral. The enforcement officer who has issued the referral may extend this time limit for an acceptable reason. According to the preparatory works of the Enforcement Code the threshold of an acceptable reason is rather high.[14] If the party fails to file the action within the time limit, they may no longer invoke the same claim in the pending enforcement proceedings. The possibility to invoke the same claim in other proceedings is not precluded.

The competent District Court is determined according to the same rules as in enforcement appeal matters. The court must handle an enforcement dispute as an urgent matter. The District Court's judgment may be appealed to a Court of Appeal subject to a permit granted by the Court of Appeal and further to the Supreme Court subject to a leave to appeal granted by the Supreme Court.

The enforcement officer must stay the enforcement upon issuing a referral to file for an enforcement dispute until two weeks after the time limit for filing the action. The court handling the enforcement dispute may issue an order to stay the enforcement upon a request by a party or on its own motion applying the same rules as in the case of an appeal. Also, the rules on the duration of the stay and its impact on the enforcement are the same as in the context of an appeal.

After the enforcement dispute has been decided, the enforcement must be continued or cancelled as required by the judgment.

[D] Administrative Complaint

An illegal act or omission of enforcement authorities may be complained in writing to the Central Administration of the Authority. The matter will be decided by the Director General of the Authority. They may refer the case to one of the Chief Enforcement Officers. A complaint that concerns a matter that is more than two years old will not be handled unless there is a particular reason to do so.

An administrative complaint does not remedy the illegal act or omission in the individual case at hand. The decision may only point out the decision-maker's view on the requirements of the law or, if the former is not sufficient, include a reminder to the authority under supervision. In case more severe measures under some other procedures provided by law would be warranted, the complaint will be dropped.

14. Government Proposal to the Parliament on Amending the Legislation on Enforcement Authorities and Appeal in Enforcement Matters HE 106/1995 vp. 77.

§7.07 PARTICULARITIES WITH RESPECT TO SPECIFIC ORDERS

In the below certain basic principles are laid out regarding the UPC orders vis-à-vis the Finnish system. However, it is acknowledged that as no practice exists as of yet of the UPC orders, only the future practice of the UPC in the specific formulation of its orders and in applying the measures available to it, e.g., regarding securities and penalty payments, and the consequent enforcement practices will establish the practical framework in the interplay between the UPC and national competence in enforcement questions.

[A] Permanent Injunctions, Article 63 UPCA

A permanent injunction in itself is considered under Finnish law to be an obligation not to do something (i.e., an injunction). Consequently, when enforcing the order, the Authority would instruct the defendant to comply with the obligation ordered by the UPC and enforce such order in the event of non-compliance with the order (e.g., through preventing the use of equipment, interrupting work, and the like). In the Finnish system, if the defendant failed to comply with the order, the Authority may order compliance with the penalty of a fine (unless already ordered by the Court). However, as noted above, in the UPC, the UPC has the competence to set forth recurring penalty payments for deterring non-compliance (UPCA 63) on its own motion or on the request of the other party. Thus, while the competence for such penalty payments vests with the UPC instead of the Authority, the Authority should be deemed to have the competence at least to enforce the collection of such payments as monetary claims. With respect to legitimacy of the proper party and the role of UPC, see above §7.03[B].

[B] An Order to Produce Evidence, Article 59 UPCA

An order to produce evidence should be considered under Finnish law an obligation to act and should be enforceable under the Finnish enforcement rules set forth above. It is noteworthy that in the Finnish system the order to produce evidence is combined with the possibility for the Authority, e.g., to search premises to locate the relevant evidence. However, the developing practice will establish whether under the UPC system such enforcement activities would require also an order under Article 60 UPCA. What is stated above regarding possible recurring penalty payments ordered by the UPC should apply also with respect to orders to produce evidence. With respect to legitimacy of the proper party and the role of UPC, see above §7.03[B].

[C] An Order to Preserve Evidence and to Inspect Premises, Article 60 UPCA

An order to preserve evidence and to inspect premises should be considered under Finnish law an obligation to act and/or an obligation to let another party to do something and should be enforceable under the Finnish enforcement rules set forth above. The actual enforcement measures, however, will depend on the formulation of the order. However, what is stated above regarding possible recurring penalty payments and below (with respect to preliminary injunctions) regarding lodging of a security ordered by the UPC should apply also with respect to orders to preserve evidence. It is notable that under the Finnish practice, an order to preserve evidence is typically handled as a precautionary measure (similar to preliminary injunction; see below). With respect to legitimacy of the proper party and the role of UPC, see above §7.03[B].

[D] Freezing Orders, Article 61 UPCA

A freezing order should be considered under Finnish law an obligation to act and/or as an injunction and as a precautionary measure (similar to preliminary injunction; see below). What is stated above regarding the enforcement of an injunction, possible recurring penalty payments ordered by the UPC, and the lodging of a security should apply also with respect to freezing orders. However, as with the other orders, the enforcement practice will essentially depend on the formulation of the order by the UPC and on any accompanying obligations ordered by the UPC (e.g., regarding RoP 352 and 213). With respect to legitimacy of the proper party and the role of UPC, see above §7.03[B].

[E] Preliminary Injunction, Article 62(1) UPCA

A preliminary injunction should be considered under Finnish law an obligation not to do something (i.e., an injunction) and as a precautionary measure (Chapter 7 of the Finnish Code of Judicial Procedure). The enforcement of precautionary measures under the Finnish system (Chapter 8 of the Finnish Enforcement Code) requires the placing of a security by the applicant of the precautionary measure. Moreover, under the Finnish system, the applicant must lodge the main action within one (1) month from the preliminary injunction decision in order for the preliminary injunction to remain in effect (Chapter 7 of the Finnish Code of Judicial Procedure).

The enforcement of the (preliminary) injunction itself follows the principles outlined above regarding injunctions. However, as noted above, with respect to orders by the UPC, the UPC has the competence to set forth recurring penalty payments for deterring non-compliance also with respect to preliminary injunctions (UPCA 62). Further, it is acknowledged in the UPCA (UPCA 82) that the enforcement of a decision may be subject to the provision of a security and the UPC itself is also competent to order the placement of security (UPCRoP 352). Further, under RoP 213 the applicant is required to start the proceedings on the merits within 31 calendar days or 20 working days (whichever is the longer) of the UPC's order or otherwise the provisional measures are revoked or otherwise cease to have effect upon the request of the defendant without prejudice to the damages which may be claimed. Thus, while the UPC has the competence for such penalty payments and securities, the Authority should be deemed to have the competence at least to enforce the collection of such payments as monetary claims and the placement of securities as obligations to act. With respect to legitimacy of the proper party and the role of UPC, see above §7.03[B].

[F] Seizure or Delivery up of Infringing Products, Article 62(3) UPCA

A seizure or delivery up of infringing products should be considered under Finnish law, depending on the exact formulation of the order, an obligation to act, an injunction, and/or an obligation to let another party to do something. It is notable that under the Finnish practice, a such an order is typically handled as a precautionary measure. What is stated above regarding preliminary injunctions as precautionary measures should thus also apply with respect to seizures and delivery ups of infringing products. With respect to legitimacy of the proper party and the role of UPC, see above §7.03[B].

[G] Precautionary Seizure of Movable and Immovable Property, Article 62(3) UPCA

A precautionary seizure of movable and immovable property by the UPC should be enforceable under the Finnish enforcement rules set forth above. It is notable that under the Finnish practice, a such an order is typically handled as a precautionary measure. What is stated above regarding preliminary injunctions as precautionary measures should thus also apply with respect to seizure of movable and immovable property. With respect to legitimacy of the proper party and the role of UPC, see above §7.03[B].

[H] Recalling from the Channels of Commerce, Article 64(2) lit (b) UPCA

An order to recall from the channels of commerce should be considered under Finnish law an obligation to act and/or an obligation to let another party to do something and should be enforceable under the Finnish enforcement rules set forth above. What is stated above regarding possible recurring penalty payments ordered by the UPC should apply also with respect to such orders for recalling from the channels of commerce. With respect to legitimacy of the proper party and the role of UPC, see above §7.03[B].

[I] Depriving the Product of Its Infringing Property, Article 64(2) lit (c) UPCA

An order to deprive the product of its infringing property should be considered under Finnish law an obligation to act and/or an obligation to let another party to do something and should be enforceable under the Finnish enforcement rules set forth above. What is stated above regarding possible recurring penalty payments ordered by the UPC should apply also with respect to such orders for depriving the product of its infringing property. With respect to legitimacy of the proper party and the role of UPC, see above §7.03[B].

[J] Removing from the Channels of Commerce, Article 64(2) lit (d) UPCA

An order to remove from the channels of commerce should be considered under Finnish law an obligation to act and/or an obligation to let another party to do something and should be enforceable under the Finnish enforcement rules set forth above. What is stated above regarding possible recurring penalty payments ordered by the UPC should apply also with respect to such orders for removing from the channels of commerce. With respect to legitimacy of the proper party and the role of UPC, see above §7.03[B].

[K] Destruction, Article 64(2) lit (e) UPCA

An order to destruct should be considered under Finnish law an obligation to act and/or an obligation to let another party to do something and should be enforceable under the Finnish enforcement rules set forth above. What is stated above regarding fines possible recurring penalty payments ordered by the UPC should apply also with respect to such destruction orders. With respect to legitimacy of the proper party and the role of UPC, see above §7.03[B].

[L] Communication of Information, Article 67 UPCA

An order to communicate information should be considered under Finnish law an obligation to act and/or, in some occasions, an obligation to let another party to do something and should be enforceable under the Finnish enforcement rules set forth above. What is stated above regarding possible recurring penalty payments ordered by the UPC should apply also with respect to such orders for communicating information. However, the actual enforcement measures would depend on the formulation of the order. With respect to legitimacy of the proper party and the role of UPC, see above §7.03[B].

Chapter 8

France

Marc Lauzeral, Emmanuel Gougé, Jules Fabre and Nevyn Fournel

§8.01 SOURCES OF LAW FOR ENFORCEMENT

According to Article 82(3) of the Agreement on a Unified Patent Court ('UPCA'), enforcement of Unified Patent Court ('UPC') decisions and orders is governed by the law of the Contracting Member State where the enforcement takes place and under the same conditions as a decision from a court of that Member State.

Enforcement of court decisions in France is primarily governed by the Code of civil procedure ('*Code de procédure civile*' or 'CPC') and the Code of civil enforcement procedures ('*Code des procédures civiles d'exécution*' or 'CPCE'). In addition, the Code of judicial organisation ('*Code de l'organisation judiciaire*' or 'COJ'), which sets out the rules for the internal organisation, functioning and competence of French courts, contains provision relevant for the enforcement of court decisions.

Enforceable titles are listed in Article L. 111-3 CPCE. This provision was amended by Order No. 2018-341 of 9 May 2018[1] relating to the unitary patent and UPC (which contains several provisions aimed at adapting French law to the unitary patent regulations and the UPCA) to add UPC decisions to the list of enforceable titles. This change entered into force the same date the UPCA will enter into force, i.e., on 1 June 2023.

Hence, as of 1 June 2023, Article L. 111-3 CPCE reads as follows:

> Only the following are enforceable titles:
>
> 1° Decisions of judicial or administrative courts when they are enforceable, as well as agreements to which these courts have conferred enforceability;

1. Order No 2018-341 of 9 May 2018 on the European patent with unitary effect and the unified patent court: https://www.legifrance.gouv.fr/jorf/id/JORFSCTA000036887990.

> 2° Foreign acts and judgments as well as arbitration sentences declared enforceable by a decision that is not subject to an appeal suspending enforcement, without prejudice to applicable provisions of European Union law;
>
> 2° bis Decisions handed down by the Unified Patent Court; ...

Therefore, UPC decisions are directly enforceable in France, as if they had been handed down by a French court, in line with Article 82(3) UPCA. Although Article L.111-3 (2bis) CPCE does not distinguish between decisions and orders, unlike in the UPCA, we believe that the term 'decision' should be understood in a broad sense, i.e. as referring to both UPC decisions and UPC orders.

Hence, subject to provisions on enforcement which are contained in the UPCA and the UPC Rules of Procedure, UPC decisions and orders will be enforced in France under the same rules as decisions from French courts.

§8.02 OVERVIEW OF AUTHORITIES CARRYING OUT ENFORCEMENT IN FRANCE

In France, bailiffs (since July 2022 '*Commissaires de justice*', previously '*huissiers de justice*') are the main authority responsible for the enforcement of court decisions and other enforceable titles, although in specific areas other persons or authorities can be competent for enforcement. Bailiffs are authorised to seek the assistance of the police force and public prosecutor when enforcing a decision. It should be noted that any party with an enforceable title can appoint a bailiff. There is no need to use a locally qualified attorney for that purpose.

In case of issues with the enforcement, parties can seize the competent Enforcement Judge ('*Juge de l'exécution*' or 'JEX') who, under Article L. 213-6 COJ 'has exclusive competence to handle difficulties relating to enforceable titles and disputes arising in the context of enforcement'. We believe that the JEX will retain such competence in relation to issues arising in the context of enforcing decisions from the UPC (see section VI below).

Only a locally qualified attorney may refer a case to the JEX, except where the amount at stake does not exceed EUR 10,000, in which case legal representation is not required. In most patent disputes, the party seeking judicial help to enforce a decision has to use a locally qualified attorney to seize the JEX.

Attorneys are granted a certificate which allows them to access a virtual platform called '*e-barreau*' via a private network, the 'RPVA'. This private network enables them to communicate amongst them or with the French jurisdictions. Typically, attorneys will seize the JEX by filing a complaint on '*e-barreau*'.

[A] French Bailiff's Monopoly on Enforcement

Under Article L. 122-1 CPCE, bailiffs have an exclusive competence in France for executing the enforcement of, *inter alia*, court decisions and protective seizures.

Therefore, bailiffs will be the authority primarily responsible for the enforcement of UPC decisions in France and will thus be competent to enforce orders to preserve evidence and inspect premises (Article 60 UPCA), freezing orders (Article 61 UPCA), protective measures such as the seizure of delivery up of allegedly infringing products or precautionary seizure or movable and immovable property of an alleged infringer (Article 62(3) UPCA), or the destruction of the infringing products (Article 64(2)(e) UPCA). Bailiffs will also be competent for enforcing orders to pay damages or other financial remedies, as well as recurring penalties, notably with the following procedures available under French law:

- the '*saisie-vente*', a procedure to seize and sell the debtor's goods (Articles L. 221-1 and R. 221-1 CPCE) ; and
- the '*saisie-attribution*', a procedure to seize a debt in the hand of a third party, such as a bank where the debtor has an account (Articles L. 211-1 and R-211-1 CPCE).

Moreover, when bailiffs are faced with an issue or obstacle when executing enforcement, they are entitled to refer the issue directly to the JEX (Article R. 151-1 CPCE).

[B] Other Persons Qualified to Carry out Enforcement

As an exception to the bailiffs' monopoly, under Article L. 122-3 CPCE, other persons can be authorised to carry out enforcement and perform protective seizures, in specific areas.

[1] Directorate-General of Public Finance

Agents of the Directorate-General of Public Finance ('*Direction Générale des Finances Publiques*'), which is the French tax authority, are competent for the recovery public debts (Article R. 122-2 CPCE). If the party seeking to enforce a UPC decision is a French public body, agents of the Directorate-General of Public Finance may therefore be competent for certain enforcement measures, without the need to instruct a bailiff.

[2] Customs Officers

Article 368 of the Customs Code provides that 'customs officers may perform, in customs matters, all acts of execution and other legal acts that bailiffs are usually required to perform'.

That being said, the role of customs officers in the enforcement of measures ordered by the UPC is likely to remain limited.

[C] The Assistance of the Police Force and Public Prosecutors

[1] The Police Force

According to Article L. 153-1 CPCE 'the State is required to assist in the enforcement of judgments and other enforceable titles.' Article R.153-2 CPCE further states that bailiffs can 'request the assistance of police officers'.

Assistance of police officers is typically sought by bailiffs if they anticipate or are faced with resistance from the party against which the measures are being enforced (for instance, in the context of a seizure).

[2] Public Prosecutors

Under Article L. 121-5 CPCE, public prosecutors have a general responsibility to 'ensure the enforcement of judgments and other enforceable titles'.

However, in civil patent litigation cases, public prosecutors usually do not play a role in the enforcement of judgments in practice, as they prioritise criminal matters.

[D] Enforcement Judges

JEXs have an exclusive jurisdiction to hear issues related to the enforcement of, *inter alia*, court decisions. They can be seized by either party, as well as bailiffs. In view of Article 82(3) UPCA, we believe that the exclusive competence of the JEX in enforcement matters also apply to UPC decisions (see section VI below).

JEXs are notably competent for granting protective measures and hearing disputes relating to their enforcement (Article L. 213-6 al. 2 COJ). Protective measures available are the '*saisie-conservatoire*', a protective seizure and the '*sûreté judiciaire*', a judicial security (Article L.511-1 CPCE).

JEXs also have jurisdiction over claims for compensation in cases of a harmful enforcement or lack of enforcement (Article L. 213-6 al. 4 COJ).

JEXs also have the power to grant measures including recurring penalties and grace periods.

[1] Recurring Penalties

The main measure used to enforce injunctive relief in France is the recurring penalty and, even in cases where the judgment orders an injunction but does not order the payment of a recurring penalty if the injuncted party fails to comply, JEXs have the power to impose a penalty payment (they can do so in relation to the compliance with any measures in a decision issued by any court) (Article L. 131-1 CPCE).

JEXs can impose a recurring penalty to put pressure on a party and force them to comply with several measures foreseen by the UPCA, including:

- an order to produce evidence (Article 59 UPCA);
- a recall of products from the channels of commerce (Article. 64(2)(b) UPCA);
- an order to deprive a product of its infringing property (Article 64(2)(c) UPCA);
- an order to remove products from the channel of commerce (Article 64(2) lit (d) UPCA);
- an order to communicate information (Article 67 UPCA).

JEXs are exclusively competent to order the payment of a recurring penalty, unless proceedings are still pending before the relevant court or if the latter has reserved the right to calculate the recurring payment and order its payments (Article L. 131-3 CPCE).

[2] Grace Periods

JEXs can also order a grace period, to delay the enforcement of a measure, upon request from the party against which enforcement is being sought (Article 510 CPC).

§8.03 GENERAL REQUIREMENTS FOR ENFORCEMENT

[A] General Rules to be Observed before Enforcing a Civil Court Order

Article 502 CPC provides that, save exceptions, only copies of decisions to which an order for enforcement (‘*formule exécutoire*’) is appended are enforceable. The order for enforcement is an order made on behalf of the French Republic giving power to all bailiffs to enforce the decision and to all police force officers to assist such enforcement where required, manually signed by or on behalf of the Presiding Judge and bearing the official stamp of the court.

We understand that for UPC decisions this requirement will be satisfied under Article 82(1) UPCA which provides that ‘an order for enforcement of a decision shall be appended to the decision by the Court’.

Under Article 503 CPC, and unless a party voluntarily enforces a decision, decisions are only enforceable after they have been notified to the party against which enforcement is sought.

In French civil proceedings, notification of decisions is normally made by the parties, not by the court.

The notification must be made directly to the party by a bailiff in accordance with and under the forms of the French legal rules on service of documents by bailiffs (Article 675 CPC). In proceedings where representation is mandatory, a prior notification between parties’ representatives is also required (Article 678 CPC).

However, for UPC decisions, Rules 6 and 276 of the UPC Rules of Procedure provide that the Registry shall serve orders and decisions directly to the parties. In addition, Rule 354 provides that UPC decisions and orders are directly enforceable ‘from their date of service’.

Therefore, and although this remains to be confirmed, it is arguable that the service of UPC decisions by the UPC Registry satisfies the prior notification requirement of Article 503 CPC and thus that no additional service by the enforcing party is required for enforcement to take place in France.

Regarding translation requirements, Rules 270 et seq. and Regulation (EU) 2020/1784 on the service in the Member States of judicial and extrajudicial documents in civil or commercial matters (service of documents) apply.

Under Rule 271(7) and Article 12 of Regulation (EU) 2020/1784, the party against which a UPC decision is served (either by the UPC Registry or by the other party) is entitled to refuse service if the decision is not written in, or is not accompanied by a translation into, either a language they understand, or an official language of the Member State where service is being made.

Rule 271(7) provides for a short period for the addressee to notify the refusal (one week, instead of two weeks under Article 12 of Regulation (EU) 2020/1784) and states that, should a refusal be notified, the enforcing party shall provide a translation to the Registry.

Finally, under Article L. 111-4 CPCE there is a time lime of ten years (from the date of the decision) to enforce court decisions. This rule will now apply to the enforcement of UPC orders and decisions in France.

[B] Limitations as to Who is Entitled to Seek Enforcement in France

Under French law, court decisions can be enforced by any party who is the creditor of an obligation ordered in the decision.

It is likely (but subject to discussion) that this also includes the UPC itself when a penalty payment has been ordered against a party, under Rule 354(3), given that such payment is payable to the UPC and not to the other party (contrary to the French practice on penalty payments which are normally payable to the other party, not the court).

As mentioned above, the main authority responsible for carrying out enforcement of court decisions in France are bailiffs (Article L122.1 CPCE). Bailiffs have a territorial competence in France, thus any party (or the UPC) seeking to enforce a UPC decision in France should instruct a bailiff established within the territorial jurisdiction of the Court of Appeal where the enforcement measures will be performed.

If enforcement is sought by both a party and the UPC (regarding penalty payments), it would probably be advisable to instruct two different bailiffs to avoid any risk of a potential conflict of interest.

§8.04 OVERVIEW OF PROCEEDINGS

As noted above, it is not necessary for a party seeking to enforce a judicial decision to hire an attorney in order to apply to a bailiff. Legal representation is only mandatory if the party encounters enforcement issues that would force them to lodge a complaint with the JEX.

Moreover, under the Villers-Cotterêts Act of August 1510, the legal language to be used for all legal proceedings in France is French. In consequence, it is possible to notify the debtor of an obligation in a foreign language, but an addressee who does not know the language in which the document is written may refuse service and request a French translation at the sender's expense (Article 688-5 CPC). In addition, as already mentioned (see section III.1 above), Rule 271(7) and Article 12 of Regulation (EU) 2020/1784 also provides that the party against whom a UPC decision is served is entitled to refuse service if the decision is not written in, or is not accompanied by a translation into, either a language they understand, or an official language of the Member State where service is being made.

When a case is brought before a court, including the JEX's court, the French Civil Procedure Code provides that the judge does not have to use a professional translator if they understand the language in which the parties are speaking (Article 23 CPC).

Subsequently, regarding the enforcement measures themselves, they can be classified in two categories depending on their object: *personal* or *real* property.

Regarding *real* property, the seizure of real estate is a procedure which 'aims at the forced sale of the debtor's real estate or, where applicable, of the third-party holder with a view to the distribution of its price' (Article L. 311-1 CPCE).

Regarding *personal* property, which includes the debtor's movable goods, the main procedures are the '*saisie-vente*', and the '*saisie-attribution*'. These two proceedings are explained in further details below as they are the most common measures undertaken by creditors.

The '*saisie-vente*' consists in seizing and selling the debtor's goods (Articles L. 221-1 and R. 221-1 CPCE). Once the decision is enforceable (see section III.1 above), the '*saisie-vente*' starts with the bailiff sending a notice to the debtor. Such notice can be sent on paper or electronically but is in any case mandatory, otherwise the seizure is void. The notice must refer to the enforcement title (i.e. the UPC decision) on the basis of which enforcement is sought, and contain an order to pay within *eight days*, failing which the debtor may be compelled to pay with the proceeds of the forced sale of their goods. The seizure of the goods must take place within *two years* after the notice, otherwise a new notice with a new order of payment is required.

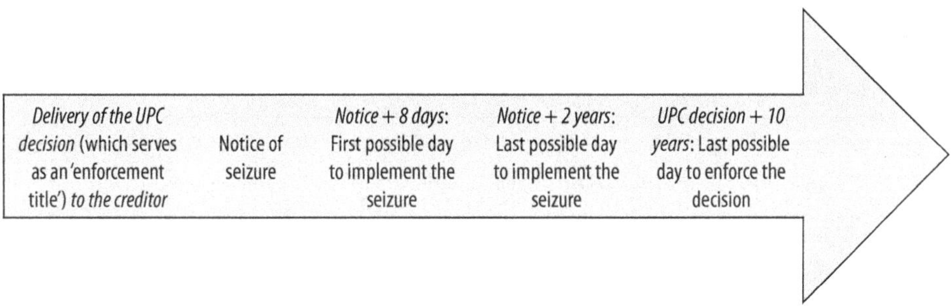

As to the seizure itself, it must comply with certain formalities. First, if the debtor attends the seizure, the bailiff must verbally reiterate the order of payment and inform the debtor of their obligation to disclose which goods have already been the object of another seizure, if any. While they are conducting the seizure, the bailiff writes a report of the seizure (the '*acte de saisie*', Article R. 221-16 CPCE) which describes all the measures undertaken and provides for an inventory of the seized goods. If the debtor does not attend the seizure, the bailiff sends them a copy of the report, with an injunction to disclose any anterior seizure of their goods. The bailiff undertakes similar steps when the debtor' goods are with a third party. The third party is obliged to declare the assets that belong to the debtor. They are financially liable for any refusal to answer and/or for any inaccurate or untruthful declaration (Articles R. 221-21 and R. 221-22 CPCE).

The '*saisie-vente*' continues with the sale of the debtor's assets. According to Article L. 221-3 CPCE, the debtor has *one month* to sell their goods out-of-court, starting from the notice of seizure. Debtors willingly selling their goods must inform the bailiff of the offers they receive, together with the name, address and time period in which the potential buyer intends to pay for the goods. From the moment the bailiff informs the creditors of these elements, they have *fifteen days* to accept or refuse the offers. The absence of a reply is deemed to be an acceptance (Article R. 221-31 CPCE). The transfer of property depends on the payment of the price. In case of non-payment within the time limit, the bailiff shall proceed with the auction of the debtor's property. The auction can take place only after completing public display formalities to ensure that potential buyers are aware of it (Article R. 221-34 CPCE).

The bailiff informs the debtor about the auction *eight days* before it starts. The creditor who initiates the seizure must notify other creditors who have a perfected security interest in the seized property of the upcoming disposition of their collateral (Article R. 221-36-1 CPCE). The other creditors then have *fifteen days* to claim their security interest (by communicating its nature and amount) otherwise they lose their right to their share in the proceeds of the sale.

The goods go to the highest bidder. If there is only one creditor, they receive the proceeds of the sale either *one month* after the auction or *one month* after the out-of-court sale. If there are several creditors, the proceeds are distributed amongst them (Article R. 251-2 CPCE).

Step 1: Seizure

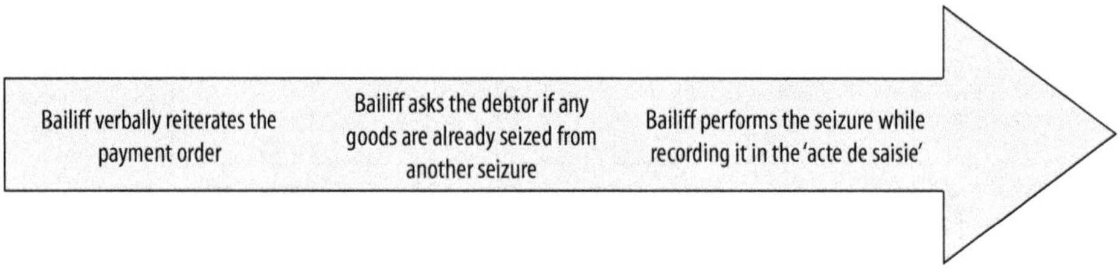

Step 2: Sale of the seized goods

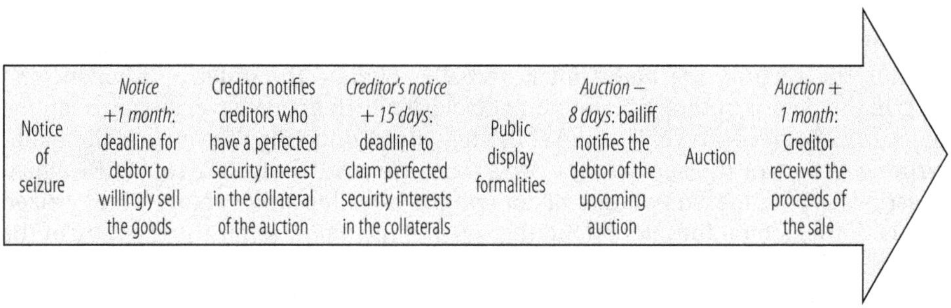

The '*saisie-attribution*' consists in seizing an amount from a deposit account owned by the debtor (Articles L. 211-1 and R-211-1 CPCE). Hence, it involves three parties: the enforcing creditor, the debtor and the third party who detains the debtor's money, typically the debtor's bank.

The procedure starts with a request to the bailiff for a writ of attachment ('*acte de saisie*') specifying the goods to be seized. The bailiff communicates this writ to the debtor's bank (Article R. 211-1 CPCE), who must disclose all the required information. The bailiff then notifies the debtor of the seizure within *eight days* (by an '*acte de dénonciation*', Article R. 211-3 CPCE), failing which the seizure is void. According to Article R. 211-3 CPCE, this notification must also indicate in very visible characters that any challenge must be brought within *one month* following service of summons and the corresponding date. If no dispute is lodged in that time, or before if the debtor states that they are not willing to raise any challenge, the third party executes the payment upon presentation of a certificate issued by the bailiff certifying that no challenge has been raised.

In any event, if the parties encounter any difficulty in carrying out the enforcement measures, for example if the debtor refuses to pay the sums owed by the debtor, or if the creditor exceeds their enforceable title, they can seize the JEX (see section VI). For the recall, legal representation by an attorney is mandatory in most cases before the JEX.

§8.05 COSTS

Lawyers' fees are *freely determined* and usually charged on the basis of an hourly rate (French ethical rules limit the possibility of setting up success fees).

Regarding bailiffs, their fees include:

- *fixed fees* set by decree;
- *freely fixed fees*, intended to cover the bailiff's preparatory diligences that may be more substantial in the event of a complex case or, for instance, difficulty in locating the assets to be seized or blockage from the debtor.

The French Commercial Code regulates most of the fixed fees incurred by the official intervention of a bailiff (Articles L. 444-1, R. 444-1 and A. 444-10 et seq.).

The debtor shall bear the cost of enforcement, although the creditor can be required to pay a provision to the intermediaries involved in the enforcement measures.

Where enforcement involves the seizure of monies, the bailiff can directly collect the amounts due to them as fees.

If proceedings are launched before the JEX, one party may recover part of the costs incurred for the need of these proceedings. These expenses include translation fees, jurisdictional taxes, bailiff's fees and witness compensation (Article 695 CPC). This rule aims to ensure equal and effective access to justice. Furthermore, French courts may apply the principles of equity to order a party to pay additional costs not included in Article 695 CPC in a discretionary fashion (Article 700 CPC). This enables a party, for example, to recover at least part of the lawyers' fees incurred.

The bailiff's costs for *prior notification* of a decision to a debtor (Article 503 CPC) are usually around EUR 80 (not including external lawyers' fees for instructing the bailiff).

Enforcing a *permanent or preliminary injunction* would mainly result in imposing a recurring penalty either directly or by the JEX or the court, which will incur lawyers' fees. It is common practice in France to instruct a bailiff to issue a certified report acknowledging that the injunction is not being complied with (for instance an online or onsite purchase report to show the injuncted products are still being sold). Bailiff's fees for the drafting of such report are freely set and usually amount to about EUR 350. This does not include external lawyers' fees which will depend on the difficulty of the case and the defence raised by the infringer.

Once the recurring penalty is settled or liquidated, or if damages have been awarded (Article 68 UPCA), the bailiff's fees for seizing the corresponding sums on the debtor's bank account usually amounts to EUR 400–500 (it being specified that the payment of an initial fee up to EUR 270 may also be required if this is the first enforcement measure).

The same would apply to enforcing *an order to produce evidence* which would result in imposing a recurring penalty.

The enforcement of an *order to preserve evidence and to inspect premises* requires the intervention of a lawyer and a bailiff and may require a patent attorney and a technical expert (e.g., a computer expert to seize documents in the alleged infringer's information system), although this will depend on the UPC practice. Patent attorneys and technical experts' fees are freely set up. The amount of fees incurred can vary depending on the number of patents involved, the technicality of the case and the strategy elected, for instance if inspections are simultaneously conducted in different places, or the technical difficulty in seizing or describing part of a process invention.

The enforcement of a *freezing order* will require the bailiff to affix seals on the alleged infringing products to temporarily prevent the debtor from selling or moving them. The cost of a such act usually amounts to EUR 400–500.

As to *seizure or delivery up of infringing products order*, the cost will depend on the volume and number of products. The bailiff can proceed with their seizure or report their delivery up for an fee of approximately EUR 400–500.

A bailiff can proceed in a *precautionary seizure of movable or immovable goods* for fees of approximately EUR 300. Additional diligence will be necessary however to convert this measure into a definitive one and to proceed with the sale of the concerned property.

If an (alleged) infringer subject to a *recall from the channels of a commerce order* does not comply, the creditor may have the continued marketing of the concerned products certified by means of a bailiff report, notably in order to enforce a recurring penalty. The bailiff's fees for such a report usually amount to EUR 300–400.

The same would apply to the enforcement of a decision that would order to *deprive the product of its infringing property*.

In case of non-compliance with a decision that orders *the removal from the channels of commerce of the infringing products*, two scenarios must be considered:

- if the infringing products are stored in a *single location* and can be seized by the bailiff and provided that the court allows it, the bailiff can proceed for a fee of approximately EUR 400–500 depending on the extent of the seizure;
- if the infringing products are *not* stored in a single location, the creditor may have the continued marketing of the products concerned certified by means of a bailiff's report, notably in order to enforce a penalty.

Destruction can be certified by way of a bailiff's report. The corresponding fees depend on the time spent by the bailiff in carrying out or supervising the destruction and drafting of the related report. If necessary, a specialised company can also intervene to destroy the goods.

As to the *enforcement of a communication of information order*, it would mainly result in imposing a recurring penalty either directly or by the JEX and, once liquidated, in a seizure.

§8.06 COUNTERMEASURES ON ENFORCEMENT

It is important to note that the scope of JEX's jurisdiction is wide but not unlimited. Article L. 213-6 COJ states that JEX have 'exclusive jurisdiction over difficulties relating to enforceable titles and disputes arising in connection with enforcement, even if they relate to the merits, *unless they fall outside the jurisdiction of the judicial order*.'

This means that as long as issues raised in the context of enforcement fall within the French judicial order, only JEXs have jurisdiction to hear them, whereas if the dispute involves an issue falling within the jurisdiction of the administrative order, JEXs do not have jurisdiction and will have to order a stay until an administrative court decides on the issue. Regarding difficulties relating to the enforcement of a UPC decision and UPC orders, one could query whether the UPC belongs to the French judicial order and thus whether it falls outside the exclusive competence of the JEX (in which case, parties would have to go back to the UPC, not the JEX, to decide on any issues relating to enforcement in France). However, our view is that the UPC must be viewed as being part of the judicial order (i.e. not the administrative order) within the meaning of Article L. 213-6 COJ and thus that JEXs are competent. This interpretation would also be in line with Article 82(3) UPCA which clearly states that UPC decisions shall be enforced under the same conditions as national decisions and that enforcement procedures shall be governed by national law (with the exception under Article 82(4) UPCA that the UPC retains the power to grant recurring penalties if a party does not comply with an order from the UPC).

JEXs can take various measures with different purposes.

As a reminder (see Section II), JEXs can order measures to ensure the proper performance of the execution. In that regard, JEXs can order penalties if the 'circumstances of the case appear to require it' (Article L. 131-1 CPCE), under the condition that the jurisdiction which issued the decision did not expressly reserve the right to order penalties. If the court that issued the decision has ordered a penalty payment, the default rule is that JEXs have jurisdiction to calculate it (Article L. 131-3 CPCE). JEXs can also order grace periods if they deem it necessary (Article 510 CPC). JEXs will hear the disputes in connection with these orders linked to the performance of the execution measures (Article L. 213-6 COJ).

Secondly, JEXs will have jurisdiction over claims of invalidity of the enforcement procedures. As seen above, there are numerous requirements to comply with in order to implement enforcement measures.

For example, the debtor may challenge the validity of a seizure of their goods (in the case of a '*saisie-vente*') on formal or substantive grounds until the sale of the seized goods (Article R. 221-54 CPCE). If the invalidity is ordered after the sale but before the distribution of the price, the debtor may request the reinstatement of the proceeds of the sale (Article R. 221-54 al. 2 CPCE). Nevertheless, an application for invalidity does not suspend the seizure operations unless the judge decides otherwise (Article R. 221-56 CPCE). In addition to the debtor, a third party who claims to be the owner of a seized good may ask the JEX to order the segregation of such good. The request must specify the evidence on which the ownership right claimed is based (Article R. 221-51 CPCE). According to Article R. 221-52 CPCE, third parties must assert their rights of ownership before the sale of the goods, otherwise a specific action to claim ownership is the only possible option.

As to the '*saisie-attribution*', the debtor may ask the judge for the release of the seizure if it is unjust or useless, while requesting damages (Article L. 121-2 CPCE). According to Article R. 211-11 CPCE, disputes relating to the seizure shall be lodged within a period of one month from the date of notification of the seizure to the debtor.

In any case, the judgments from JEXs can be appealed before the court of appeal.

§8.07 PARTICULARITIES WITH RESPECT TO SPECIFIC ORDERS

There are no additional particularities specific to the following orders.

(a) permanent injunctions, Article 63 UPCA;
(b) an order to produce evidence, Article 59 UPCA;
(c) an order to preserve evidence and to inspect premises, Article 60 UPCA;
(d) freezing orders, Article 61 UPCA;
(e) preliminary injunction, Article 62(1) UPCA;
(f) seizure or delivery up of infringing products, Article 62(3) UPCA;
(g) precautionary seizure of movable and immovable property, Article 62(3) UPCA;
(h) recalling from the channels of commerce, Article 64(2) lit (b) UPCA;
(i) depriving the product of its infringing property, Article 64(2) lit (c) UPCA;
(j) removing from the channels of commerce, Article 64(2) lit (d) UPCA;
(k) destruction, Article 64(2) lit (e) UPCA;
(l) communication of information, Article 67 UPCA.

Chapter 9

Italy

Gualtiero Dragotti and Carlo M. Faggioni

---

§9.01 SOURCES OF LAW FOR ENFORCEMENT

General provisions on enforcement are contained in the Italian Code of Civil Procedure ('CCP'). The enforcement procedure is governed, in particular, by Articles 474 et seq. CCP. In particular, Articles 474–482 regulate the requisites of the executive title and of the formal request for payment; Articles 483–490 provide the rules generally applicable to all the enforcement proceedings, while the subsequent provisions regulate the different measures available to proceeding party, including the movable assets garnishment (Article 518 et seq. CCP), the third-party assets garnishment (Article 543 et seq. CCP) and the real estate property garnishment (Article 555 et seq. CCP).

Some additional rules are provided by the implementing provisions of the CCP. Other rules indirectly affecting the enforcement are included in the Italian Criminal Code (CC).

Specific rules regarding intellectual property ('IP') are provided in the Italian Code of Industrial Property ('IPC'), in particular in Article 124, which lists the measures and remedies available to the right owner, Article 127 that regulates the criminal sanctions, Articles 130 and 131, regulating the judicial description, the seizure and the injunction. Article 137 regulates the garnishment of IP rights and assets, while Article 144-bis introduces the seizure of goods and other assets of the infringer to guarantee the payment of damages due to the infringement of IP rights. Some additional measures available to fight IP piracy are regulated by Article 146 IPC.

It is worthwhile to mention that in 2022 a major reform of the Italian Code of Civil Procedure was enacted; the majority of the changes entered in force on 1 March 2023. It is too early to fully appreciate the effects of the reform, which modified a significant number of provisions and introduced relevant changes, not directly affecting the provisions immediately relevant for the purpose of this work. Unless otherwise specified, in the following discussion no reference has been made to the changes related to the reform.

§9.02 OVERVIEW OF AUTHORITIES EXECUTING ENFORCEMENT IN ITALY

In Italy the main authorities and entities involved in the process of the enforcement of a judicial decision, in particular those referring to intellectual property rights ('IPRs'), are the following:

- enforcement divisions of ordinary civil courts;
- IP divisions of ordinary civil courts;
- bailiffs;
- criminal courts and police;
- Italian Revenue Agency.

With specific reference to the IP divisions of ordinary civil courts, they were originally established in twelve main courts; subsequently they become twenty-two, but only eleven of them, i.e. Bari, Cagliari, Catania, Genova, Milano, Napoli. Roma, Torino, Venezia, Trento and Bolzano are competent to deal with disputes involving foreign parties.

It must be noted that actually those divisions are not really involved in the enforcement of decisions in the narrow sense, but rather they can be invoked in all those cases where disputes arise in connection with the execution of the measures, as per Article 124(7) IPC. In particular, any challenge which should arise during the execution of the measures provided by the IPC, shall be decided by the same judge who issued the decision containing those measures, by a ruling not subject to appeal, after hearing the opinions of the parties. In these cases, the judge who issued the order can be asked by the party interested in the enforcement of the granted measures to better clarify *how* the infringer shall comply with the order. Major scholars maintain that all the disputes referred to the *an, quantum* and *quomodo* of the measure granted to protect IPRs should be managed and solved by the competent IP division.

All other cases, especially the enforcement of an order to pay money in connection with penalties, are within the jurisdiction of enforcement divisions of the ordinary Italian courts (which also set the specific manner of direct enforcement). The competent enforcement division is determined on the basis of the criteria set forth in Article 26 CCP, according to which the competent forum corresponds to the location of the goods or assets on which the execution must take place, or the location where the obligation to do or not to do something must be fulfilled (quite frequently, the debtor's domicile).

Turning to the actual enforcement actions, they are usually carried out by a bailiff, chosen on the basis of the place where the activity must take place. If necessary the bailiff could be assisted by the police to overcome difficulties that may arise in the course of the enforcement.

Lastly, criminal courts are involved in the application of criminal sanctions in the event of non-compliance with a (civil) court's order, for example when an injunction or an order to cease and desist is wilfully ignored or violated, as provided by Article 388(3) of the Italian Criminal Code ('CC'), which reads as follows:

> The same penalty [imprisonment up to three years or a fine from EUR 103 to 1,032] applies to anyone who eludes the enforcement of a court order prescribing injunctions or corrective measures for the protection of industrial property rights.

§9.03 GENERAL REQUIREMENTS FOR ENFORCEMENT

According to Italian law, once a decision suitable for enforcement, i.e. an executive title (*'titolo esecutivo'*) has been obtained from the competent court, enforcement proceedings against the debtor/recipient of the court's order can be started.

Depending on the content of the order and on the nature of the measures to be enforced, different paths can be followed, as better detailed in the following.

Usually, the main difference lies between payment orders and all the other measures (obligation to do something and orders not to do something). It is worth mentioning that it is not unusual, and is indeed common in IP proceedings, that non-monetary measures are assisted by penalties, aimed on the one side to cause the debtor to comply with the measure and on the other side to ease the enforcement in case of non-compliance. As a matter of facts, some orders, in particular those including an obligation to do something, cannot be enforced without the cooperation of the debtor; the penalty is a strong and usually effective means to obtain such cooperation.

For payment orders, including the payment of the penalties just mentioned, the measure can be immediately enforced by serving upon the debtor a formal request for payment (*'precetto'*). Such a request is usually drafted by the creditor's attorney and should clearly identify, *inter alia*, the amount due and the executive title supporting the credit. Moreover, the request for payment shall contain the declaration of the residence or the election of the domicile by the creditor in the same municipality as the court competent for the enforcement proceedings.

In all the other cases, a formal application before the enforcement division of the civil court shall be sought, according to Articles 612 et seq. CCP.

The subject entitled to request the enforcement is either the creditor, in case of payment orders, or the entity in favour of which the Court's order was issued.

An application to the Enforcement Division of the civil court initiates a formal judicial procedure that requires the assistance of a locally qualified attorney.

The proceedings are and must be conducted in Italian (some exceptions may apply in certain multilingual regions of the country); therefore, it is necessary to have an Italian translation of the relevant documents, especially the decision to be enforced.

The procedure provides for limited use of the electronic or remote filing and management system, now adopted for main proceedings but not fully available for enforcement proceedings.

As for the timings, there are no specific time limits on the enforcement of a (civil) court order, except for statutory limitation after *res judicata* which amounts to ten years. Only some provisional remedies – such as seizure – require to be enforced within a specific term.

It is deemed that the same general requirements will be applied by national authorities upon orders of the UPC (this being equivalent to a national court).

§9.04 OVERVIEW OF PROCEEDINGS

In order to start enforcement proceedings, an executive title shall be issued. Any decision issued by a judicial authority entailing an order is suitable for this purpose. This applies also to provisional orders.

With reference to IP disputes, court decisions can usually entail various measures which differ significantly, from a cease and desist order to the destruction of the infringing goods, from the order of withdrawal from the marketplace to the seizure of goods. Some of these measures are usually accompanied by a penalty, which means that the court usually provides for a fixed sum due by the infringer for any future violation of the order or for any delay in complying with it. This is a kind of *astreinte*, which aims at making it inconvenient for the infringer not to comply with the order issued by the court.

As anticipated in §9.01 above, for the purposes hereof, the executive titles can be distinguished between those pertaining to payment orders and those entailing different obligations, mainly to do or not to do something.

As for enforcement of the penalty clause, as above stated, the creditor can immediately ask the debtor for the payment of the sum due, without going back to the judge for clarifications, unless doubts related to the *quantum* or to the scope of the violation arise – in such cases, pursuant to Article 124(7) IPC it is possible to ask the IP Judge who issued the order for an explanation. Apparently, such an option is not available for doubts on UPC orders, whose interpretation is presumably not subject to any intervention by the Italian IP divisions of civil courts.

Otherwise, in order to start the enforcement proceedings, the creditor – in IP litigation usually the IPR owner, assisted by a local attorney- shall serve the debtor – in IP litigation usually the infringer – with a formal notice (so-called '*precetto*') requesting the payment of the due sums within ten days from the service date.

According to the general rules of Italian civil proceedings, the '*precetto*' should be in the Italian language; it should also be accompanied by the executive title, again translated into Italian.

Should the debtor fail to comply, the creditor can satisfy its credit by attaching the assets of the debtor through serving on the debtor a writ of garnishment no later than ninety days after the service of the notice for payment. Italian law provides for three different types of garnishment, depending on the assets that the creditor intends to attack:

(1) movable assets garnishment, by which, pursuant to Article 518 et seq. CCP, the creditor can attach debtor's movable properties (it shall be considered that Article 514 CCP prohibits attaching, *inter alia*, some primary assets indispensable for the debtor either to live – such as clothes or essential furniture – or to carry out his profession);
(2) third-party assets garnishment, by which, pursuant to Article 543 et seq. CCP, the creditor can attach the credits that the debtor has against third parties, typically the bank(s) used by the debtor;
(3) real estate property garnishment, by which, pursuant to Article 555 et seq. CCP, the creditor can attach the debtor's real estate properties.

The procedural steps vary slightly depending on the specific garnishment procedure that the creditor opts for; the same applies to the criteria for determining the competent court. In general terms, it can be considered that, as for the movable and immovable assets garnishment, the court of the place where the assets are located is identified as the competent court. Whereas for the enforcement of credits, including third-party assets garnishment, the court of the place where the debtor has his residence, domicile, abode or seat is generally competent.

All these procedures aim to get control of some of the debtor's assets and sell them to the public in order to obtain sufficient funds to pay the creditor. The procedures take place under the control of the court, often operating through external agencies and professionals. Any dispute is ultimately subject to a decision of the court.

Once the garnishment is in place, the court schedules a hearing in which either the sale or the assignment of the garnished assets can be ordered.

With reference to the timing, third-party garnishment is usually the fastest procedure, as it can be usually carried out in six or seven months. In order to successfully execute this garnishment, the creditor must identify in advance the third parties holding the debtor's assets; most frequently they are the banks where the creditor has its accounts or any other funds.

For non-monetary measures, according to Article 612 CCP, in order to obtain the enforcement of a judgment for breach of an obligation to act or not to act, – after the service of the executive title along with the formal notice ('*precetto*') upon the infringer – the applicant must file an application with the enforcement judge asking for directions on the specific execution of the order. In this case, for the enforcement of obligations to act or not to act, the court of the place where the obligation must be performed has jurisdiction.

The judge issues the directions, in the form of an enforcement decision, after hearing the opposing party. In the enforcement decision, the judge designates the bailiff who is to proceed with the execution and the persons who are to provide for the completion of the unperformed obligation or the disposal of what had been performed. Further to that, it is up to the bailiff to carry out the execution as indicated in the order, without prejudice to the right to ask the enforcement judge, pursuant to Article 613 CCP, to intervene to overcome any obstacles incurred during the execution.

Lastly, it is worth mentioning that in any case the party against whom the enforcement is sought can lodge an objection, as better outlined in §9.06.

For an overview of the proceedings please refer to Figure 1.

§9.05 COSTS

Court fees related to enforcement proceedings in Italy are negligible (presently they vary from EUR 139 for movable assets garnishments to EUR 278 for real estate property garnishments).

Most of the actual costs therefore correspond to attorney fees. Under Italian law, attorney fees are usually determined through a private agreement which the client and the attorney are free to stipulate as they wish.

If there is no agreement between the client and the attorney, a compulsory fixed tariff system will apply, based on activity carried out in the proceedings and depending on the jurisdiction and the value of the proceeding. In this latter case the cost estimation (attorney fees) is usually provided according to Ministerial Decree 55/14 and depends on the value of the dispute.

By way of example, said Decree indicates that the average legal fees due for commencing the execution by drafting and serving the '*precetto*' (see §9.04 above)

Figure 1.

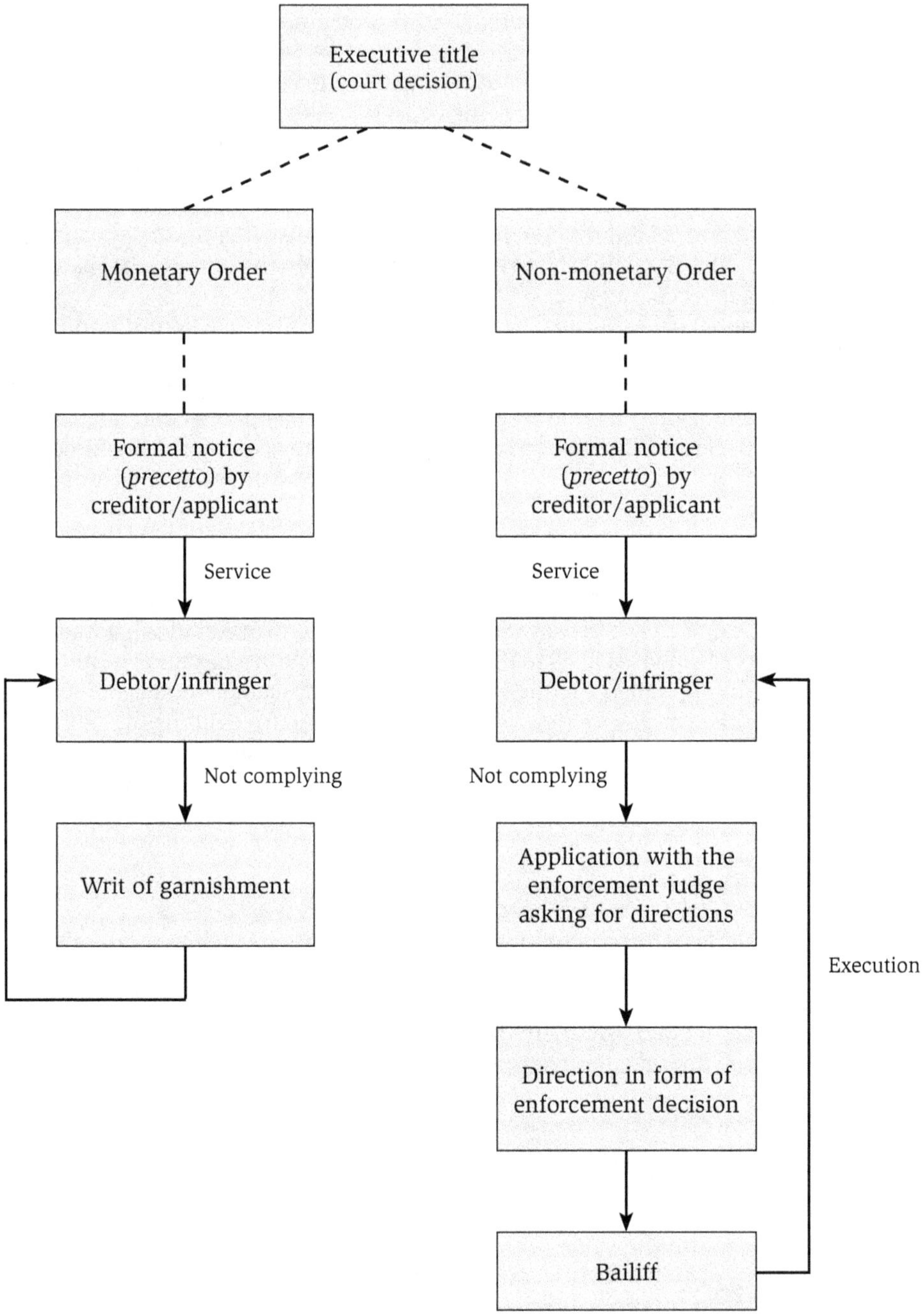
Executive title
(court decision)
Monetary Order
Non-monetary Order
Formal notice (*precetto*) by creditor/applicant
Formal notice (*precetto*) by creditor/applicant
Service
Service
Debtor/infringer
Debtor/infringer
Not complying
Not complying
Writ of garnishment
Application with the enforcement judge asking for directions
Execution
Direction in form of enforcement decision
Bailiff

could vary from as little as EUR 400 to around EUR 1,100, assuming that the credit is in the range EUR 520,000–1,000,000.

The fees for the movable assets garnishment proceedings related to a credit in the above range would vary from as little as EUR 1,600 to almost EUR 5,000.

In case of third-party assets garnishment the range would be EUR 2,700–8,000; slightly lower fees would apply for real estate property garnishment.

The figures provided by Ministerial Decree 55/14 are used by the courts in the award of costs which, according to Article 91 CCP, the losing party in a proceeding must in most cases reimburse to the winning party. The resulting figures of a decision on awarding costs are often low, except where substantial costs for a bailiff or expert appointed by the court are incurred.

The above provisions on costs and fees are relevant for a number of different enforceable measures, such as permanent injunction (Article 63 UPCA), an order to preserve evidence and to inspect premises (Article 60 UPCA), freezing orders (Article 61 UPCA), preliminary injunctions (Article 62(1) UPCA), seizure or delivery up of infringing products (Article 62(3) UPCA), precautionary seizure of movable and immovable property (Article 62(3) UPCA), recalling from the channels of commerce (Article 64(2) lit (b) UPCA), and destruction (Article 64(2) lit (e) UPCA).

In connection with an order to produce evidence (Article 59 UPCA) there is usually no cost, since it cannot be delivered out of or after decision of a lawsuit on the merits.

Moreover, according to Article 96.2 CCP when the judge assesses that the right, for which a preliminary injunction was executed or an execution proceeding commenced or accomplished does not exist, upon request by the party who was damaged as a consequence of it, the petitioner of the proceeding who acted without due diligence must compensate the damaged party for the damages suffered by the latter.

The recent reform of the CCP introduced the possibility for the judge to order the party in the cases mentioned above also to pay a fine, not lower than EUR 500 and not higher than EUR 5,000, to a specific fund of the court (*'Cassa delle Ammende'*). In this case the competent body for the enforcement of the decision is the Italian Revenue Agency.

§9.06 COUNTERMEASURES ON ENFORCEMENT

The party against whom enforcement is sought has two main remedies: opposition to the enforcement proceedings (*'opposizione all'esecuzione'*), which is governed by Article 615 CCP, and opposition to the enforcement acts (*'opposizione agli atti esecutivi'*), which is governed by Article 617 CCP.

[A] Opposition to the Enforcement Proceedings

Opposition to the enforcement proceedings is aimed at challenging the right of a party to seek the enforcement of a decision, for example because there is not a valid executive title, the debtor has already fulfilled the obligation set by the decision, the party against whom the enforcement is sought is not the debtor, or because the movable assets garnishment is sought with regard to assets that cannot be attached (see §9.04 above). The CCP does not provide for a time within which the party has to start the opposition proceedings, but they cannot be started after the decision issued at the outcome of the enforcement proceedings. If enforcement proceedings have already started, the opposition shall be lodged before the seised judge. If enforcement proceedings have not been yet started (e.g. after the service of the formal notice – '*precetto*' – but before the service of the writ of garnishment), the opposition shall be lodged before the judge of the place of the enforcement (see Article 615 CCP). In case the '*precetto*' served by the creditor did not contain the declaration of residence or the election of domicile in the same municipality of the judge competent for the enforcement proceedings, the opposition shall be filed before the judge of the place where the request of payment has been served (see Article 480(3) CCP).

If serious reasons exist, upon the interested party's request the judge can stay the enforcement action until the end of the opposition proceedings.

[B] Opposition to the Enforcement Acts

Opposition to the enforcement acts is aimed at challenging the formal regularity of the executive title or of the '*precetto*' (see §9.04 above), or of other specific acts of the enforcement proceedings.

If enforcement proceedings have already started, the opposition shall be lodged before the judge of the enforcement. If enforcement proceedings have not yet started (i.e. if the formal irregularities concern the executive title or the '*precetto*'), the opposition shall be lodged before the judge who would be competent for the enforcement.

The proceedings have to be started within twenty days from the service of the executive title or the '*precetto*', or within the same term from the date when the opposed act was accomplished.

In addition to the above, since a party against whom enforcement is sought can also be a third party whose goods are at stake in the enforcement proceedings, that party can also bring an opposition before the court ('*opposizione di terzo*', governed by Article 619 CCP).

§9.07 PARTICULARITIES WITH RESPECT TO SPECIFIC ORDERS

Most of the measures and orders that can be granted by the UPC have corresponding measures provided by the IPC or by the CCP. It is reasonable to guess that those national measures, and the related enforcement rules and practice, are going to be relevant and also applied for the enforcement of the corresponding UPC measures.

In the following paragraphs we therefore indicate the IPC or CCP provisions regulating the corresponding Italian measures, if any.

[A] Permanent Injunctions, Article 63 UPCA

Corresponding Italian measure: see Article 124(1) IPC.

Permanent injunction orders under current national law are generally enforced through an *ex ante* determination of the sum that the party against which enforcement shall be enacted must pay for each time it fails to respect the mentioned order (Article 124(2) IPC).

Under Italian law, in case a party fails to comply with an injunction, the other party may directly enforce the penalty set by the Judge together with the injunction, without first asking the Court to determine the exact amount of the credit (see Article 615-*bis* CCP). The party against whom the enforcement is requested can file an opposition to the enforcement proceedings (see §9.06). The seised civil court is competent to ascertain the actual violation of the order, if contested.

Against this background it is important to point out that Rule 354(4) of the Rules of Procedure of the Unified Patent Court ('RoP UPC') seems to require a decision of the UPC on the existence of the violation of the injunction order. Therefore, it is questionable whether the national judge competent for the opposition to the enforcement will be allowed, in turn, to verify the existence of the violation of the injunction order.

Moreover, according to Article 63(2) UPCA, the penalty payment is due to the court, hence only the latter would be entitled to enforce the payment order in case of non-compliance. This highlights an important difference between the penalty provided by Article 63(2) UPCA and the national *astreinte*, provided by Article 131(2) IPC, due to the IP right owner.

The enforcement of the latter, outlined in §9.04 above, is left to the party in favour of which the penalty is given. Such a person would, however, not have the right to enforce a payment order provided in favour of a different entity, i.e. the UPC. It is reasonable to expect therefore that the court will enforce those orders with the cooperation of the agencies usually competent to enforce payment orders due to the public administration.

An injunction can also be enforced according to Article 612 CCP (see §9.04), to the extent that it is necessary to destroy what the breaching party accomplished in violation of the order not to act.

The competent body is the enforcement division of the ordinary civil court.

A criminal court could also be regarded as competent to apply the criminal sanctions linked to the order violation pursuant to Article 388(3) CC.

[B] An Order to Produce Evidence, Article 59 UPCA

Corresponding Italian measures: see Articles 116 and 210 CCP, Articles 121 and 121-bis IPC.

There are no specific rules for this order, which cannot be enforced in case the party against whom it is issued does not comply with it.

However, according to Article 116(2) CCP, the judge may infer circumstantial evidence from the parties' behaviour during the proceeding. There is a similarity, here, with the provisions set by Rules 172 and 190(7) RoP UPC.

For IPR litigation, the same principles are set forth in Article 121(4) IPC. Also, Article 121-bis IPC provides that the judge can order a party to supply information on the origin and distribution network of infringing goods/services. The relevant proceeding is regulated by Articles 249, 250, 252, 255 and 257 CCP.

Moreover, according to Article 210 CCP as recently amended, the court may issue a fine in case a party does not comply, without justified reasons, to the court order. There is a similarity, here, with the provisions set by Articles 63(2) UPCA (see above).

[C] An Order to Preserve Evidence and to Inspect Premises, Article 60 UPCA

Corresponding Italian measures: see Articles 129 and 130 IPC; see also Articles 670 and 696 CCP.

Articles 129 and 130 IPC provides for rules similar to Article 60 UPCA and Rules 192–199 RoP UPC, which should be applicable.

An order to preserve evidence or inspect premises can be enforced directly through a bailiff, who may also be assisted by the police in case the party against whom the order is issued does not cooperate. When there are technical issues to be considered during access or inspection (for example, the need to identify specific infringing goods amongst others or the need to preserve the confidentiality of some documents/articles of the defendant), the bailiff is usually assisted by a technical expert appointed by the court and operations involving taking evidence are made also under supervision of the plaintiff.

The enforcement proceeding is governed by Article 677 CCP.

[D] Freezing Orders, Article 61 UPCA

There are no specific rules regarding freezing orders. Assuming that Article 61 UPCA and Rule 200 RoP UPC will be interpreted as entailing an obligation not to do something, and not a seizure of the assets of the party against whom the order is issued, the order should be enforceable according to Article 612 CCP, regulating the execution of obligations to do or not to do something. The relevant procedure, outlined in §9.04 above, is supervised by a judge of the Italian civil court, selected on the basis of the general criteria on territorial competence, with the support of the competent bailiff.

If the court provides for a penalty to be payable in the event that the party does not comply with the terms of the freezing order (see Rule 354 RoP UPC), the penalty should be enforceable according to Article 615-*bis* CCP (see, however, Rule 354.4 RoP UPC and §9.07[A] above).

[E] Preliminary Injunction, Article 62(1) UPCA

Corresponding Italian measure: see Article 131 IPC.

From the enforcement point of view, preliminary injunctions and permanent injunctions should not present relevant differences. See §9.07[A] above.

[F] Seizure or Delivery up of Infringing Products, Article 62(3) UPCA

Corresponding Italian measure: see Articles 129 and 130 IPC, as well as Articles 670 et seq. CCP.

According to Article 677 CCP, the judicial seizure is executed pursuant to Articles 605 et seq. CCP, to the extent that they are compatible. In short, the competent bailiff accesses the premises where the goods to be seized are located, with the power to extensively search for them. Once the goods have been identified - possibly with the assistance of a technical expert appointed by the court - the bailiff formally seizes them and appoints a person as custodian. It is not unusual that the appointed custodian is indeed the owner of the goods (i.e. the infringer), who however can no longer have control over them anymore and is liable for any loss of the goods.

The delivery up of the products is executed pursuant to Articles 605 et seq. CCP, hence according to the same blueprint, but for the delivery of the products to the proceeding party instead of their seizure. In both cases, the competent subject for materially enforcing the order is the bailiff.

[G] Precautionary Seizure of Movable and Immovable Property, Article 62(3) UPCA

Corresponding Italian measure: see Articles 678 and 679 CCP.

Precautionary seizure of movable and immovable property aimed at preventing circumstances likely to endanger the recovery of damages (Article 62(3) UPCA) can be enforced in accordance with Articles 678 and 679 CCP. The proceedings differ depending on whether the assets to be seized are movable or immovable; in both cases, the seizure shall be executed within thirty days from the decision (see Article 675 CCP).

Under Article 678 of the CCP, the seizure of movable property shall be executed pursuant to the provisions governing the attach of the assets at the debtor's premises or at a third party's premises (Articles 513 et seq. CCP and Articles 543 et seq. CCP). In this last event, with the seizure petition, the proceeding party shall summon the third party to appear before the competent court of the place where the third party has his/her residence in order to make a declaration under Article 547 of the CCP (i.e. the declaration specifying which assets or sums he/she has and when he/she shall pay or deliver to the debtor). The competent body is the enforcement division of the civil court.

Under Article 679 CCP, the seizure of immovable property shall be enforced by transcribing the judge's decision in the land registrar's office at the place where the assets are located.

[H] Recalling from the Channels of Commerce, Article 64(2) lit (b) UPCA

Corresponding Italian measure: see Article 124 IPC.

An order to recall the products from the channels of commerce can be enforced pursuant to Article 612 CCP (see §9.04 above).

[I] Depriving the Product of Its Infringing Property, Article 64(2) lit (c) UPCA

See §9.07[H] above.

[J] Removing from the Channels of Commerce, Article 64(2) lit (d) UPCA

See §9.07[H] above.

[K] Destruction, Article 64(2) lit (e) UPCA

See §9.07[H] above.

[L] Communication of Information, Article 67 UPCA

See §9.07[B] above.

Chapter 10

The Netherlands

Mark van Gardingen and J.C. Sebastian Pinckaers

§10.01 SOURCES OF LAW FOR ENFORCEMENT

[A] Introduction: When is Dutch Enforcement Law Applicable

[1] UPC Orders and Decisions to be Enforced

The Unified Patent Court ('UPC') is 'a court common to the Contracting Member States' for the settlement of disputes relating to European patents and European patents with unitary effect (Art. 1 of the Agreement on a Unified Patent Court ('UPCA'). In case of 'unitary patents', UPC decisions shall cover all countries which have ratified the UPCA (Art. 3(2) Unitary Patent Reg.) and in the case of a European patent, the UPC's decisions shall (in principle[1]) cover the territory of those countries which have ratified the UPCA for which the European patent has effect (Art. 34 UPCA).

Enforceable orders the UPC may grant (on an *ex parte* or *inter partes* basis) can be found in Chapter IV, Articles 56 and further (Powers of the Court) of the UPCA, and i.a. include preliminary and permanent injunctions, protective seizures and damages.

According to Article 62(1) and Article 63(2) UPCA, injunctions may be ordered 'where appropriate' subject to a recurring penalty payment. Article 82(4) UPCA extends the possibility for the UPC to sanction a party with a recurring penalty for any (term of an) order of the UPC a party fails to comply with. Penalty payments for not complying with UPC orders are payable to the UPC. This is different from Dutch practice, where penalties for violating a Dutch order are common and normally payable to the claimant.

1. Possibly subject to any carve-outs for the territory of national jurisdictions where national proceedings may have been initiated before the UPC action started.

[2] *Service of Orders and Decisions by the UPC*

Article 82(1) UPCA provides that '[d]ecisions and orders of the Court shall be enforceable in any Contracting Member State.' Rule 354(1) of the Rules of Procedure of the UPC ('UPCARoP') clarifies that 'decisions and orders of the Court shall be directly enforceable from their date of service in each Contracting Member State' (see further §10.03).

Pursuant to Rule 6(1)(a) UPCARoP, orders and decisions of the UPC shall be served on the parties by the Registry of the UPC, 'as soon as practicable', applying Part 5, Chapter 2 (Rules 270 and further) UPCARoP. This is different from Dutch practice, where service of decisions is normally done by the claimant (by instructing a bailiff to execute the service – see below).

For service within the Contracting Member States of the UPCA, these rules include service by electronic means (email) or any other means referred to in Regulation (EU) 2020/1784 (Rule 276 jo. Rules 270–271). For service outside the Contracting Member States of the UPCA, the Registry shall serve orders and decisions by any method provided by Regulation (EU) 2020/1784, the Hague Service Convention, or through diplomatic or consular channels from the UPCA Contracting Member State in which the sub-registry of the relevant UPC division is established (Rule 276 jo. Rule 274). Alternative service methods may be used if the aforementioned methods cannot be effected (Rule 275).

It seems therefore that for decisions and orders to be 'in force' between the parties, appropriate and proper service of the relevant decision or order by the Registry should be sufficient. But what if a party does not comply with a decision or order that has been served? What enforcement options does a party have in the Netherlands to then force the other party to comply with UPC decisions? This will be discussed below.

[3] *Orders to Preserve Evidence*

According to Rule 196(3) UPCARoP, orders for preserving evidence, which may be rendered *ex parte*, shall be enforceable *immediately* (i.e. can be executed on the parties affected by the order, without prior service), unless the Court decides otherwise. For the execution of such measures, Rule 196(4) and (5) refer to national law of the place where the measures are executed.

[4] *Enforcement Procedures Governed by National Law*

Article 82(3) UPCA provides that '[w]ithout prejudice to this Agreement and the Statute, enforcement procedures shall be governed by the law of the Contracting Member State where the enforcement takes place. Any decision of the Court shall be enforced under the same conditions as a decision given in the Contracting Member State where the enforcement takes place.' Rule 354(1) UPCARoP clarifies that '[e]nforcement shall take place in accordance with the enforcement procedures and conditions governed by the law of the particular Contracting Member State where enforcement takes place.'

Therefore, if enforcement is necessary to make a party comply in the Netherlands with decisions or orders of the UPC that have been properly served by the UPC's Registry (e.g. to actually force a party to stop violating an injunction or any other order, and/or to force a party to pay penalties or awarded damages or cost orders), Dutch national law governs the relevant enforcement procedures and conditions that can be applied in the Netherlands. Dutch national law also applies to the execution of orders to preserve evidence.

As will be set out in more detail below, this requires instructing a Dutch judicial bailiff to enforce the relevant decisions and orders in conformity with the relevant Dutch procedures and conditions.

[B] The Statutory Framework on the Enforcement of UPC Decisions in the Netherlands

In its Memorandum of Explanation of the Law to approve the UPC Agreement, the Dutch government stated:

> The UPC's decision can be directly enforced. This is done according to the rules applicable in the respective Member State for the enforcement of national judgments (Article 82 UPC Agreement). These provisions also reflect the fact that the UPC, as a court common to the contracting Member States, is on an equal footing with a national court. (2016 Parliamentary Papers 34411, No. 3, p. 17)

Therefore, the Dutch government has not proposed or implemented any specific or new statutory provisions in addition to those already in place for enforcing national decisions prior to the ratification of the UPC Agreement.

Enforcement of decisions in the Netherlands is regulated by the Dutch Code of Civil Procedure (*Wetboek van Burgerlijke Rechtsvordering*; 'DCCP'). In general, enforcement of court decisions in the Netherlands is exclusively executed by a *judicial bailiff* (*gerechtsdeurwaarder*) on the basis of an 'enforcement title' (the operative part of a court decision, containing the orders, qualifies as such as 'title'), at the request and on behalf of the interested party.

The DCCP includes various provisions on enforcement of decisions by way of conservatory/preservative and executory attachment measures (e.g. seizures and/or public sale of (im)movable property and other assets). Below, the sections of the DCCP that may be (partly) relevant to the enforcement of UPC orders will be discussed. These sections are in Book 2 of the DCCP, on judicial enforcement of judgments, orders and authentic instruments.

[1] Book 2, 1st Title: General Rules (Arts 430–438c DCCP)

The first title contains the general rules for the enforcement of enforcement titles within the meaning of Article 430 DCCP. Judgments and orders rendered in the Netherlands and authentic deeds executed in the Netherlands can be enforced throughout the Netherlands (Art. 430 (1) DCCP) after service on the party which is subject thereof (Art. 430 (3) DCCP). Judgments given by foreign courts cannot be enforced within the Netherlands, unless there is a legal basis for the enforceability in the Netherlands in a treaty or law in accordance with Articles 985–994 DCCP (Art.

431 DCCP). Moreover, Article 438 DCCP is relevant to execution disputes and will be discussed in more detail in the next sections.

[2] *Book 2, 2nd Title: Judicial Execution on Non-registered Property (Arts 439–500 DCCP)*

The second title of Book 2 consists of four sections. The first section deals with the execution on movable not-registered property (Arts 439–474 DCCP). The attachment of movable not-registered property must be preceded by a bailiff's writ containing an order to comply with the enforceable title within two days (Art. 439 DCCP). The attachment is made by a bailiff's report that must comply with the conditions set out in Article 440 DCCP. The second section is on executory attachment under third parties (e.g. banks) (Arts 475–479a DCCP). The attachment of claims which the judgement debtor may have against third parties or will acquire directly from a legal relationship existing at the time of the attachment shall be effected by a bailiff's writ. The writ must comply with the conditions set out in Article 475 DCCP. The third section of the second title is on the distribution of proceeds of execution (Arts 480–490d DCCP). Lastly, the fourth section deals with the execution to surrender movable not-registered property (Arts 491–500 DCCP).

[3] *Book 2, 3rd Title: Judicial Execution on Immovable Property (Arts 502–562 DCCP)*

The third title contains the provisions relevant for the attachment of immovable property. The attachment of immovable property is similar to that of movable property. The attachment must be preceded by a bailiff's writ containing an order to comply with the enforceable title within two days, after which the attachment can be made (Art. 502 DCCP).

[4] *Book 2, 4th Title: Execution of Ships and Aircraft (Arts 562a–584 DCCP)*

The fourth title of Book 2 contains a separate regime for the recovery of ships and aircraft. Pursuant to Article 8:1 of the Dutch Civil Code, ships are understood to be all things, other than aircraft, which, according to their construction, are intended to float and float or have floated. Aircraft are devices that can be held in the atmosphere as re result of forces exerted on it by the air (Art. 8:8 Dutch Civil Code).

§10.02 OVERVIEW OF AUTHORITIES EXECUTING ENFORCEMENT IN THE NETHERLANDS

In the Netherlands, execution of court decisions and orders (including that of the UPC) can only be performed by a bailiff, with assistance of the police if necessary (e.g. Art. 444(2) DCCP). Unlike in some other European countries, under Dutch law the bailiff will conduct both conservative measures (such as preserving evidence or inspecting premises under Article 60 UPCA or seizure of infringing products or property of the alleged infringer, including blocking of bank accounts under Article 62

UPCA) and the execution measures (such as collecting payments, if necessary by seizing and publicly selling assets).

The bailiff is a judicial officer, who acts as a public official appointed by the Crown with official duties. He has been granted, to a large extent, a monopoly position by the Judicial Officers Act ('JOA') (*'Gerechtsdeurwaarderswet'*): to the exclusion of others, the bailiff is authorized to service writs of summons under Dutch law, levy attachments, carry out compulsory evictions and perform other executions of court orders (Art. 2 JOA). In connection with the judicial officer's monopoly position, the JOA and its implementing regulations include numerous safeguards for the adequate performance of the office, such as appointment and training requirements, a ministerial duty (Art. 11 JOA) and (disciplinary) supervision (Arts 30–55 JOA). A bailiff, in principle, is not at liberty to refuse services upon request.

§10.03 GENERAL REQUIREMENTS FOR ENFORCEMENT

In the Netherlands, UPC decisions and the orders, which will be 'appended' to the UPC decision (Rule 350(2) UPCARoP), should qualify as 'enforcement titles', since they are *directly* enforceable in the Netherlands (Art. 82(1) UPCA, Rule 354(1) UPCARoP and 2016 Parliamentary Papers 34411, No. 3, p. 17)). UPC decisions will have to be treated in the Netherlands in the same way as decisions of Dutch courts. No special or separate recognition and enforcement rules apply, unlike for instance in respect of 'foreign' court decisions. This also follows from the Brussels I bis (recast) Regulation on jurisdiction and the recognition and enforcement of judgments in civil and commercial matters (Regulation (EU) 1215/2012), which stipulates in Article 71d, last sentence: 'where recognition and enforcement of a judgment given by a common court [like the UPC] is sought in a Member State [like the Netherlands] party to the instrument establishing the common court [the UPCA], any rules of that instrument on recognition and enforcement [Article 82 UPCA] shall apply instead of the rules of this Regulation.'

This may also explain why the Dutch government has not proposed or implemented any statutory provisions in relation to enforcement measures in addition to those already in place prior to the ratification of the UPC Agreement. The Dutch Act of 29 June 2016 approving the UPC Agreement (Stb. 2016, 314) and Act of 30 October 2019 amending the 1995 Dutch Patent Act in connection with the UPC Agreement and Unitary Patent Regulation No. 1257/2012 (Stb. 2019, 476) do not contain any amendments of the DCCP or JOA.

Pursuant Rule 118(8) UPCARoP, orders shall be enforceable on the defendant only after (i) the claimant has notified the UPC which part of the orders he intends to enforce, (ii) a certified translation (Rule 7 UPCARoP) of the orders into the official language of a Contracting Member State in which the enforcement shall take place has been provided by the claimant (i.e. a translation (also) into Dutch if the orders are to be (also) enforced in the Netherlands), and (iii) the said notice and translation have been served on the defendant by the Registry.

Note: this does not apply to orders to preserve evidence. As mentioned above, according to Rule 196(3) UPCARoP, such orders shall be enforceable immediately, unless the Court decides otherwise.

In respect of the proper service on the defendant, as mentioned above, Rule 6(1) (jo. Rule 276) UPCARoP provides that the UPC Registry (i.e. the sub-registry of the relevant UPC division) shall as soon as practicable serve orders and decisions of the UPC on the parties. As also mentioned above, this service may be conducted via e-mail or any other means referred to in Regulation (EU) 2020/1784 or the Hague Service Convention. After proper service, and as of that moment, the UPC orders should be enforceable.

In view of Article 82(3) UPCA ('Without prejudice to this Agreement and the Statute) and Article 71d Brussels I bis recast, these UPCA rules for service/enforcement of UPC decisions in Contracting Member States of the UPC take precedent over any different Dutch national rules for service/enforcement of *Dutch* court decisions, which require service of the decision upon the defendant (Article 430(3) DCCP) by a bailiff (Article 2 JOA). For a UPC decision to be enforceable in the Netherlands, service by the UPC Registry upon the defendant would be sufficient.

The UPCA and UPCARoP do not contain any provisions about the subsequent execution of enforceable UPC decisions in the Netherlands, should that be necessary or appropriate (e.g. to collect penalties for violations of any of the orders, or to collect damages a defendant was ordered to pay). For such enforcement actions in the Netherlands, Dutch law must be applied in accordance with the proceedings described below.

§10.04 OVERVIEW OF PROCEEDINGS

In general, the process of enforcement of a UPC order in the Netherlands consists of the following steps:

Making a UPC order enforceable in the Netherlands:

- the UPC renders its enforceable order(s) appended to its decision (Art. 82(1) UPCA);
- the claimant notifies the UPC which part of the order(s) he intends to enforce (Rule 118(8) UPCARoP);
- the claimant provides the UPC with a translation of the order(s) into Dutch if the enforcement shall (also) take place in the Netherlands (Rules 7 and 118(8) UPCARoP);
- the UPC Registry serves the order on the defendant (Rule 6(1)(a) UPCARoP);
- if the UPC has subjected its order to a security to be given by the claimant (whether by deposit or bank guarantee or otherwise) to the other party, the execution can only start after such security has been rendered (Art. 82(2) UPCA and Rule 352(1) UPCARoP). Article 438c DCCP provides that if a financial guarantee is required for the enforcement of an order in the Netherlands, an equivalent guarantee lodged with a bank or insurer established in another Member State of the European Union shall be recognized.

As mentioned above, according to Rule 196(3) UPCARoP, orders to preserve evidence are enforceable immediately, i.e. without the steps of Rule 118(8) UPCARoP. For the subsequent actual enforcement or execution of such orders, the following actions are required:

- the UPC decision and enforceable orders to preserve evidence must be handed over to a bailiff in the Netherlands (this will probably have to be done by the UPC Registry; the claimant should inform the UPC Registry about the relevant contact details of the bailiff, and the details of any independent and impartial expert the claimant would like the bailiff to be assisted by; see Rule 196(4) and (5) UPCARoP);
- the bailiff subsequently performs the actual execution of the order.

If the claimant (or the UPC itself) finds out that the defendant has not fully complied with a (condemnatory) order of the UPC that has been served on the defendant, such as the order for a provisional injunction (Art. 62(1) UPCA), a permanent injunction (Art. 63(2) UPCA), or an order to disclose information (Art. 67(1) UPCA), the UPC may decide on the amount of forfeited penalty payments upon the request of the plaintiff or of its own motion (Rule 354(4) UPCARoP). In such 'penalty proceedings', the defendant shall be given an opportunity to be heard and the UPC may request both parties to provide written submissions within a specified period and/or shall or may invite the parties to an oral hearing (Rule 354(4) jo. Rule 264 UPCARoP). If the UPC orders the defendant to pay a specific penalty for not complying with its order(s), this order will again have to be served upon the defendant by the UPC Registry, and can subsequently be executed by a bailiff in the Netherlands.

In case of execution of an order to pay damages, legal costs, or penalty sums, the UPC will have to send the enforceable order to a bailiff in the Netherlands, who can then take the appropriate execution measures (e.g. seizure and public sale of the defendant's assets in the Netherlands). What the appropriate measures actually are, is something the claimant will want to discuss with the bailiff beforehand. Moreover, the execution itself will take place in Dutch. It seems advisable therefore that the claimant's counsel, including Dutch counsel familiar with the details of enforcement options in the Netherlands, will take the initiate to contact the bailiff to discuss proper execution steps.

The handing over by the UPC of the enforceable title (the decision with enforceable orders), the execution of which is desired, to the bailiff, authorizes him to carry out the *entire execution* in that case resulting from that title (Article 434 DCCP). The bailiff may collect payment for the claim from all the debtor's goods. The execution aims to collect a monetary claim through the forced execution of one or more of the debtor's goods. The bailiff shall be free to seize any attachable property to which he is entitled to recover his claim (Art. 3:276 Civil Code and Art. 435(1) DCCP). However, such executorial attachment may not be levied on goods intended for public service (Art. 436 DCCP). In general, the value of what is seized should not be exorbitantly greater than the claim for which recovery is sought. Should a defendant believe this requirement is violated, it may be possible for the defendant to try to get the attachments lifted or limited by means of an 'enforcement dispute' arguing abuse of attachment law rules ('vexatious' attachment) (e.g. Netherlands Supreme Court 24 November 1995, ECLI:NL:HR:1995:ZC1894, NJ 1996/161) (below) (see below §10.06[C]). The language the bailiff applies in the course of this execution is normally Dutch, and it can be expected that this will also be the case for execution of UPC decisions and orders (although in appropriate cases the bailiff may perhaps want to include translations).

The further procedural rules that apply depend on the type of goods that will be executed. In case of executory seizure of *movable property*, the execution must be preceded by a (in principle: Dutch) writ of the bailiff ordering the executed party to comply with the enforcement order *within two days* (Art. 439(1) DCCP). This rule exists to give the executed person one last opportunity to voluntarily comply with the order. Only after expiry of this period may the execution attachment be levied. Further, the enforcing party (executor) must elect domicile at the office of the bailiff until the end of the enforcement or at the office of a lawyer in the Netherlands (Art. 439(3) DCCP). The bailiff must serve his official report of the seizure (in principle: in Dutch) on the executed party *within three days* of the seizure (Art. 443 DCCP). Either at the time of service of his report or by a separate writ *no later than three days later*, the day and time of the sale must be served on the executed party (Art. 449 DCCP). The sale of the seized goods may not take place before *four weeks* from the day of service of the report referred to in Article 443 DCCP. The sale itself is regulated by Articles 463470 DCCP. The distribution of the proceeds is determined by Articles 480490d DCCP. The bailiff is responsible for the proceeds. From the proceeds he pays the enforcement costs (Art. 474 DCCP).

In case of executory garnishment, the executory third-party attachment is made by service of a garnishment notice by a bailiff on the *third party* (such as banks). Within *eight days* of the levying of attachment, the attachment must be served on the executed party (Art. 475i DCCP). After the lapse of maximum *four weeks* from the levying of attachment, the third party must declare what he has in his possession from or owes to the executed party (Art. 476a DCCP).

Executory attachment of *immovable property* must be preceded by a writ containing an order to comply with the enforceable order *within two days* (Art. 502 DCCP). The legal effects of the seizure only take effect once the bailiff's report is registered in the Dutch public registers. No later than *three days* after registration, a copy of this record must be served on the executed party (Art. 505(1) DCCP). If it appears upon registration that the immovable property is mortgaged, the attachment must be served on the mortgagee *within four days* of registration (Art. 508 DCCP). The sale of the immovable property itself is regulated by Article 514529 DCCP. It takes place in public in the presence of a civil-law notary (Art. 519 DCCP). If the notary has not already been designated in the record of seizure, the designation of the responsible notary shall be made by writ to the executed party. This notary shall fix the day, time and place of the sale *within fourteen days* of his designation and he shall notify this to the executed party (Arts 514 and 515 DCCP). The notary shall be responsible for the proceeds; from them, he pays, in the first place, the execution costs (Art. 524 DCCP). The distribution of the rest of the proceeds is determined by Articles 551553 DCCP.

Article 3:324(1) Civil Code provides that the power to enforce a judicial order in the Netherlands shall lapse *twenty years* from the commencement of the day following that on which the order was rendered. However, the prescription of this term can be interrupted under Article 3:325 Civil Code (e.g. service of the order or any act of enforcement).

Since the UPC Agreement and Rules of Procedure do not contain any provisions on the *transfer* of enforcement titles (the UPC orders), Article 431a DCCP is applicable in this respect. It provides that if the authority to execute an enforceable title is transferred to another person, execution may not be commenced or continued until this transfer has been served on the person (to be) executed.

Article 611g(1) DCCP provides that a penalty payment shall lapse six months after the day on which it is forfeited and this forfeiture was reasonably known. The UPCA does not provide for such a limitation, and it is questionable therefore if this national rule applies to forfeited penalties for violating a UPC order.

§10.05 COSTS

The costs of bailiffs are standardized in the Dutch Decree on fees for official acts of bailiffs (*'Besluit tarieven ambtshandelingen gerechtsdeurwaarders'*). The standard costs of fulfilling service under Dutch law amount to approximately EUR 100–300. The costs can be much higher in practice though, especially in the case of complex attachment orders, e.g. to preserve evidence. In such cases additional hourly rates of the bailiff may apply for preparations and the work the bailiff needs to do to describe the evidence preserved or findings of his inspection in a written report (Rule 196(4) UPCARoP). In complex cases additional costs may also include the costs of third parties assisting the bailiff in the execution, such as an independent technical expert (Rule 196(5) UPCARoP). If conserved evidence or seized goods or documents are taken into the bailiff's custody or in the custody of a third party custodian, extra costs will also be made for that. Therefore, costs of enforcement depend heavily on the complexity of the specific case. In principle, under Dutch law, such costs must be advanced by the creditor, but the costs may be reimbursed by the debtor if the creditor 'wins' his claim (Art. 237 DCCP). Such a cost order then provides the successful party with an enforceable title for the recovery of the legal costs, but also for the recovery of the costs of enforcement (the Netherlands Supreme Court, 19 March 2010, NL:HR:2010:BL1116 and the Netherlands Supreme Court, 10 June 2022, ECLI:NL:HR:2022:853). For UPC decisions, it seems most appropriate to request the UPC to order the compensation of such enforcement costs.

§10.06 COUNTERMEASURES ON ENFORCEMENT

[A] Appeal

In view of Article 82(3) UPCA ('Without prejudice to this Agreement ...') the UPCA and UPCARoP provisions prevail over national law, also as to the enforcement procedure. UPC orders are enforceable and an appeal shall, in principle, *not* have *suspensive effect* unless the Court of Appeal decides otherwise at the motivated request of one of the parties (Art. 74(1) UPCA). Therefore, lodging an appeal does not have suspensive effect unless the Court of Appeal grants suspensive effect on an application (Rule 223 UPCARoP).

An appeal may always be brought before the Court of Appeal (Art. 73(2) UPCA) by a party adversely affected against final decisions and the following orders of the Court of First Instance: an order to produce evidence, an order to preserve evidence, an order to freeze assets, an order for a provisional injunction, an order of the provisional seizure or delivery up of infringing products or the final order to disclose information about the infringing acts and goods (Art. 73(2)(a) UPCA and Rule 220(1)(c) UPCARoP). However, an order to pay a forfeited penalty payment can only be appealed where the UPC grants leave to appeal, within fifteen days of the notification of the UPC's decision to that effect (Art. 73(2)(b)(ii) UPCA and Rule 220(2) UPCARoP). In case of a refusal of the Court of First Instance to grant leave within fifteen days of the UPC order, a request for a discretionary review to the Court of Appeal may be made within fifteen calendar days from the end of that period (Rule 220(3) UPCARoP). In all other cases, the appeal against the order must be lodged together with the appeal against the final decision of the court of first instance.

[B] Countermeasures if the Patent that is the Basis for the Executed Order is Subsequently Varied or Revoked

According to Articles 60(9), 61(2) and 62(5) UPCA, when measures to preserve evidence or inspect premises, freezing measures or provisional/protective measures (including provisional injunctions) are revoked, or where they lapse due to any act or omission by the applicant, or where it is subsequently found that there has been no infringement or threat of infringement of the patent, the Court may order the applicant, at the defendant's request, to provide the defendant with appropriate compensation for any damage suffered as a result of those measures.

Furthermore, Rule 354(2), first sentence, UPCARoP provides that where 'during an action' an enforceable decision or order of the Court is subsequently varied or revoked, the UPC may order the party, which has enforced such decision or order, upon the request of the party against whom the decision or order has been enforced, to provide appropriate compensation for any injury caused by the enforcement. The determination of such damages may be the subject of separate UPC proceedings (Rule 125 UPCARoP).

If however, according to Rule 354(2), third sentence, UPCARoP, 'following the conclusion of the action', the patent is amended or revoked, the UPC may order, upon the request of the party against whom the decision or order would be enforceable, that the decision or order *ceases to be enforceable*. For this situation (revocation or amendment of the patent *after* completion of the UPC action), the UPCA and UPCARoP contain no provisions about liability for damages caused by the enforcement. However, pursuant to Article 82(2) UPCA, where appropriate, the enforcement of a decision may be subject to the provision of security or an equivalent assurance to ensure compensation for any damage suffered, in particular in the case of injunction. It may be possible therefore that UPC decisions or orders themselves, in particular in the case of injunctions, contain a provision about security for compensating for damages in case the patent is revoked or amended after completion of the UPC action.

The UPC Agreement does not seem to provide for competence (let alone exclusive) of the UPC with respect to a claim for damages or unjust enrichment based on 'wrongful' enforcement of a patent, which is, after completion of the UPC action, subsequently invalidated with retroactive effect, or for a claim for reimbursement of forfeited penalties after revocation of the patent. Arguably, for such actions the Dutch national court may remain competent (Art. 32(2) UPCA), and the Dutch national court may have to deal with this under Dutch national law. Under Dutch law, enforcement measures based on a non-final decision are taken *at the risk of the executor*, meaning that if the enforcement title, such as a UPC order, is subsequently annulled or otherwise set aside, the executed party may claim damages under Dutch tort law: with hindsight, the executor in such a case has acted unlawfully towards the executed party (e.g. Netherlands Supreme Court 13 January 1995, ECLI:NL:HR:1995:ZC1608, NJ 1997/366). However, Dutch law makes an exception for forfeited penalty sums due to violation of a court order: forfeited penalty sums can only be set side on appeal. A later case, even a merits case following a preliminary injunction, has no effect on forfeited penalties (Netherlands Supreme Court 22 December 1989, ECLI:NL:HR:1989:AD0992, NJ 1990/434). Ratio behind this is the prevailing interest that court orders (also in summary proceedings) have to be followed. It is not ruled out that the Dutch court may award a claim for damages or unjust enrichment as a result of enforcement of *final* decisions.

[C] Execution Dispute to Stop the Execution by a Bailiff under Dutch Law

The execution of an enforceable order in the Netherlands can be challenged under Dutch law in a so-called *execution dispute* (normally summary proceedings), but the threshold to successfully do so is very high. It requires that the interest in a suspension of the affected party pending an appeal, substantially outweighs the principle/starting point that the executing party has a right and strong interest in executing a court order. In practice, this requires that the affected party shows that it may not survive the execution, and/or that the decision is based on 'immediately evident/manifest errors'. The execution dispute judge does not have the power to assess the correctness of the underlying judicial order beyond obvious errors, and is not allowed to take the 'chances of success on appeal' into consideration. The Supreme Court of the Netherlands held that the finding that a judgment to be enforced is based on a manifest error of law or fact does not necessarily imply that the one who enforces it is abusing his powers (the Netherlands Supreme Court, 24 April 2020, ECLI:NL:HR:2020:806).

Execution disputes can be initiated before the district court (in practice: the summary proceedings judge of the court) in whose jurisdiction the execution takes place or will take place, pursuant to Article 438(1) and (2) DCCP. Article 438 DCCP covers the disputes arising in connection with an imminent or pending execution. Such proceedings can be initiated by the affected party, but also by the executing bailiff who encounters an objection requiring an immediate remedy, or third parties affected by the execution (Article 438(5) and (6) DCCP and the Netherlands Supreme Court 14 January 1983, ECLI:NL:HR:1983:AG4519).

Pursuant to Article 438(3) DCCP, the court can (without prejudice to its other powers) suspend the execution, order the provision of security, lift attachments, order to restore omitted formalities and order that a third party cooperates in the execution or tolerates the execution. In the event of suspension, the enforcement measures already taken shall remain in force, but further enforcement shall be suspended. Article 438 DCCP can no longer be applied after the execution has ended.

[D] Enforcement Issues about the Scope of an Injunction

Under current Dutch practice, if a claimant obtained an injunction strengthened with a penalty clause and served that decision on the defendant, and if the claimant subsequently believes the defendant has forfeited the injunction, e.g. by continuing the forbidden offers or sales or by offering or selling a slightly amended product, which according to the claimant still falls under the injunction, the claimant can simply instruct a bailiff to start collecting payment of penalty sums. It would then be up to the claimant to initiate (summary) execution dispute proceedings to get a court decision about whether his continued acts fall within or outside the scope of the injunction. If a defendant wants clearance that his amended product falls outside the scope of an injunction beforehand, to avoid the risk of having forfeited penalties, he should obtain confirmation about the claimant beforehand. If the plaintiff refuses to confirm that the new product falls outside the scope of the injunction and (thereby) reserves the right to start collecting penalties, the defendant can start execution dispute proceedings based on threat of arguably wrongful enforcement.

This is different under the Rules of the UPCA. Under the Rules of the UPCA, collecting payment of penalties is only possible after the UPC has decided, having heard both parties, that orders have indeed been violated and penalties have been forfeited (Rule 354(4) UPCARoP). Although the Rule does not explicitly state that a defendant could start such proceedings himself to get clearance about the scope of an injunction and associated penalties, there seems to be no good reason to apply the Rule restrictively and not allow a defendant to get such clearance pro-actively.

Chapter 11

Portugal

Gonçalo de Sampaio

§11.01 SOURCES OF LAW FOR ENFORCEMENT

To date, there have been no specific national rules or legislation related with the Unified Patent Court ('UPC') and enforcement of UPC orders.

Without any specific rules, one must apply and follow the relevant and general provisions that are contained in the Portuguese Civil Procedure Code and additional applicable legislation, namely the Portuguese Industrial Property Code. Considering how the rules are established and the basis under which the same were written, it would be relevant and assist in legal certainty to have specific rules for the enforcement of UPC rules, but that is not the case, at least at the present moment.

Looking at enforcement procedure in Portugal, this is governed by Articles 703 et seq. of the Civil Procedure Code.

Considering the contents of the Agreement of the Unified Patent Court as well as UPC Rules of Procedure, regarding enforcement, UPC decisions will be subject to the same enforcement rules as decisions from a Portuguese national court. Therefore, the decisions of the UPC may be directly enforced by the Portuguese courts without the need of any procedure, namely any prior validation or recognition, as happens with decisions of 'foreign courts'.

A revision of the Industrial Property Code, which specifically regulates all matters related to the creation of the UPC, related to the enforcement of the respective decisions is awaited, but not yet foreseen.

§11.02 OVERVIEW OF AUTHORITIES EXECUTING ENFORCEMENT IN PORTUGAL

According to Portuguese Law 62/2013 (Judicial Organization Law), the judicial authority to execute enforcement regarding intellectual property ('IP') cases in

Portugal is the Intellectual Property Court (*Tribunal da Propriedade Intelectual*, 'IP Court'). The IP Court is based in Lisbon and presently has three judges.

Decisions from the IP Court may be appealed to the Second Instance Court of Lisbon (*Tribunal da Relação de Lisboa*).

The Portuguese legal system provides a further level of appeal, the Supreme Court of Justice. However, this level is extremely restricted regarding industrial property rights, thus one should not consider it in most cases. In fact, the requirements for an industrial property right case to be appealed to the Supreme Court are extremely demanding, thus the possibility of using such an exception is very limited and should not be considered in regular cases.

According to Article 45 of the Industrial Property Code, there is no appeal from the decision of the Second Instance Court of Lisbon to the Supreme Court of Justice, except in cases where such an appeal is always admissible.

According to Article 629 Civil Procedure Code, an appeal to the Supreme Court of Justice is always admissible in the following situations:

(a) on grounds of infringement of the rules of international jurisdiction, the rules of jurisdiction according to subject matter or rank, or infringement of *res judicata*;
(b) against decisions regarding the merits of a case or of incidents on the grounds that their value exceeds the jurisdiction of the court against which the appeal is brought;
(c) a decision rendered in the field of the same legislation and on the same fundamental question of law against the uniform jurisprudence of the Supreme Court of Justice;
(d) a decision of the Court of Appeal that is in contradiction with another decision of the same or a different Court of Appeal, in the same area of legislation and on the same fundamental question of law, and from which no ordinary appeal is possible for reasons beyond the court's jurisdiction, unless a court decision has been issued that conforms to it.

It is important to note that Portuguese industrial property law foresees the criminalization of certain infringements of industrial property rights. In these cases, which are actual criminal offences, the competent court for the respective judgment is the criminal court, and not the Intellectual Property Court. It is also up to the criminal courts to enforce penalties. Portuguese law admits court decisions that condemn any violator of IP rights to prison.

This criminal route, although operating via the criminal courts, has the same principles as enforcement in civil proceedings.

§11.03 GENERAL REQUIREMENTS FOR ENFORCEMENT

Under Portuguese law, court decisions can be enforced by those that are creditors of an obligation ordered in the decisions.

Article 53 of the Civil Procedure Code establishes that enforcement must be requested by the entity that is creditor based on a court decision. This means that the entity wishing to enforce a court decision must take an active role and not wait for any third party to take action. It is up to the entity to promote the actions required for the enforcement to take place.

The enforcement must be based on a formal written request (on the form provided for this purpose), made by the entity interested in said enforcement before the competent court.

The application must be filed electronically via the electronic platform of the court system ('Citius')

As for the formalities regarding the enforcement procedure, these may be filed in electronic format and may also be filed on paper. However, it is important to note that whenever the creditor has a lawyer, the application must be filed electronically via Citius. Since lawyers must be registered to be able to use the electronic platform, this platform will automatically use the electronic signature from the lawyer signing the request.

A Portuguese lawyer appointed by the entity must be duly registered with the Portuguese Lawyer Association (*Ordem dos Advogados*).

All contact with the court, including statements to be filed before the court and notifications issued by the court, will be communicated through said electronic platform. In fact, all written contacts between the parties involved in the enforcement procedure must be made using said official electronic platform.

An enforcement procedure filed before a Portuguese national court must be filed in Portuguese and the language of the procedure must be Portuguese. Portuguese is the only language that may be used before national courts, it is not possible to communicate with the court or judge in English.

Irrespective of the court understanding English, any documents to be used and that a party wishes to be considered by the judge should be filed in its original language and a translation must be filed. The translation of the document need only be of the relevant parts. Text that is not translated into Portuguese will not be considered by the court.

The same rules apply for possible witnesses that the party wishes to be heard by the court.

A party presenting a witness who is not fluent in Portuguese is obliged to guarantee the presence of a translator, to ensure that all the questions are made and answered in Portuguese.

The enforcement of a court decision has a time limit of twenty years from the date of the final decision.

It is relevant to note that, as regards translation requirements, Regulation (EU) No. 2020/1784 on the service in a Member State of judicial and extrajudicial documents in civil or commercial matters shall apply.

This means that a party against which a UPC decision is served is entitled to refuse service if the decision is not written in, or is not accompanied by, a translation into a language they understand or the official language of Portugal, which is Portuguese.

Should this occur, the process would be delayed, so it is important to have this in mind when filing for an enforcement. To avoid any delays, the service should be made in Portuguese, otherwise the likelihood that objections will be raised is very significant.

§11.04 OVERVIEW OF PROCEEDINGS

The enforcement procedure is initiated by a statement to be filed before the competent court. This statement must be filed by the party wishing to enforce the court decision.

Said party must appoint a bailiff (*Agente de Execução*), in accordance with Article 720 Procedure Civil Code. The bailiff has legal competence to perform the following acts: service, notification, publication, access to databases, seizure and payment.

The bailiff has a predominant role in the enforcement action. According to Article 723 Civil Procedural Code, the judge is specifically responsible for:

(a) issuing a preliminary order, should this take place;
(b) deciding the opposition to execution and attachment, as well as verifying and ranking the credits, within three months of the opposition or complaint;
(c) deciding, without the possibility of appeal, on complaints against acts and challenges to decisions by the enforcement agent, within ten days;
(d) deciding on other matters raised by the enforcement agent, the parties or intervening third parties, within five days.

As regards overall deadlines it is not possible to define an accurate and reasonable time period, since this strongly depends on the particularities of each case, namely if there is opposition to the enforcement. The bailiff should be able to perform its duties in a period of a maximum of six months.

The law establishes deadlines for some actions to be taken. In fact, under Article 720(7) Civil Procedure Code, the enforcement agent must make the notifications within five days and the other acts of the enforcement within ten days, which demonstrates that the law requires that enforcement takes place in an expeditious manner.

§11.05 COSTS

In comparison with other national judicial systems in Europe, Portuguese court fees are not high, since the wish is to ensure that judicial fees are not an obstacle for any entity to have access to the judicial system.

An execution action involves a court fee of up to EUR 51, according to the regulation of court fees in Decree Law No. 34/2008 of 26 February (if the steps are not made by a bailiff but by an execution agent).

The bailiff's professional fees vary significantly and may depend on several factors making it difficult to provide an amount. But one may consider around EUR 500 for bailiff costs, although this amount must be taken as merely a guidance since the professional fees are charged based on the personal decision of the bailiff, who is not bound to any established schedule of charges. For this reason, one must consider that it is a cost that is based on the functioning of the market.

The creditor must provide the enforcement agent and pay the expenses for the steps taken. These costs, related to expenses that need to be made to ensure the execution of the enforcement request, are not included in the professional fees.

At the end of the execution, the creditor can ask for reimbursement of the expenses of the execution agent.

§11.06 COUNTERMEASURES ON ENFORCEMENT

The general principle, under Portuguese law, is that the party against whom the enforcement decision is taken may oppose the same.

An opposition must be filed within a twenty-day deadline, counting from the service of the enforcement request.

In accordance with Article 729 Civil Procedure Code, the opposition must be based on one of the following arguments:

(a) non-existence or unenforceability of the writ of execution;
(b) falsity of the process or of the copy or its infidelity, when one or the other influences the terms of the execution;
(c) lack of any procedural assumption on which the regularity of the instance of execution depends, without prejudice to its supplementation;
(d) lack of intervention of the defendant in the process of declaration, if any of the situations provided for in Article 696(e) Civil Procedure Code are verified;
(e) uncertainty, unenforceability or illiquidity of the enforceable obligation, not remedied in the introductory phase of the execution;
(f) *res judicata* prior to the judgment being enforced;
(g) any fact extinguishing or modifying the obligation, provided that it is subsequent to the conclusion of the discussion in the declaration process and is proved by documentation; the prescription of the right or obligation may be proved by any means
(h) counterclaims against the distrainor with a view to obtaining the setting off of claims;
(i) in the case of a judgment confirming confession or settlement, any cause of nullity or annulment of such acts.

Once the opposition has been filed, the judge will make a preliminary order. The opposition may be immediately dismissed if:

(a) it was filed out of time;
(b) the grounds do not comply with the provisions of Articles 729 to 731 Civil Procedure Code;
(c) it is manifestly unfounded.

Once the opposition is accepted, the party seeking the enforcement is notified to answer and present its arguments. The deadline to file this answer is twenty days.

If the facts alleged in the enforcement action are not expressly contradicted, it shall be deemed to be admitted.

Both parties may present witnesses to be heard by the judge and one or more court sessions may take place.

The court will take a decision and in case the opposition is successful, the enforcement is dismissed. If the opposition is not successful, the enforcement will proceed.

Portuguese Civil Procedure Code does not establish any deadline for the court to issue a decision, both in case an opposition is filed and in case an opposition is not filed. Accordingly, it is not possible to provide a deadline or an expected timeframe for a court decision on the enforcement request to be taken, since the timing for said decision is at the judge's discretion.

An appeal on the opposition decision may be filed.

The opposition to the enforcement does not suspend the same unless the executed entity provides a bail or, if there was an opposition, the enforceability or liquidation of the enforced obligation was contested and the judge decides, after hearing the arguments, that the suspension is justified without the provision of a bail.

§11.07 PARTICULARITIES WITH RESPECT TO SPECIFIC ORDERS

A general remark regarding the specific orders. These specific orders are regulated by Portuguese IP Code, in Articles 337 et seq., and the comments made on the enforcement procedures apply to these specific orders. Again, to date there has been no proposal to adapt these Articles to the enforcement of UPC orders.

These legal provisions follow the European Union directives and respect the principles inscribed therein.

In accordance with Portuguese law, namely the rules established in Article 350 of the Industrial Property Code, court decisions on the enforcement measures may be published.

In fact, at the request of the prejudiced party and at the expense of the infringer, the court may order publication of the final decision. Said publication may be made through the Industrial Property Bulletin or through disclosure in any media deemed appropriate, such as newspapers. The publication is an extract containing the elements of the sentence and conviction, as well as identification of the agents.

[A] Permanent Injunctions, Article 63 UPCA

Permanent injunctions are regulated by Article 349 IP Code ('*medidas inibitórias*').

The IP Court decision may also impose on the offender measures aimed at inhibiting the continuation of the verified infraction.

The measures provided may comprise:

(a) the temporary interdiction of the exercise of certain activities or professions;
(b) deprivation of the right to participate in fairs and markets;
(c) temporary or permanent closure of the establishment.

Also it is noted that this is applicable to any intermediary whose services are being used by third parties to violate industrial property rights or trade secrets.

The IP Court may impose a penalty payment to ensure the enforcement of decisions ordering the cessation of an illicit activity. The amount of said penalty is at the IP Court's discretion. Due to the specifics of Portuguese jurisprudence, the amounts tend to be not very high.

[B] An Order to Produce Evidence, Article 59 UPCA

Orders to produce evidence are regulated by Article 339 IP Code ('*medidas para obtenção de prova*').

Whenever evidence is in the possession, dependence or under the control of the opposing party or of a third party, the interested party may request the IP Court to produce it, provided that he presents sufficient evidence of violation of industrial property rights or trade secrets to support his claim.

When acts carried out on a commercial scale are at issue, the claimant may also request the IP Court to produce banking, financial, accounting or commercial documents that are in the possession, dependency or under the control of the opposing party or a third party.

The IP Court, ensuring the protection of confidential information, will order the respondent, within the designated time limit, to present the evidence in its possession, stating the resulting actions in case of non-compliance.

Accordingly, this request must be made before the IP Court that notifies the party (or a third party) to present the requested evidence.

It is important to note that the IP Court may take all required measures in case the party does not fulfil the order.

Where delay in applying the measures would cause irreparable harm to the applicant, or where there is a serious risk of evidence being destroyed or concealed, the measure may be ordered without hearing the respondent. In this case, the respondent is notified only of the decision, and has ten days to comply.

This measure may be made conditional, by IP Court decision, on the lodging of a security by the applicant.

[C] An Order to Preserve Evidence and to Inspect Premises, Article 60 UPCA

Orders to preserve evidence and inspect premises are regulated by Article 340 IP Code (‘*medidas para preservação da prova*’).

Whenever there is a violation or justified fear that another party may cause serious injury to an industrial property right or trade secret that is difficult to repair, the interested party may request urgent and effective provisional measures to preserve evidence of the alleged violation.

Measures for preservation of evidence may include detailed description, with or without taking of samples, or actual seizure of the goods suspected of infringing industrial property rights or trade secrets and, whenever appropriate, of the materials and instruments used in the production or distribution of those goods, as well as the documents relating thereto.

It is required that the party requesting this order is capable of proving that there is a violation or well-founded fear that another person will cause serious or irreparable harm to his rights.

Where delay in applying the measures would cause irreparable harm to the applicant, or where there is a serious risk of evidence being destroyed or concealed, the measure may be ordered without hearing the respondent. In this case, the respondent is notified only of the decision, and has ten days to comply.

This measure may be made conditional, by IP Court decision, on the lodging of a security by the applicant.

[D] Freezing Orders, Article 61 UPCA

There are no specific issues regarding freezing orders in Portuguese law.

[E] Preliminary Injunction, Article 62(1) UPCA

Preliminary injunctions are regulated by Article 345 IP Code.

Whenever there is violation or founded fear that a third party will seriously, and with difficult reparability, injure the industrial property right or commercial secret, the IP Court, at the request of the interested party, may order the appropriate measures to:

(a) inhibit any imminent infringement; or
(b) prohibit the continuation of the infringement.

The IP Court requires that the party applying for the measure provides evidence to demonstrate that it is the owner of the industrial property right or trade secret, or that it is authorized to use it, and that an infringement has occurred or is imminent.

Injunctions may also be ordered against any intermediary whose services are being used by third parties to violate industrial property rights or trade secrets.

The IP Court may, of its own motion or at the request of the plaintiff, order a penalty payment to ensure the execution of the measures.

At the request of the alleged infringer, the injunction may be replaced by a bond, provided that the bond, after hearing the applicant, is adequate to ensure compensation for the holder.

When determining the measures provided for in this Article, the IP Court shall take into consideration the nature of the industrial property rights or trade secrets, safeguarding the possibility of the holder continuing to exploit his rights without any restriction.

It is important to note that in cases where there is a violation, and the same is proven before the IP Court, there is no need to prove the irreparability of the damage. The need to prove said irreparability only applies for cases where, in the event of no violation, there is a founded fear of said violation.

Such has long been the jurisprudence of Portuguese courts when it comes to IP rights. Violation of the IP right is sufficient ground to grant a preliminary injunction. If there is no present violation, but a grounded fear of the same to occur, the IP Court shall require evidence of the irreparability of the damages that it may cause.

[F] Seizure or Delivery up of Infringing Products, Article 62(3) UPCA

Seizure is regulated by Article 346 IP Code.

In case of actual or imminent infringement on a commercial scale, and whenever the interested party proves the existence of circumstances susceptible of compromising the collection of damages, the IP Court may order the preventive seizure of the movable and immovable assets of the alleged infringer, including the contents of his bank accounts. The judge may also order the communication of or access to banking, financial or commercial data and information concerning the alleged infringer.

Whenever there is an infringement of industrial property rights or commercial secrets, the IP Court, at the request of the interested party, may order the seizure of the goods that are suspected of infringing those rights or secrets, including imported goods, to prevent their entry into circulation in the market, or the instruments that can only be used in the practice of the illicit act.

The IP Court shall also require that the requesting party provide all reasonably available evidence to demonstrate that it owns the industrial property right or trade secret, or that it is authorized to use it, and that a violation has occurred or is imminent.

[G] Precautionary Seizure of Movable and Immovable Property, Article 62(3) UPCA

See section §11.07[F] above.

[H] Recalling from the Channels of Commerce, Article 64(2) lit (b) UPCA

Recalling from the channels of commerce is regulated by Article 348 IP Code.

The IP Court decision of merit shall, without prejudice to the award of damages, and at the request of the injured party and at the expense of the infringer, determine measures concerning the destination of goods in which there has been an infringement of industrial property rights or trade secrets.

These measures must be appropriate, necessary and proportional to the gravity of the violation and may include destruction, withdrawal or definitive exclusion from commercial circuits, without awarding any compensation to the infringer.

When applying these measures, the IP Court must take into consideration the legitimate interests of third parties, in particular of consumers.

Instruments used in the manufacture of goods for which there is evidence of infringement of industrial property rights or trade secrets shall also be subject to additional sanctions.

[I] Depriving the Product of Its Infringing Property, Article 64(2) lit (c) UPCA

See section §11.07[H] above.

[J] Removing from the Channels of Commerce, Article 64(2) lit (d) UPCA

See section §11.07[H] above.

[K] Destruction, Article 64(2) lit (e) UPCA

See section §11.07[H] above.

[L] Communication of Information, Article 67 UPCA

Communication of information is regulated by Article 344 IP Code.

The interested party may request the provision of detailed information on the origin and distribution networks of the goods or services suspected of infringing industrial property rights or trade secrets, namely the names and addresses of the producers, manufacturers, distributors, suppliers and other previous possessors of the goods or services, as well as the receiving wholesalers and retailers and information about the quantities produced, manufactured, delivered, received or ordered, as well as the price obtained for the goods or services.

These may be ordered from the alleged infringer or any other person who has been found in possession of the goods or using or providing the services, on a commercial scale, which are suspected of violating industrial property rights or trade secrets or has been indicated by a person as having participated in the production, manufacturing or distribution of the goods or in the provision of the services suspected of violating industrial property rights or trade secrets.

The provisions of this Article do not prejudice the application of other legislative or regulatory provisions that: confer on the interested party the right to more extensive information; regulate its use in civil or criminal proceedings; regulate liability for abuse of the right to information; grant the right to refrain from making statements that may obligate any of the people referred to above to admit their own participation or that of close family members; grant the right to invoke professional secrecy, the protection of confidentiality of information sources or the legal regime of protection of personal data.

Chapter 12

Sweden

Louise Jonshammar

§12.01 SOURCES OF LAW FOR ENFORCEMENT

The Swedish Patents Act dates from 1967. In October 2012, the Swedish Government appointed a Committee to review and suggest changes in the Swedish legislation needed to implement the unitary patent system and the Unified Patent Court ('UPC'). The Committee was also tasked with performing a full review of the Swedish Patents Act and the Patents Decree.

The first report from the Committee was published in June 2013, identifying changes in the current Patents Act which were necessary to comply with and implement the unitary patent system and the new UPC. The changes were proposed to the Swedish Parliament in 2014, and entered into force on 1 June 2023. Simultaneously, changes to the Patents Decree were made, regarding entries in the Swedish patent register.

Regarding enforcement, a new Section 70a of the Swedish Patents Act has been decided but is not yet in force. The new section reads (in translation from Swedish):

> A ruling by the [Unified Patent Court] is enforced in this country as a corresponding Swedish ruling.

The preparatory works on this new section mention that 'ruling' means a judgment, decision or injunction referred to in Article 82 of the Agreement on a Unified Patent Court ('UPCA'), which also includes interim decisions. The UPC may combine its orders with a fine and the fines are imposed directly by the UPC pursuant to Articles 62.1, 63.2 and 82.4 of the UPCA. A decision to impose a fine is also covered by the provision in Section 70a of the Swedish Patents Act. In the preparatory works, it was specifically noted that the UPC's jurisdiction is limited to protective measures and sanctions under civil law, and that the UPCA does not grant the UPC jurisdiction to handle criminal matters or impose sanctions based on criminal law. Patent infringement can be prosecuted as a criminal act under Swedish law, and property which is subject to a criminal action can be confiscated. Thus, Swedish courts will still have jurisdiction over criminal matters relating to infringement and forfeiture of property in such matters, also as regards European patents with unitary effect.

Further, the legislator has noted that, pursuant to Article 82 UPCA, the decisions of the UPC shall be enforceable in all Contracting Member States under the same conditions as a decision given in the Contracting Member State where the enforcement takes place, and that a decision on enforceability shall be attached to the Court's ruling. Therefore, the preparatory works clarify that to comply with the UPCA, a ruling by the UPC shall be enforceable in Sweden without any national declaration of enforceability and no translation of the decision can be required.

Enforcement in Sweden is governed by the Enforcement Code (1981:774), a national Swedish legislation applicable to all acts of enforcement, and the Enforcement Ordinance (1981:981) which sets out certain details of the procedure.

Pursuant to Chapter 1 Section 1 of the Enforcement Code, the Code applies to matters concerning the enforcement of all enforcement titles, whether it regards an obligation to pay or other obligation, and also applies to matters concerning enforcement of decisions on provisional attachment or other similar security measures. Enforcement of an obligation to pay is implemented through attachment and enforcement of another obligation or security measure is implemented either by the Enforcement Authority ordering the defendant to fulfil his/her/its obligations or to observe a prohibition or other regulation, or by the Authority itself implementing the necessary measures. If the Authority considers it appropriate, it may, subject to a request from the claimant, transfer the implementation of the measures to the claimant.

Pursuant to Rule 354.1 of the Rules of Procedure, decisions and orders by the UPC have a binding effect and are directly enforceable. Under the Swedish Enforcement Code, an application for enforcement of a judgment which concerns an obligation to fulfil a payment may be enforced immediately, even if the judgment has been appealed or while appeal is still available, and can be pursued *provided the debtor has not deposited with the Enforcement Authority the corresponding amount* (including any accrued interest for the debt on the day the deposit takes place), together with administration costs. The debtor may also pledge the amount with corresponding credit balances at a bank together with the interest that runs on the credit balance for the period thereafter, to avoid immediate enforcement actions while an appeal is tried.

Currently, there are no planned amendments to the Swedish patent or enforcement law, which specifically addresses enforcement in Sweden for penalty payments payable to the UPC. Compared to penalty fees imposed by the Swedish patent courts, such fees are owed to the Swedish Government and will therefore be enforced directly by the Enforcement Authority, on behalf of the Government. As the UPC is not a part of the Swedish governmental or municipal institutions, it must be assumed that without an amendment to the legislation, the Enforcement Authority will not enforce a UPC judgment on penalty payments without the UPC applying for enforcement under the enforcement provisions of a private case. It must be further assumed that it is in the interest of the winning party that a penalty fee decided by the UPC is in fact enforced. If it is not enforced, the decision of the UPC is likely to be of less value, as the penalty fee is an important factor to the enforcement of a decision to perform the underlying obligations of the losing party when such actions do not involve payment of money to the winning party. If the winning party cannot control enforcement of a decision which relates to penalty payment, it is rather in the hands of the UPC to enforce its decision for it to be useful to the winning party.

§12.02 OVERVIEW OF AUTHORITIES EXECUTING ENFORCEMENT IN SWEDEN

An application for enforcement in Sweden shall be addressed directly to the Enforcement Authority (in Swedish: '*Kronofogden*'). The authority has several office locations across Sweden with a main office in Sundbyberg, just outside Stockholm. The Authority is headed by the Chief Enforcement Director. The claimant shall file the application for enforcement with the Enforcement Authority office in the jurisdiction where the respondent has his/her residence or (for companies) its registered statutory seat. The Enforcement Authority provides a search engine on its website where the postal code of the respondent can be entered and the site indicates which of the authority's office locations the application for enforcement should be filed with. The customer service of the Enforcement Authority is also available to assist with finding the correct office for jurisdiction purposes.

The Enforcement Authority is the public authority in Sweden that helps a person who requests enforcement (referred to as 'the claimant') and those who must pay. It is also the exclusive enforcement authority for performance of other actions, such as enforcement of an order for destruction of goods or execution of infringement investigations. The procedure involves the claimant requesting the Enforcement Authority's assistance in enforcing the order and the Enforcement Authority deciding on attachment of property or other proper means of action for the enforcement. The Enforcement Authority collects payment from the obligated party for distribution to the claimant.

If the Enforcement Authority expects to be met with resistance when performing an enforcement procedure, it may request assistance from the police authority.

§12.03 GENERAL REQUIREMENTS FOR ENFORCEMENT

Enforcement cases are dealt with as private cases or public cases. Simply put, public cases are cases concerning funds to which the State or a municipality is entitled, and which may be enforced without a preceding judgment and other similar claims that the State or a municipality is entitled to, such as payable taxes. All other cases are considered private cases. Under current legislation, as the UPC is not an authority under the Swedish Government, any enforcement of, for example, penalty payment to the UPC must be understood to be a private case before the Enforcement Authority, just like enforcement of payment to the patentee of damages for infringement is a private case before the Enforcement Authority.

Effective enforcement of a debt in Sweden requires that the obligated party/ debtor either resides in Sweden or has assets in Sweden.

Enforcement of decisions and orders by the UPC is directly available under the rules and procedures set out in the Swedish Enforcement Code and Enforcement

Ordinance, pursuant to the legal provision in the new Section 72a of the Swedish Patents Act.

If the UPC has ordered discontinuation subject to a penalty fee should the order/discontinuation be not complied with by the infringing party, the Enforcement Authority cannot decide on a matter of non-compliance. If the claimant (patentee) wants to raise a matter of non-compliance, it must be raised with the UPC under Rule 354.4 of the Rules of Procedure, and the UPC shall decide whether the order has been complied with or not, and whether the penalty fee shall be paid or not, and – upon request by the claimant – whether the order shall be subject to a new penalty fee. Enforcement of a penalty fee, under current Swedish legislation, must be understood as subject to a claim from the UPC to the Swedish Enforcement Authority, to be handled as an ordinary private case.

The claimant should be mindful of time as the general Swedish statute of limitations applies for enforcement of monetary claims. The clock will start on the date of decision or judgment by the UPC. The ordinary limitation for enforcement of a judgment is ten years.

§12.04 OVERVIEW OF PROCEEDINGS

A claimant wanting to enforce a judgment by the UPC in Sweden shall lodge an application for enforcement with the Swedish Enforcement Authority. The appropriate form for filing the enforcement application is available also in English on the website of the Enforcement Authority (www.kronofogden.se). (See also Appendix 1 below.) The form for application of enforcement includes a detailed description of how to complete the form, and the form is available both for downloading to complete onscreen and downloading to print and complete by other means.

The application shall state

(i) the action requested;
(ii) the claimant's name;
(iii) company registration number or personal identification number;
(iv) postal address; and
(v) telephone number.

If the claimant has appointed an agent for representation, the representative's name, postal address and telephone number shall be stated.

Regarding the obligated party/debtor, the application shall include such party's name, occupation (if physical person and if known to claimant), company registration number or personal identification number, domicile, postal address, and address of workplace (if known to claimant) and, where applicable, another address where the obligated party/debtor can be found for service by a bailiff. Further, the application shall include information on the obligated party's/debtor's home telephone number and about the workplace and other conditions of importance known to the claimant. If the obligated party/debtor does not have a known address, information must be provided about the claimant's investigation carried out to determine this.

The application shall include as an attachment the decision, order, or judgment on which the application is based, and the order for the enforcement which the UPC has attached to the decision.

Figure 1. Description of enforcement procedure

The party seeking enforcement in Sweden ('the claimant') shall proceed as follows.

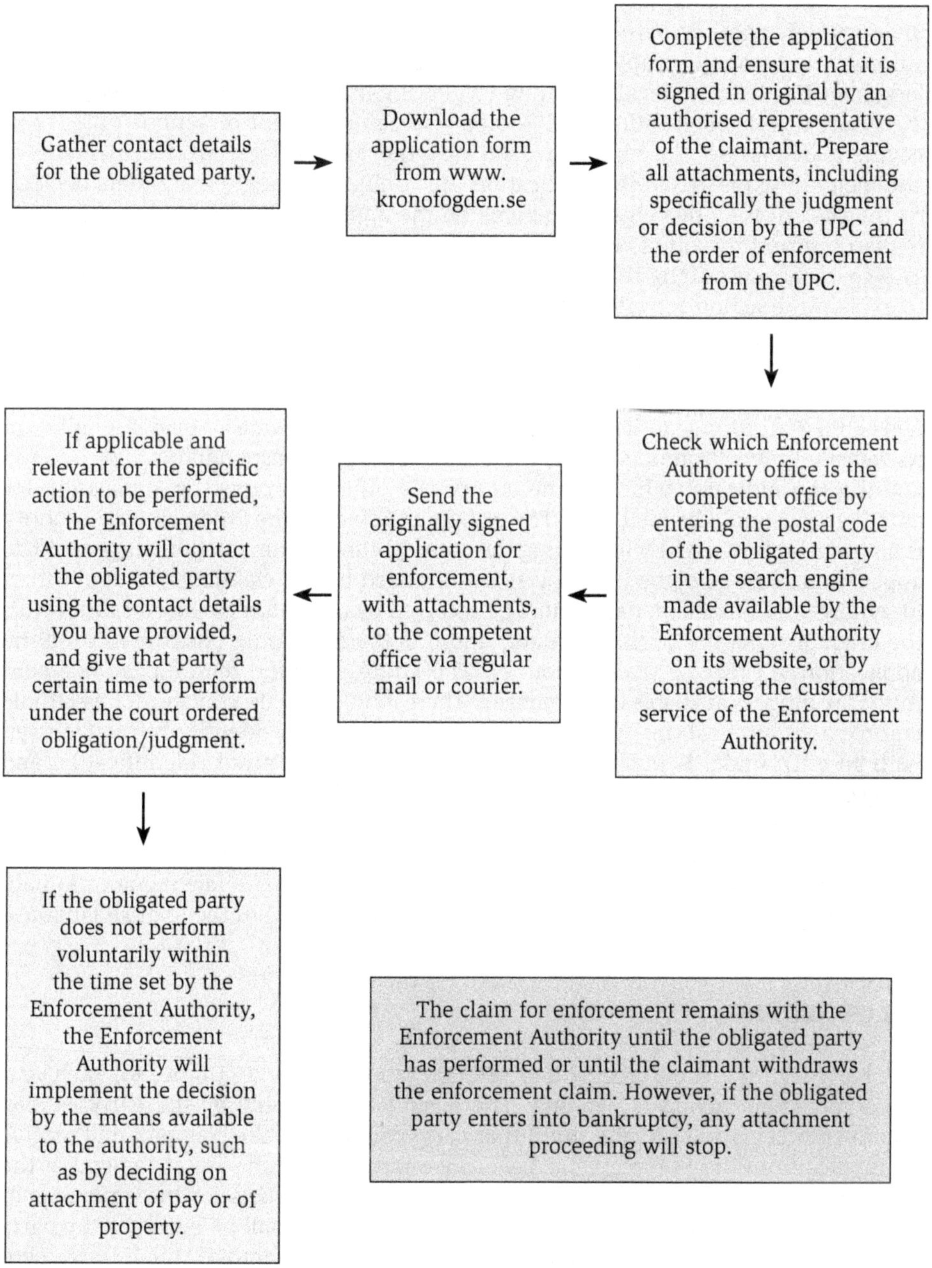

If several parties (jointly and severally) are responsible to fulfil/adhere to the same claim, the claimant must submit one application per party. In such case, the applications shall be lodged with the same Enforcement Authority office, even if one person belongs to another office.

The same application form can be used to apply for enforcement of a judgment under which another party is obligated to do something. Such decision can be enforced by measures implemented by the Enforcement Authority only when the judgment has become legally binding (when it can no longer be appealed) unless the Court has decided differently. To apply for enforcement of actions other than payment of money, the claimant shall tick the appropriate box for the type of enforcement requested in the application. It is unlikely, though, that orders decided by the UPC fit the pre-suggested actions on the application form, and the claimant is then referred to complete the box 'Other' under the heading 'The application'. The space for describing the action is limited, and the claimant may find it useful to explain the action for which enforcement is applied in a separate appendix and refer to this appendix in the box 'Other'.

The application shall be lodged with the Enforcement Authority office in the jurisdiction where the respondent has his/her residence or (for companies) its registered statutory seat. The Enforcement Authority provides a search engine on its website (www.kronofogden.se) the postal code of the respondent can be entered and the site indicates which of the authority's office locations the application for enforcement should be filed with. The customer service of the Enforcement Authority is also available to assist with finding the correct office for jurisdiction purposes. The application must be signed by a person authorised by the claimant. An application for enforcement made on paper must be received by the Enforcement Authority with the original signature of the claimant, and it is therefore only possible to send the application via regular mail or courier. The address for the relevant Enforcement Authority office is available on its website. There is an e-service available for electronic enforcement applications, which requires the claimant to identify himself/herself with an e-ID, under Regulation (EU) No. 910/2014 on electronic identification and trust services for electronic transactions in the internal market (eIDAS). The e-service is accessible via the webpage www.kronofogden.se.

Questions regarding the application or the enforcement procedure can be directed to the Enforcement Authority's Customer Service via telephone or e-mail. The contact details are available on the website. Knowledge of the English language can be expected.

§12.05 COSTS

The basic fee for any enforcement is SEK 600 (approximately EUR 60) for each year the enforcement action is pending. The basic fee is payable by the party against whom enforcement is sought, but if that party cannot pay, the claimant will receive an invoice from the Enforcement Authority and must pay the fee at the end of the enforcement proceeding. If the authority has additional costs for the enforcement action, for instance a cost for storage of goods, that cost shall be borne by the party against whom enforcement is sought, but if that party cannot pay, the Enforcement Authority will charge the claimant for the cost.

For each case application of enforcement, one basic fee is payable.

The only enforcement action for which the basic fee is higher than SEK 600 is for infringement investigations, which may compare to an order to preserve evidence or inspect premises under Article 60 of the UPCA, for which the basic fee is SEK 5,000 (approximately EUR 500).

Other costs for the enforcement action may accrue depending on how the decision is to be enforced. If the Enforcement Authority has costs for transporting goods or selling attached property for example, such costs are payable by the obligated party, as a main rule. However, if the costs are not paid by the obligated party, the claimant is responsible for paying the costs. If the Enforcement Authority finds it necessary, it may require the claimant to pay costs in advance, for instance if it is deemed beforehand that the costs for enforcement will be high.

If money is received in the case from, for example, attachment, the claimant will get the fee paid reimbursed from the money received.

The enforcement matter is ongoing until it is fully paid or remedied. If the claimant does not want the Enforcement Authority to continue processing the enforcement case, the claimant must withdraw it. If the case is withdrawn, the claimant will receive an invoice for the unpaid fees.

There are no rules relating to reimbursement of attorney fees for assistance in the enforcement matter.

§12.06 COUNTERMEASURES ON ENFORCEMENT

Although the enforcement title (in this case the judgment or order of the UPC) cannot be tried in the Swedish legal system, a decision by the Enforcement Authority regarding attachment of property or other means of action for the collection of a debt under the enforcement title, can be appealed. The appeal shall state the requested change of the decisions and the grounds for appeal, for example that certain property which has been made subject to attachment is exempt from attachment. An appeal shall be lodged with the Enforcement Authority and will be tried by the District Court in the jurisdiction of the debtor/obligated party, pursuant to the rules of Chapter 17 Section 1 of the Enforcement Ordinance.

The obligated party can also oppose enforcement on the basis of having already fulfilled the obligation. If the obligated party proves that the obligation has been fulfilled, the judgment shall not be enforced. If the obligated party claims that he or she has a counterclaim based on a different but enforceable judgment or another written proof of claim, and the legal conditions of a counterclaim are fulfilled, the judgment shall not be enforced. The obligated party can also present other circumstances regarding the situation between the claimant and the obligated party to oppose enforcement of the judgment. If the opposition cannot be disregarded by the Enforcement Authority, enforcement shall not be pursued. Decisions by the Enforcement Authority to not enforce a judgment can be appealed to the District Court in the jurisdiction of the debtor/obligated party, pursuant to the rules of Chapter 17 Section 1 of the Enforcement Ordinance.

§12.07 PARTICULARITIES WITH RESPECT TO SPECIFIC ORDERS

[A] Permanent Injunctions, Article 63 UPCA

If non-compliance with a permanent injunction against an infringer has been made subject to a recurring penalty payment payable to the UPC, and the infringer does not comply with the permanent injunction, the patentee cannot enforce the penalty payment against the infringer by filing an action with the Swedish courts or Enforcement Authority. The decision to impose the penalty fee on the infringer lies with the UPC pursuant to Rule 354.4 of the Rules of Procedure and the patentee must therefore file a motion with the UPC that the penalty fee be imposed. Although no specific provisions are currently in force, it is expected that a decision by the UPC for payment of penalty fee can be enforced by the UPC against the infringer also under Swedish enforcement laws and procedures.

[B] An Order to Produce Evidence, Article 59 UPCA

The preparatory works of the new Section 70a of the Swedish Patents Act, which states that a ruling by the UPC is enforced as a corresponding Swedish ruling, state that pursuant to this new Section, the regulations and procedures applicable for the Enforcement Authority in corresponding national rulings shall also apply for orders by the UPC. Corresponding Swedish regulations may be found in Chapter 38 of the Swedish Code of Judicial Procedure. An order to produce evidence is enforceable by the Enforcement Authority, but it may be noted that in a governmental report from 2017 (SOU 2017:100), enforcement of such orders where the evidence is digitally stored may be encounter certain difficulties if the information is in fact stored on a server outside Sweden or it is unknown where the information is stored.

[C] An Order to Preserve Evidence and to Inspect Premises, Article 60 UPCA

In the Swedish Patents Act, Sections 59f–59h, there are provisions regarding infringement investigation, which may be understood to correspond to an order to preserve evidence and/or to inspect premises. The preparatory works of the new Section 70a of the Swedish Patents Act, which states that a ruling by the UPC is enforced as a corresponding Swedish ruling, states that pursuant to this new Section, the regulations and procedures applicable for the Enforcement Authority in corresponding national rulings shall apply also for orders by the UPC. Thus, when the Swedish Patents Act states that an order for an infringement investigation is executed by the Enforcement Authority in accordance with the conditions prescribed by the court and pursuant to Chapters 1 to 3, Chapter 17, Articles 1 to 5, and Chapter 18, of the Enforcement Code, this is to apply to orders by the UPC to preserve evidence and to inspect premises under Article 60 of the UPCA. The Swedish Patents Act states that the (enforcement) claimant's opposing party shall be informed about the execution only if the order (to preserve evidence and to inspect premises) has been issued after hearing the opposite party. The Enforcement Authority has the right to take photographs and to make video and sound recordings of such objects for which it is authorised to search. Further, the Enforcement Authority also has the right to make copies of, and extracts from, such documents for which it is authorised to search.

Pursuant to Section 59g of the Swedish Patents Act, the opposing party has the right to summon an attorney when an order (to preserve evidence and to inspect premises) is to be executed. The execution must not commence before the attorney has arrived. This does not, however, apply if the investigation is thereby unnecessarily delayed, or there is otherwise a risk that the purpose of the measure will not be achieved. The purpose of prohibiting unnecessary delay is to prevent the opposing party exercising obvious techniques to delay the proceeding. What may qualify as 'unnecessary delay', or rather what is a reasonable time for the attorney to appear, is to be determined on a case-by-case basis. The preparatory works mention that, under normal circumstances, an hour is sufficient time for the attorney to appear. In the course of the execution, the Enforcement Authority is authorised to engage, as necessary, the services of an expert.

The Enforcement Authority may permit the (enforcement) claimant or a representative of the claimant to attend the proceedings in order to provide information. If such permission is granted, the Enforcement Authority shall see to it that the claimant or the representative is not being informed about the findings at the proceedings to a larger extent than can be justified by the execution. Photographs and video and sound recordings of objects as well as copies of, and extracts from, documents shall be listed and shall be held available for the claimant and the opposite party.

[D] Freezing Orders, Article 61 UPCA

The preparatory works of the new Section 70a of the Swedish Patents Act, which states that a ruling by the UPC is enforced as a corresponding Swedish ruling, state that pursuant to this new Section, the regulations and procedures applicable for the Enforcement Authority in corresponding national rulings, shall apply also for orders by the UPC. Swedish regulations corresponding to freezing orders may be found in Chapter 15 of the Swedish Code of Judicial Procedure. A freezing order is enforceable by the Enforcement Authority, and such decisions shall be enforced urgently.

[E] Preliminary Injunction, Article 62(1) UPCA

A preliminary injunction to prevent any imminent infringement is enforceable in Sweden just like a permanent injunction. If non-compliance with a preliminary injunction has been made subject to a recurring penalty payment payable to the UPC, and the obligated party does not comply with the injunction, the patentee cannot enforce the penalty payment against the obligated party by filing an action with the Swedish courts or Enforcement Authority. The decision to impose the penalty fee on the obligated party lies with the UPC pursuant to Rule 354.4 of the Rules of Procedure and the patentee must therefore file a motion with the UPC that the penalty fee is imposed. Although no specific provisions are currently in force, it is expected that a decision by the UPC for payment of penalty fee can be enforced by the UPC against the obligated party also under Swedish enforcement laws and procedures.

[F] Seizure or Delivery up of Infringing Products, Article 62(3) UPCA

It is to be expected that enforcement of an order for seizure or delivery up of infringing goods is subject to payment of costs, as the Enforcement Authority shall not bear the burden of such costs. Pursuant to Section 59 paragraph 6 of the Swedish Patents Act, actions relating to infringing goods shall be borne by the defendant, unless there is a special reason to decide otherwise. This aligns with the Enforcement Code, under which the costs for enforcing an order are payable by the obligated party. If the costs are not paid by the obligated party, the claimant is responsible for paying the costs and the Enforcement Authority may even require the claimant to pay costs in advance, for instance if it is deemed beforehand that the costs will be high. Since the Patents Act specifically places the burden of paying the costs for enforcement of the action on the defendant, it is assumed that the claimant can claim reimbursement of such costs from the defendant if the claimant nevertheless is obligated to pay the Enforcement Authority for the enforcement action.

Because seizure may also involve the act of transporting and even temporarily storing the infringing goods, costs may accrue which are payable by the party imposed with the seizure but will be charged to the claimant if not paid by the imposed party. If non-compliance with the order has been made subject to a recurring penalty payment payable to the UPC, and the infringer does not comply with the order, the patentee cannot enforce the penalty payment against the infringer by filing an action with the Swedish courts or Enforcement Authority. The decision to impose the penalty fee on the infringer lies with the UPC pursuant to Rule 354.4 of the Rules of Procedure. Although no specific provisions are currently in force, it is expected that such decision by the UPC can be enforced by the UPC against the infringer also under Swedish enforcement laws and procedures.

[G] Precautionary Seizure of Movable and Immovable Property, Article 62(3) UPCA

Enforcement of precautionary seizure of products is handled under the same procedure as enforcement of seizure. It is to be expected that enforcement of an order for precautionary seizure of movable and immovable property can be subject to payment of costs, as the Enforcement Authority shall not bear the burden of such costs. Pursuant to Section 59 paragraph 6 of the Swedish Patents Act, actions relating to infringing goods shall be borne by the defendant, unless there is a special reason to decide otherwise. This aligns with the Enforcement Code, under which the costs for enforcing an order are payable by the obligated party. If the costs are not paid by the obligated party, the claimant is responsible for paying the costs and the Enforcement Authority may even require the claimant to pay costs in advance, for instance if it is deemed beforehand that the costs will be high. Since the Patents Act specifically places the burden of paying the costs for enforcement of the action on the defendant, it is assumed that the claimant can claim reimbursement of such costs from the defendant if the claimant nevertheless is obligated to pay the Enforcement Authority for the enforcement action.

For seizure involving the blocking of bank accounts and other assets, corresponding Swedish regulations are found in Chapter 15 of the Swedish Code of Judicial

Procedure. Precautionary seizure is enforceable by the Enforcement Authority, and such decisions shall be enforced urgently (Chapter 15 Section 1 of the Enforcement Ordinance).

[H] Recalling from the Channels of Commerce, Article 64(2) lit (b) UPCA

The Swedish Patents Act includes corresponding provisions, which allow for courts to order that infringing goods are recalled from the channels of commerce. However, there are no special provisions regarding enforcement of such orders. If the obligated party does not comply with the order of the Court and is sanctioned with a recurring penalty payment, enforcement of such penalty payment cannot be applied for by the patentee by filing an action with the Swedish courts or Enforcement Authority. The decision to impose the penalty fee on the infringer lies with the UPC pursuant to Rule 354.4 of the Rules of Procedure. Although no specific provisions are currently in force, it is expected that such decision by the UPC can be enforced by the UPC against the infringer also under Swedish enforcement laws and procedures.

[I] Depriving the Product of Its Infringing Property, Article 64(2) lit (c) UPCA

The Swedish Patents Act includes a rather wide catalogue of correctional actions available to handle infringing goods, as the recital of actions includes also the notion of 'any other action'. There are no special provisions regarding enforcement of such orders. It must be understood however, that enforcement will require that the action to be performed is very specific and detailed for the Enforcement Authority to be able to actually enforce it. In this respect, it may be noted that if a ruling is considered to be so unclear or incomplete that it cannot be concluded what the Court has decided, the Enforcement Authority shall refer the claimant to seek judicial review (Chapter 5 Section 2 of the Swedish Enforcement Ordinance).

If the obligated party does not comply with the order of the Court and is sanctioned with a recurring penalty payment, enforcement of such penalty payment cannot be applied for by the patentee by filing an action with the Swedish courts or Enforcement Authority. The decision to impose the penalty fee on the infringer lies with the UPC pursuant to Rule 354.4 of the Rules of Procedure. Although no specific provisions are currently in force, it is expected that such decision by the UPC can be enforced by the UPC against the infringer also under Swedish enforcement laws and procedures.

[J] Removing from the Channels of Commerce, Article 64(2) lit (d) UPCA

Although there are corresponding provisions in the Swedish Patents Act, which allow for courts to order that infringing goods are removed from the channels of commerce, there are no special provisions regarding enforcement of such orders. If the obligated party does not comply with the order of the Court and is sanctioned with a recurring penalty payment, enforcement of such penalty payment cannot be applied for by the patentee by filing an action with the Swedish courts or Enforcement Authority. The decision to impose the penalty fee on the infringer lies with the UPC pursuant to Rule 354.4 of the Rules of Procedure. Although no specific provisions are currently in force, it is expected that such decision by the UPC can be enforced by the UPC against the infringer also under Swedish enforcement laws and procedures.

[K] Destruction, Article 64(2) lit (e) UPCA

It is to be expected that enforcement of an order for destruction of goods and materials is subject to payment costs, as the Enforcement Authority shall not bear the burden of such costs. Pursuant to Section 59 paragraph 6 of the Swedish Patents Act, actions relating to infringing goods shall be borne by the defendant, unless there is a special reason to decide otherwise. This aligns with the Enforcement Code, under which the costs for enforcing an order are payable by the obligated party. If the costs are not paid by the obligated party, the claimant is responsible for paying the costs and the Enforcement Authority may even require the claimant to pay costs in advance, for instance if it is deemed beforehand that the costs will be high. Since the Patents Act specifically places the burden of paying the costs for enforcement of the action on the defendant, it is assumed that the claimant can claim reimbursement of such costs from the defendant if the claimant nevertheless is obligated to pay the Enforcement Authority for the enforcement action.

[L] Communication of Information, Article 67 UPCA

Although there are corresponding provisions in the Swedish Patents Act, which allow for courts to order the communication of information, there are no special provisions regarding enforcement of such orders. If the obligated party does not comply with the order of the Court and is sanctioned with a recurring penalty payment, enforcement of such penalty payment cannot be applied for by the party having requested the information by filing an action with the Swedish courts or Enforcement Authority. The decision to impose the penalty fee on the infringer lies with the UPC pursuant to Rule 354.4 of the Rules of Procedure. Although no specific provisions are currently in force, it is expected that such decision by the UPC can be enforced by the UPC against the infringer also under Swedish enforcement laws and procedures.

APPENDIX 1

Kronofogden
The Enforcement Authority

Application for Enforcement

Date

The Enforcement Authority

Is your personal information protected?
If your personal information is protected, you must always notify the Enforcement Authority of this. Before you send in an application or submit information, you are welcome to contact us to find out which information is necessary to submit to your case, and which information is not necessary. Keep in mind also that sensitive information may be found on other documents you send to us. For more information, visit **www.kronofogden.se**.

Applicant (Creditor)	Name			Personal ID number/Company Registration Number
	Complete address			
	Plus/Bank giro	Bank account: Clearingnumber / Account number		Phone number (including area code)
Representative for applicant	Name			
	Complete address			
	Plus/Bank giro	Bank account: Clearingnumber / Account number		Phone number (including area code)
Debtor	Name			Personal ID number/Company Registration Number
	Complete address			Phone number (including area code)

The application	☐ Attachment ☐ Sequestration ☐ Eviction ☐ Repossession	Other Goods that are to be repossessed			
The applicant's claim upon requested attachment/ sequestration - amount and currency	Capital	Interest	Interest added at %	From and including	until payment made
	Collection cost	Interest	Interest added at %	From and including	until payment made
	Procedural cost	Interest	Interest added at %	From and including	until payment made
Applicant's claim upon requested repossession - amount and currency	Unpaid part of credit claim	of which due / Late payment interest	Interest added at %	From and including	until payment made
	Compensation for applicant's costs	Repair cost upon hire-purchase in certain cases, according to annex			
Applicant refers to	☐ Order to pay (decision)	☐ I request the Enforcement Authority to produce the decision		Decision number	
	☐ Decision ☐ Judgment	Others			
	Court			Date	
Other information that can be of value for the handling of the matter by the Enforcement Authority	E.g. your reference number or details of debtor's occupation, employer (name, address, telephone), banking connection and assets such as property etc.				
Annexes	☐ Cited documents ☐ Instruments of debt ☐ Leasing agreement	Others			

Signature

Signature	Print name here

KFM 9329 23 en web 01

How to fill in the form

Once you have a judgment or other basis for the application, you can submit an application for enforcement to the Enforcement Authority: Enforcement means that you will have assistance in enforcing what has been decided in the judgment/decision/verdict. If you have a judgment or decision, you can ask us to collect the debt before it has become legally binding, i.e., while it can still be appealed. However, we cannot disburse any money before the judgment or decision has become legally binding. This means that money is disbursed when the judgment can no longer be appealed.

You can use this form to apply for enforcement of attachment, eviction, sequestration, repossession, or otherwise. See explanations under Section 4.

1. Applicant (e.g., the person to be paid)

The applicant is the person who makes a claim against someone (the debtor) to pay or do something else, such as move.

2. Representative of the applicant, if any

You shall only fill in information about a representative if you, as the applicant, have a representative in your dealings with the Enforcement Authority. If so, all communication goes through the representative. If so, you must enclose a power of attorney for the person who will act as your representative, and possibly a power of attorney to receive money on your behalf.

If the applicant is under 18, the legal guardian(s) must act as representative(s).

3. Debtor (the person to whom the claim is addressed)

The person against whom the claim is directed is called Debtor. It is important that you fill in the debtor's details carefully so that the case can be processed as quickly as possible.

If several persons (debtors) are jointly liable for a debt, you must submit an application for each debtor against whom you want to request enforcement. In this case, it is important that you send all applications to the same office, even if a debtor lives in another part of the country. You only need to enclose one copy of the judgment or decision. See Section 7.

4. The application concerns

Tick the box for the type of enforcement requested in the application.

- Attachment means that we seize assets from the debtor, such as a car or part of their salary, to pay the debt. If the investigation shows that the debtor owns a real property, we will ask you if you want to request attachment thereof. Such an attachment may entail additional costs.
- Eviction
- Sequestration is a temporary measure ordered by a court, whereby property is taken as security for a certain debt pending a judgment.
- In some cases, repossession means that the seller can get goods back if the buyer does not fulfil their part of the purchase agreement, for example if they fail to pay instalments.
- Other, such as removal of property or transfer of movable property. For example, someone has closed a road without permission, or someone is withholding an object or something else belonging to you.

5. Applicant's claim in the event of a requested attachment/sequestration

Enter the amounts still to be recovered out of the amount determined by decision or judgment. You can calculate the interest rate until the application date at www.kronofogden.se. You may only use the interest rate set out in decision, judgment, or verdict.

6. Applicant's claim in the event of a requested repossession

Enter the unpaid part of the credit claim. Interest on arrears shall be calculated on the amount due. You can calculate the interest rate up to the application date at www.kronofogden.se. You may only use the agreed interest rate.

7. The applicant invokes (refers to)

The Enforcement Authority needs to see the document you are invoking, i.e., referring to, as a basis for your application. The document may be an order to pay, judgment, decision, or other. In the case of an order to pay, you must either attach the decision or ask the Enforcement Authority to produce it.

If you are appealing a judgment, decision or other, you must always attach the document.

If the official document you are referring to is a court decision or a verdict, we need proof that the document has taken effect (can no longer be appealed against) in order for us to be able to pay out any funds relating to this case. You can apply for enforcement before the decision/verdict has taken effect, in which case you must afterwards provide proof that the decision/verdict has taken effect.

You can request proof of having taken effect from the entity that issued the document, such as a court verdict.

8. Other things that may be of value

Enter information that may be helpful for your case. For example, this could include assets that you know the payer has, telephone numbers of the payer or contact details of their employer. If there is not enough space on the form, you can complete the information on another piece of paper and enclose it.

9. Appendices

State which appendices you are attaching. If the debt refers to a Negotiable Promissory Note, this must be attached to the application.

Appendix can also be a power of attorney to act as representative and to receive money payable to you as applicant.

10. Signature

The application must be signed by you as applicant or by the representative. If you are represented by a representative, the representative must sign.

Fee

When applying for enforcement, a fee is charged, a so-called basic fee. An enforcement case has no time-limit and the Enforcement Authority charges a fee for each year of processing. In addition, other enforcement costs may arise. To stop the processing, you as applicant must withdraw your application.

Read more at www.kronofogden.se or contact the Enforcement Authority if you wish to know more about our fees.

How we process personal data

At www.kronofogden.se there is more information about how we process your personal data and how you can ensure your rights are met. You can also order written information by calling us on **0771-73 73 00**.

KFM 9329 23 en web 01

AIPPI LAW SERIES

1. Sanna Wolk, Kacper Szkalej (eds), *Employees' Intellectual Property Rights*, Second Edition, 2018 (ISBN 978-90-411-9230-1).
2. Jochen Bühling (ed.), *Patent Protection for Second Medical Uses*, Second Edition, 2020 (ISBN 978-94-035-0935-8).
3. Christopher V. Carani (ed.), *Design Rights: Functionality and Scope of Protection*, Second Edition, 2022 (ISBN 978-94-035-3210-3).
4. Eléonore Gaspar (ed.), *Genuine Use of Trademarks*, Second Edition, 2021 (ISBN 978-94-035-2833-5).
5. Jürgen Meier, Oswin Ridderbusch (eds), *Antibody Patenting: A Practitioner's Guide to Drafting, Prosecution and Enforcement*, Second Edition, 2023 (ISBN 978-94-035-3626-2).
6. Christian Czychowski, Jan Bernd Nordemann (eds), *Law of Raw Data*, 2021 (ISBN 978-94-035-3280-6).
7. John C. Todaro, Martin Bensadon, Brigitte Carion-Taravella (eds), *Pharmaceutical Test Data Exclusivity: A Multi-Jurisdictional Survey*, 2022 (ISBN 978-94-035-0106-2).
8. Jonathan P. Osha (ed.), *Artificial Intelligence and Patents: An International Perspective on Patenting AI-Related Inventions*, 2023 (ISBN 978-94-035-2215-9).
9. Christof Augenstein, Johanna Flythström (eds), *Enforcement of Decisions of the Unified Patent Court: A Survey of Participating Member States*, 2023 (ISBN 978-94-035-4846-3).

www.ingramcontent.com/pod-product-compliance
Lightning Source LLC
Chambersburg PA
CBHW071245230926
51849CB00001B/230

9789403548463